A) 293

60p

# Fifty Years of

# Political & Economic Planning

## Looking Forward 1931–1981

*16 Queen Anne's Gate: PEP's headquarters from 1933–63.*

# Fifty Years of
# Political & Economic Planning
## Looking Forward 1931–1981

The Authors
**LORD ROLL**
**MAX NICHOLSON · KENNETH LINDSAY**
**OLIVER ROSKILL · MICHAEL YOUNG**
**RAYMOND GOODMAN · RICHARD BAILEY**
**JOHN PINDER · A. R. ISSERLIS**
**SIR CHARLES CARTER**

Edited by
**JOHN PINDER**

HEINEMANN · LONDON

Heinemann Educational Books Ltd
22 Bedford Square, London WC1B 3HH

LONDON EDINBURGH MELBOURNE AUCKLAND
HONG KONG SINGAPORE KUALA LUMPUR NEW DELHI
IBADAN NAIROBI JOHANNESBURG
EXETER [NH] KINGSTON PORT OF SPAIN

ISBN 0 435 83690 0

Filmset by Northumberland Press Ltd
Gateshead, Tyne and Wear
Printed in Great Britain by Richard Clay (The Chaucer Press) Ltd
Bungay, Suffolk

# Biographical Details of Authors

**Lord Roll of Ipsden, KCMG, CB** Former Professor of Economics; Permanent Secretary of the Department of Economic Affairs; now Chairman of S. G. Warburg & Co. Author of *A History of Economic Thought*. Joint-President of Policy Studies Institute.

**Kenneth Lindsay** Former Civil Lord of the Admiralty and Parliamentary Secretary to the Board of Education; MP 1935–50. Author of books on education and on Europe. General Secretary of PEP, 1931–5.

**Max Nicholson, CB, CVO** Former senior civil servant and Director-General of the Nature Conservancy. Author of *The System*. General Secretary of PEP, 1935–40; member of PEP governing body, 1931–78.

**Oliver Roskill** Founder and former Chairman, O. W. Roskill Industrial Consultants; former President, Institute of Management Consultants. Author of many PEP reports; member of PEP Industries Group, then Executive, 1931–75.

**Michael Young** Lord Young of Dartington. Former Chairman of Social Science Research Council; Director, Institute of Community Studies, since 1953. Author of *The Rise of the Meritocracy* and of books on family, kinship and class in London. Secretary of PEP, 1942–5.

**Raymond Goodman** Vice-President Operations, the World Bank. Director of PEP, 1946–53.

**Richard Bailey** Economist and writer; former Special Adviser to National Economic Development Office; Associate of Sir Alexander Gibb and Partners, engineering consultants. Director of PEP, 1954–64.

**A. R. Isserlis** Former Principal Private Secretary to the Prime Minister and senior civil servant. Director of the Centre for Studies in Social Policy, 1972–7; Senior Fellow at PSI.

**John Pinder, OBE** Former International Director of the Economist Intelligence Unit. Author of books on European and international affairs. Director of PEP then PSI since 1964.

**Sir Charles Carter, FBA** Vice-Chancellor, University of Lancaster for 16 years from its foundation in 1963. Chairman of the Northern Ireland Economic Council; President-Elect of the British Association for the Advancement of Science. Author of books on economics, education and technology. Chairman of the Centre for Studies in Social Policy, 1972–8; Chairman of PSI Research Committee since 1978.

# Contents

# Editor's Note

One day a definitive history will surely be written of the life of Political and Economic Planning and its eventual marriage, near the age of fifty, with the Centre for Studies in Social Policy to form the Policy Studies Institute. To commemorate the fiftieth anniversary of PEP's birth, however, we thought it better that those who were at the centre of activity during each period of its development should tell the story in their own words, and thus convey not only the essential facts but also what it felt like to be involved in this remarkable organisation.

We have not tried, therefore, to iron out differences of style or of perspective. But we have adopted some common rules which it may help the reader to know at this point. Authors have referred to PEP or PSI if it is the initials that spring to mind, without spelling out Political and Economic Planning or Policy Studies Institute. People have been named as the authors think of them, with any subsequent titles usually given only in the Select Biographical Data. (Names are also listed in the main index which gives the pages on which people are mentioned.) PEP's publications have been identified by title or subject and date, and the reader will find the precise reference in the annexed list. References to documents or events have not been given when it is clear enough that they can be found in PEP's archives, which are kept at the British Library of Political and Economic Science at the London School of Economics.

Finally, I am happy to thank those who have made this book possible: my co-authors, for their extraordinary helpfulness in dealing with the demands of timetable and editorial inquisition; all those who read the drafts on the periods when they were active in PEP and made numerous valuable suggestions; Susan Johnson, who followed countless trails to complete the Select Biographical Data; Irena Belloni and others who typed the repeatedly amended drafts; Caroline Anstey, who helped with facts and documents; and our publisher, who adopted the book with so much enthusiasm.

J.P.

JANUARY 1981

# Introduction

# The Rt. Hon. Lord Roll of Ipsden,
## KCMG, CB

It gives me great pleasure to write the introduction to this commemorative volume on Political and Economic Planning's fiftieth
anniversary.

The chapters that follow deal with various phases and aspects of
PEP's history and its work in relation to the problems of our country
during the half-century of its life – in the most recent past as one
of the two constituents of the Policy Studies Institute. Here I want
to say something general about the purposes that have inspired PEP
and the methods which it has employed to achieve them, and to
reflect on the bearing of its work on the present-day problems of
our country.

Drawing on my own experience of PEP (and now of PSI) during
the more than twenty years that I have been associated with it, and
comparing that experience with the early history of PEP in the 1930s,
what is particularly striking to me is to find how much continuity
there has been in the principles that have guided our work. The first
of these I would call relevance. From its earliest to its latest publication PEP has tried to choose for study subjects that are important
in the life of the country. From the press to race relations; from
the problems of Ulster to those of the training and retraining of
adults; from the inadequacy of investment in industry to the relations
of trade unions and government; from the employment of overseas
doctors in the National Health Service to the problems of the
European Community and our membership of it, PEP has always
tried to ensure that its work can be useful to those who have the
task of making policy or to those who, as responsible citizens, wish

to be in a position to form a valid judgement on the issues of the day and the policies pursued by those who are responsible for them.

The second principle has been that the work should be of the highest quality. This in turn has meant maintenance of three important characteristics: scholarship, independence and impartiality; and I should like to say a word on each of these. It is generally acknowledged that the academic quality of PEP's work has been sustained throughout, and many of its publications have in fact become standard works on their subjects. PEP has always insisted on independence, and had it ever been subjected to any improper pressure (which it has not) be it from government, be it from providers of funds or from any sectional interests, it would certainly have rejected that as incompatible with its purposes. This also means that PEP has always insisted on a non-partisan approach to every chosen field of study. It has had, wherever appropriate, close contacts with successive governments of all political persuasions. It has had on its governing bodies backbenchers from all the political parties. It has maintained close contact with officials, many of whom have served on its Council or its Executive Committee. I do not recall any instance where PEP has been accused of any political bias.

Yet PEP's work has never been bland. It has never been 'academic' in the somewhat derogatory sense in which that word is sometimes used. It has always been realistic and has endeavoured not only to present facts objectively and to provide a thoroughgoing analysis of problems, but it has also on numerous occasions presented new ideas and proposed new courses of action to which the analyses might point.

Given its unshakeable attachment to relevance, scholarship, independence and impartiality, it is not surprising that PEP (and now PSI) has always been able to attract a great variety of outstanding people from many walks of life – from business, the universities, Parliament and government departments – to its counsels and to get them to take an active part in its work, be it on its various governing bodies, be it on the advisory committees, usually anonymous, which PEP often uses, to assist those who are in charge of specific pieces of research. And again, it is a tribute to the quality of the institution that it has always been able to recruit outstanding researchers and authors.

I do not suppose that anybody would deny that the problems with which PEP has dealt in the last fifty years – economic, social and political, domestic as well as international – are any less acute than they ever were. Nor, I imagine, would anyone seriously doubt that work done by PEP has made a very substantial contribution to solving them, even if complete solutions are impossible to find. If there is one particular guiding thought that continues to underlie PSI's work, it is in my view the belief that many of our problems, particularly in the economic sphere, are to a large extent social and institutional ones; and that the main task is to find patterns of relationships between the citizens of this country that would encourage people to contribute their best at work and to find satisfaction in doing so. If we can succeed in this, there can be no doubt that the effect on the health of the economy and of our society could be enormous. With this in view, PEP has in the past, and PSI will in the future, put a good part of its research effort into the study of problems involving relations between government and industry, and within industry, between management and employees. This, I am convinced, should produce work of direct value to industry.

There are, of course, many other matters which are part of the continuing activity of PSI. There is work on the European Community, on British industry and on economic and financial problems generally, much of it in co-operation with Chatham House and the National Institute of Economic and Social Research. Indeed, PEP/PSI has been in the forefront of cultivating research in co-operation with other institutions. This is not only designed to be more economical by avoiding duplication, but also promises to produce better results by mobilising larger research resources.

PEP has always had two great concerns, and these continue within PSI: efficiency in the government and the economy; and the creation of a just and harmonious society; and it has held the view that these are not separate objectives but that they condition each other. I believe that their mutual dependence has never been more obvious than it is today. Social advance depends on efficient government and on efficient industry, and efficiency in government and industry depends on the acceptance by all concerned that the society in which we live is a fair and just one. If these concerns continue to be paramount today, then I am convinced that the qualities with which PEP/PSI approaches them are as badly needed as they ever were. Politics is necessarily partisan and one must not be surprised if from time to time, even in a stable and mature society such as ours, politics becomes polarised and apparently insurmountable ideological differences make their appearance. It is all the more necessary that while the clamour of political battle goes on, dispassionate, non-partisan, analytical yet highly relevant work directly focused on particular issues should continue to flourish.

# The Proposal for a National Plan

## Max Nicholson

PEP entered the world precipitately and unceremoniously in the spring of 1931. To understand why, it is necessary to envisage a world apparently on the point of falling apart. Just over a year earlier the Wall Street crash had led to widespread bankruptcies, mass unemployment and national economic crises in many countries. Britain was losing the struggle to remain on a gold standard related to pre-war parities. The superiority of the British way of life and of British goods, the soundness of the British Empire, and the pretence of a successful post-war revival of Britain were foundering in the bitter aftermath of the 1926 General Strike. Europe was facing both the collapse of the Versailles settlement after World War I and the alarming gains of Hitler's following in Germany. The bold and well-publicised Marxist planning initiatives in Soviet Russia, and the bombastic claims of Mussolini's Fascist Italy, were beginning to exert disturbing pulls on dissatisfied war veterans, young men of the post-war generation, and others.

While many continued blindly in their complacent ways, others perceived a mortal challenge, demanding an appropriate new British response. Most of the latter were in their thirties and forties, and were in or approaching positions of some responsibility. They had something to lose from a breakdown, or an abrupt extremist change. Many would, in an earlier decade, have been Liberals. These had been left high and dry by the split in the Liberal Party and the beginning of its protracted exclusion from power by the Conservative and Labour Parties to the right and left of it. The Liberals had a certain tradition of political studies which persisted amid growing frustration.

Early in 1930 Lord Beaverbrook's spirited but short-lived news-paper campaign for his personal nostrum of 'Empire Free Trade' had tempted the then proprietor of the long established and in-fluential *Saturday Review* to pledge its support, without consultation. The young and talented Editor, Gerald Barry, thereupon resigned, with almost all his editorial team (including me). In a miraculously short time, with new backing, they brought out a new and brighter *Week-End Review*, produced by a lively band of young contributors who set themselves to exposing the 'Old Gang' and their out-of-date, ineffectual ways of running the country. A number of young and frustrated Members of Parliament responded that such carefree sniping was not good enough: the journal should define positively what it stood for. Planning was in the air, and the Editor entrusted me with preparing, in consultation with experts, a kite-flying *Week-End Review* National Plan. After being submitted in proof to well-known figures for comments, to be published with it, this appeared under the title *A National Plan for Great Britain* as a supplement to the *Week-End Review* of 14 February 1931.

## Content of the Plan

The timing proved to be excellent, and the content of the 20,000 word Plan at once attracted and stimulated many of the leaderless but thoughtful non-partisan minority. It minced no words about the situation. Modern technology would not avail 'if most of the invisible machinery to which this is connected is a Heath Robinson con-trivance composed of the clutter of past generations and tied together with rotten bits of string'. 'The hopeless confusion of the post-war years and the extended active life of elderly men with elderly ideas' had created a risk 'that in incompetent hands this country may go drifting on either towards a sharp crisis which might have revolutionary consequences, or to dictatorship, or perhaps worse still to gradual decline ...'

The document put forward was described as the raw material for the Plan, subject to all kinds of additions, omissions and amend-ments. Some of its proposals were borrowed from specialists, others were free translations from experience abroad or in analogous con-ditions at home. 'There must be vigorous constructive argument if dynamics are to replace stagnatics as a policy for Great Britain.' Stress was laid on the need for general reorganisation of the political, social and economic structure, and for a basis of modern function.

'It must be clear that the Employer–Trade Union and State–Industry deadlocks are insoluble in present conditions.' The remedy was seen in extensive devolution from Westminster and Whitehall through flexible self-government for industry. Much less would be left directly under the thumb of the State than in the contemporary system, but on the other hand no major elements would be allowed to remain irresponsible to the community and to one another. It would be necessary to start by overhauling the machinery of government, reducing the Cabinet to ten, including Ministers for Defence and Economic Affairs as a whole, with a group of subordinate departmental Ministers, and the conversion of the Post Office and the Ministry of Works into autonomous Public Utilities. Research and the State share of Health and Education should also be hived off from Ministers. Priority should be given to building up a satisfactory structure for 'pure' and 'applied' science, and creating a Bureau of Statistics, a Standards and Design Institute and a dynamic National Museums and Libraries Trust to support putting new ideas, discoveries and methods into rapid and effective circulation. The Plan also advocated a National Roads Trust, regionally decentralised; the transfer of education from political and municipal control to a permanent Education Commission; the establishment of a Business University; provision of satellite towns; creation of a broad Green Belt for London; formation of National Parks; thorough reconstruction of the South Bank of the Thames; a programme for making the country attractive to a vastly increased number of foreign visitors and improving the trade balance through tourist spending; a Railway Corporation; a National Aviation Board; organisation of agriculture on a commodity basis, and much more. It will be noted that, despite the continuing absence of a National Plan, and of the related central institutions proposed, the intervening fifty years have confirmed the far-sightedness of the Plan by establishing in piecemeal fashion a remarkable number of the fresh organisations which it identified as necessary but missing. The timelag required for significant action has ranged from some two years, in the case of agriculture and London Transport, to nearly fifty years, or more if allowance is made for proposals which may still be implemented in the future.

The above highly incomplete account can serve merely to illustrate the kind of scope and impact aimed at by the National Plan, and its strong emphasis on fully co-ordinated modernisation within the context of British traditions and values. It claimed to be 'an elastic solution capable of adjustment to the needs of a rapidly changing situation ... not ... prophetically in advance of the times but ... abreast of them, and therefore some forty years ahead of the game of party politics as at present played at Westminster'. That rash claim can now be put to the test by those who refer back to the Plan.

In the peculiar situation described earlier it aroused a lively demand for some continuing body to be formed to carry on independent non-party discussion and study over this whole range of public affairs.

The situation in the latter part of February 1931 was therefore that the widely felt need for a new approach to reconstruction had been brought to a point of focus, and provided with a platform for starting work, by the *Week-End Review* National Plan, and that a number of experienced, determined and well-connected people were making up their minds to take this as the launching-pad for which they had been waiting. Central among them was Kenneth Lindsay, who takes up from this point the story of PEP's foundation and its organisation, structure, and people.

# 1

# PEP through the 1930s:
# Organisation, Structure, People

## Kenneth Lindsay

**Origin and Birth**

This is the story of the birth of an idea which took place within two months, has developed during 50 years and is now a national institution. The fact that it started in 1931 is important because PEP grew out of a crisis which bears comparison with the present day. PEP has always been an independent, non-party organisation, which 'has acted as a bridge between research on the one hand and policy making on the other, whether in government, the social services or industry. Its aim is a practical one: to study problems of public concern, to find out the facts, to present them impartially, to suggest ways in which the knowledge can be applied.'[1]

This introduction in 'matter moulded forms of speech' can afford little indication of the sense of excitement felt by the founding fathers; it also fails to explain why busy men of affairs, industrialists, architects, financiers, civil servants and academics, between them covering two generations of experience and thought, gave up evenings and weekends to discuss the current malaise. The early birth pangs of PEP occurred during the dying months of the second Labour government; our inception must be measured against the rapidly deteriorating condition of Britain with well over two million unemployed and the prospect of financial bankruptcy. There was also a bankruptcy of political ideas. It is difficult to recapture the national mood of the year 1931. The significance of PEP is that a

[1] These words were printed at the beginning of PEP publications for a number of years. See for example PEP, *Family Needs and the Social Services*, London, George Allen & Unwin, 1961.

group of young and not-so-young but determined people were prepared to face the challenge of the 1930s and, by dint of enthusiastic
and searching analysis, influence in some measure the course of
affairs in Britain.

PEP originated from the supplement to the *Week-End Review* of
14 February 1931, entitled *A National Plan for Great Britain*, which
has just been described by its author, Max Nicholson, who was then
the *Review*'s Assistant Editor. The Editor, Gerald Barry, later to
become the Editor of the *News Chronicle* and Director of the Festival
of Britain, also played a notable part in the formation of PEP. But
I must add here a few words about Max Nicholson. The *National
Plan for Great Britain*, which Max prepared and wrote when still
only in his twenties, was a brilliant political document. Although
many of its comprehensive proposals now seem familiar, in 1931
it belonged to the realm of political pioneering. Those of us with
more practical experience in government, industry or the social
services recognised it as a beacon in the hopeless confusion of those
post-war years. My own task as the first Secretary of PEP would
have been quite impossible without the equally brilliant succession
of broadsheets and reports largely edited, if not written, by Max
himself. He was younger and even more impatient than some of us;
he resigned more than once. But the collective wisdom of the
Executive Committee prevailed. As Lord Sieff wrote in his memoirs:

> Max represented, as nobody else quite has, what I have always
> admired; the application of the intellect to the everyday pressing
> affairs of men in a steady and unsensational attempt to leave
> them better than they were before; a service of one's fellows by
> planning, not by preaching; blue printing a path to *real* progress,
> not preaching theoretical pie in the sky.[1]

There were other associations inside and outside political parties
striving to sort out the problems of the day. But PEP developed
a fundamentally different approach. The idea of forming a
permanent research body appealed to a number of people, but they
had never met one another. First there were those who assisted with
the original draft plan; then there was a small discussion group that
met at the house of Sir Basil Blackett, who was a Director of the

---

[1] *The Memoirs of Israel Sieff*, p. 192, Weidenfeld & Nicolson, 1970.

Bank of England and chairman of many imperial and international bodies. This group included Julian Huxley, Graeme Haldane and others. I was working at the Oversea Settlement Department under Geoffrey Whiskard, later the first High Commissioner to Australia. But I had a number of other friends who were impressed by the *Week-End Review* Plan: friends from politics central and local (I had fought three national elections in the 1920s, and served three years in local government and on the Board of Guardians in Stepney); friends from university days at Oxford and the London School of Economics; friends from Toynbee Hall; and, above all, friends from America.

We all shared a common concern for the declining position of Britain, but had found no focus for our constructive energies. Conversations with a view to forming a group continued through March 1931, including two Sunday evening dinners at the Ivy Restaurant. To the second dinner, I brought along my chief, Geoffrey Whiskard, the economist Noel Hall and Lawrence Neal, a very old friend and Chairman of Daniel Neal; the title Political and Economic Planning, suggested by J. C. Pritchard, was adopted with some misgivings, and it was agreed to open an office with myself as temporary Secretary.

**The Contribution of Dartington**
During my first visit in 1922 to the United States, as leader of the first Oxford Union debating team, I had made friends with Dorothy Willard Straight. Dorothy's home in New York was the centre of discussion on educational and international matters, and the editorial staff of the *New Republic*, including Walter Lippmann, often dined there. She married Leonard Elmhirst in 1926 and together they created the unique complex of economic and cultural activities at Dartington Hall in Devonshire. Leonard was engaged in forest conservation, soil surveys, scientific farming and agricultural engineering, and, with Dorothy, was heavily involved in long-term rural planning. Between 14 February and 1 April 1931, I was in weekly correspondence with Leonard over the projected PEP. My task was to convince them that the National Plan was worth taking seriously, and that the tentative steps taken in London justified their support. Not all the correspondence published by the *Week-End Review* was flattering. For example, Walter Elliot, a firm believer in planning, remarked that it was too woolly; others feared the

implications and dangers of 'regulating industry'. Fabian groups felt that the Plan shirked the issue of capitalism versus socialism, while Liberals feared a threat to free trade. I was, however, convinced that the basic ideas behind the National Plan were sound, partly because they by-passed, as Max Nicholson wrote, 'the game of party politics as at present played at Westminster';[1] and I wrote to the Elmhirsts, 'I was never more certain that we are on the right track'.[2] Leonard and Dorothy still had reservations. Leonard expressed his doubt as to whether the country was ready for such an innovation as National Planning. Leonard and Dorothy had also to be convinced that our personnel were of the right calibre to undertake such far-reaching research projects. It was too readily and falsely assumed in those days that the Dartington Trust would support any avant-garde venture. But Dorothy had an unusually perceptive mind, which I had seen at work on many and varied schemes in the United States; and Leonard's practical wisdom was shown in his unique approach to rural planning, especially agricultural economics, on which subject he became an international leader. Although our correspondence shows how far-seeing and trusting they were during the critical period from 14 February to the weekend of 18–19 April, when the Directorate of PEP was invited to Dartington and I was made first Secretary, they were not at all easy to convince. But once persuaded, they gave an enormous stimulus to PEP. Not only did they pay the salary of the first Secretary, they also provided many invaluable Dartington weekends, when those present were able to rethink first principles. They were responsible for a series of broadsheets on rural planning and forestry which preserved the balance of rural activity with a largely London-based contingent. Moreover, in later years, mostly inspired by Dartington, PEP produced a series of broadsheets and reports on the visual arts and the film industry.

### A Start, but Stresses and Strains

On 22 March 1931 a meeting was held at University College, London, where Noel Hall was then head of the Department of Political Economy; after playing an important part in the early days of PEP he went on to found the National Institute of Economic and Social Research in 1937 and the Administrative Staff College

---

[1] *A National Plan for Great Britain*, p. i, Supplement to *The Week-End Review*, 14 February 1931.

[2] Undated, February or March 1931, PEP Archive, London School of Economics.

at Henley in 1946. A provisional Directorate was established and the aims and objectives of the organisation were agreed. Sir Basil Blackett was made Chairman and I became Secretary.

Before the meeting specific groups had begun to work on such subjects as public utilities, the machinery of government and the social services. Their meetings continued at Sir Basil Blackett's house, at the Bank of England, and at 24 Essex Street, the office of the *Week-End Review*. They were unco-ordinated and lacked definite planning. It took the spring and summer of 1931 to sort ourselves out.

The two most important steps in the process were the weekend of 18–19 April at Dartington and an Inaugural General Meeting in June. Those present when the Directorate met at Dartington, apart from Sir Basil Blackett and myself, were Gerald Barry, Leonard Elmhirst, Noel Hall, Julian Huxley, Lawrence Neal, Max Nicholson, J. C. Pritchard and Mrs Skelton. The Inaugural General Meeting of members was held on 29 June at the Royal Society of Arts, with Sir Basil Blackett in the chair. The meeting adopted a brief preamble setting out PEP's raison d'être, followed by a comprehensive set of ten resolutions which had largely been thrashed out at the Dartington weekend. The text was as follows:

Being convinced

(a)   that the reorganisation on a national basis of the political, economic and social institutions of the country on lines consistent with British traditions of personal and political freedom is an urgent necessity; and

(b)   that the failure to formulate a National Plan and in due course prepare the country for its adoption will amount to a major national danger:

I      Those present at this Meeting resolve to form themselves, with power to add to their number, into a Society called P.E.P. (Political & Economic Planning) with the object of:

(a) formulating a National Plan;
(b) at a later stage promulgating such a plan.

II     That for convenience P.E.P. adopts as the initial basis of discussion, the Draft National Plan of the *Week-End Review*.

III    That the business of P.E.P. will be to institute inquiry into selected aspects of the plan by means of small study groups e.g. Machinery of Government, Public Utilities, the Social Services, Rural Problems, Building and Town Planning, Imperial Trade, Techniques of Investment.

IV   That P.E.P. endeavours to prepare a National Plan by June 30th, 1934, and that the first year be devoted to a survey and examination of the respective fields.

V   That the study groups shall ordinarily consist of not less than 3 and not more than 10 persons.

VI   P.E.P. for the time being be limited to not more than 100 working members.

VII   That the Governing body be entitled the Directorate and consist of 9 persons, at least 4 of whom will be held responsible for maintaining liaison between the Directorate and specific groups.

VIII   That members be elected by the Directorate with reference to the needs of the work to be undertaken.

IX   That the minimum subscription for membership be 10 shillings per annum.

X   That a general meeting be called not less than twice a year and the Directorate shall have power to call an extraordinary general meeting.

More important for PEP, new personalities began to appear, most of whom had started work on specific groups. Sir Henry Bunbury, then Comptroller of the Post Office and a leader in public administration studies, was a tireless, unpaid worker in PEP for over 30 years; a second-rate document rarely passed his careful eye. Oliver Roskill, one of four famous brothers and one of the first industrial consultants in this country, was responsible, and provided the backbone, for many industrial reports, about which he writes in Chapter 3. Sir Ronald Davison, a retired civil servant, was an authority on labour and social questions. Professor A. M. Carr-Saunders and his colleague Professor Simey at Liverpool helped us on many social problems, especially when the former became Director of the London School of Economics. Then there was John Dower, architect and town planner, a devoted friend until his untimely death; Maxwell Fry, another architect; Harold Howitt of Peat Marwick Mitchell; and Miss Stella Charnaud, who gave us wise counsel and became better known to the world later as Lady Reading of the WVS. The participation of these and many others, drawn from a variety of professions, shows how quickly PEP took root in the early months of 1931 and in the next two years.

A second General Meeting was held at University College on 28 January 1932 and a third on 27 June. By this time latent differences within the Directorate and among the Working Members were beginning to reveal themselves. As Max Nicholson explains (see p. 32ff), the establishing of PEP's directive to work towards the formulation of a National Plan within three years gave rise to differences of emphasis. As early as June 1932, three weeks before the third General Meeting, at the 22nd meeting of the Directorate held at Cookham, problems concerned with publicity, with the technique of planning and with the Chairman's general approach were all coming to a head, and caused the temporary resignation of Max Nicholson.

One of the issues was the speed at which publication of our work would begin. Some members of the Directorate wanted us to rush rapidly into print and a list of pamphlets was drawn up, with names of authors and subjects, with a view to publication in the autumn of 1932. In fact they were never published and some were never written. The main objective had to be to revitalise the groups for a renewed autumn programme of work.

Perhaps more important was the difference of views on what a National Plan involved. This occurred in a climate of opinion in the country that had made some members of the group which founded PEP reluctant to include the word 'planning' in the title. As Noel Hall has put it:

There was good reason for this reluctance. The word 'planning' was at that time undergoing a subtle change of meaning and of weight ... I used to say that any economic system must be in some sense planned, but that since the Russian emphasis on its then novel five-year plans and the introduction of the Fascist controlled state in Italy, Continental writers in socio-economics and politics were increasingly using the word 'planning' as an alternative to totalitarianism. 'Planwirtschaft' spoken with the tone of a Sergeant-Major was replacing the older and quieter Anglo-Saxon word 'planning', meaning considering how you get from here to there. This implies an accurate knowledge of the advantages and disadvantages of 'Here' and as accurate an appraisal as possible of the advantages to be obtained when we get 'There'. The statistical sources and the technique of making and using forecasts were in Britain in 1931 markedly deficient. Planning the development of these was as important as mapping out carefully the pathway of change.[1]

Those who were keenest to develop a single National Plan set up a group known as TEC PLAN, chaired by J. C. Pritchard, of which Max Nicholson, who was a leading member, writes at the beginning of the next chapter. The TEC PLAN group worked very hard at their self-imposed brief, but the position of PEP was precarious. The names of John Dower and Ronald Davison had been wisely added to the Directorate. But our Working Members totalled only 70, attached to different groups, six to Industry, 11 to TEC PLAN, six to Land Planning, four to Agriculture, 15 to Social Structures, four to Public Utilities, five to Education and ten to Finance. There were about 12 effective drafters.

Even with the most perfect teamwork, 70 people could not produce a plan, especially when they were giving only their spare time. The problem was to help evolve a collection of small working groups into a collective and co-ordinated body. The beginnings of this were now evident. The Directorate became more concerned with the general architecture of the plan and apportioned definite fields of work to specific groups.

Meanwhile the divergence between the Chairman and the majority of the Directorate was becoming acute. Sir Basil Blackett had seemed a natural choice as first Chairman, in view of his top public positions in Imperial and International Communications Ltd. and the Colonial Development Fund, his past record as Finance Member of the Government of India, and his directorship of the Bank of England. As a lifelong scholar he combined with his active interests a strong taste for philosophic reflection and discussion of issues. He sometimes jarred on his PEP associates by seemingly woolly discourse about the 'Good Life' and the 'Altogetherness of Everything', and by appearing more interested in pursuing debate than in reaching a plain and constructive conclusion. When on 14 March he told the Directorate of his decision to stand as independent conservative candidate at the St Marylebone by-election he indicated his willingness to give up the chairmanship while remaining a member. His insistence on priority for imperial aspects over international, and

[1] 'Use of the word planning in the early 1930s', 2 December 1980, PEP Archive, LSE.

his attempts to commit PEP to drafts for a pamphlet which were felt to be at variance with majority views, brought to a head during 1932 latent divisions between him and his few devoted followers on the one hand and the broad centre group led by Israel Sieff, L. K. Elmhirst (who were the two main financial backers), Sir Arthur Salter and myself, with the general support of Lawrence Neal, Noel Hall, Oliver Roskill, Geoffrey Whiskard, Ronald Davison and others representing the strong retailing, economic, industrial and civil and social service elements in the uneasy mix of PEP elements. Finding himself in a minority, Blackett gradually withdrew from active participation, and eventually created a situation in which he was deemed to have relinquished his chairmanship, having gone away to South Africa without answering urgent communications or making any provision for the conduct of business in his long absence.

## A New Chairman and New Dynamism

On 5 December 1932 Israel Sieff, then Vice-Chairman of Marks & Spencer Ltd., was invited to be Chairman of the Directorate. He was vitally important for the progress and evolution of PEP. My introduction to him had come through a mutual friend, the late Sir Wyndham Deedes, a distinguished soldier, administrator and idealist, who returned to London in the 1920s to devote himself to social work, and whom I met at Toynbee Hall. I lunched with Israel at the Savoy on Saturday 18 May 1931 and for four hours unfolded our plans. He agreed to give us help, financial and otherwise. Later on, a small invited group dined with Israel in a private room and they all testified to the magnetic authority and charm of our new leader. When Israel Sieff became Chairman 18 months later he did much to shape the course of the difficult but fruitful years from 1933 onwards. He contributed greatly from his experience in industry; he gave time and counsel, and above all, dynamic leadership. At his death in 1972 he was President of PEP.

Israel Sieff became a great friend of the members but more particularly of Leonard and Dorothy Elmhirst, to whom he confided his mind, his doubts and dreams about PEP. He once wrote to Leonard:

> I have been trying to recollect what were the motives that brought me into contact with you and PEP. I think I felt that from my special and particular experience in business it might be possible

to work out some general principles for industry as a whole. I don't quite know how far that succeeded because my PEP colleagues were so fertile in their ideas and so imaginative that my first motive was edged out of place.[1]

That last sentence betrays far too much modesty about Israel's part in what he called 'the ginger group of gradualness'.[2] Another dimension of his mind is shown in a letter to the Elmhirsts: 'there are two basic ideas which superficially appear to be in conflict, but are really to be reconciled'. The first is taken from the Talmud: 'If I am not for myself who will be for me? If I am for myself only, what am I?' The other is from Thomas Jefferson: 'Nothing then is unchangeable but the inherent and inalienable rights of man'. Then Israel goes on in his letter to say:

As you know there is a continuous strife in us between the fear of isolation and powerlessness and the urge and need to assert our ego. Actually what we have to achieve in every group is to find the spirit, the values and the relationship which will combine the joy and satisfaction of association with the inalienable right of each one to play the role his mind and spirit best fit him for.

Before the Savoy Dinner at the end of March 1933 to which I will refer later, he wrote again:

A National Government has stemmed off an impending crisis but what next? There are tendencies at work today which are dangerous symptoms; one is a policy of drift and irresolution, the other is a sense of frustration of effort. If these tendencies are not checked and replaced by bold and constructive plans we shall inevitably be faced with alternative proposals of an extreme nature and hasty emotional appeals to the electorate; this would be fatal.[3]

Although J. C. Pritchard resigned in November 1932 and Max Nicholson had resigned from the Directorate in July (see p. 35), Max was present again at its meeting on 21 December and promised 'to help in whatever manner he could in the great work, particularly on the persuasion and publicity side'.[4] At the same meeting Israel

---

[1] This and subsequent quotations are from correspondence in PEP Archive, LSE.
[2] *The Memoirs of Israel Sieff*, p. 176, op. cit.
[3] Letter to Kenneth Lindsay, March 1931.
[4] Directorate meeting, 21 December 1932, minutes, PEP Archive, LSE.

Sieff promised to make sacrifices of time and energy; more precise plans were made for the fourth General Meeting on 16 January 1933, and for an important dinner in March. At last we were in the presence of leadership.

On 13 March a very full meeting of the Directorate was held under the new Chairman. Those present were Gerald Barry, Sir Henry Bunbury, R. L. Davison, John Dower, Leonard Elmhirst, Noel Hall, Julian Huxley, Lawrence Neal, Max Nicholson, Sir Arthur Salter, Sir Geoffrey Whiskard and myself.

This was to be the last General Meeting held and one of the last meetings of the Directorate. It was clear to some of us that in future we needed meetings of Working Members and a small Executive was established, comprising Israel Sieff, Leonard Elmhirst, Sir Geoffrey Whiskard and myself, and met on 5 April; Max Nicholson was included *de facto* after a few meetings. The first Working Members' Meeting took place on 25 July. As usual new members appeared, including Harold Emmerson (later Permanent Secretary of the Ministry of Labour), Hilda Matheson and James Hosken. It was now possible to discern the future shape of PEP. 1933 was the year of decision.

Between April and July 1933 a series of decisions was taken, notably to establish the Executive Committee for direction and general administration; to set up a Publicity Committee to issue Broadsheets at regular intervals; and, equally important, to form a Documents Committee with the following terms of reference:

(a) to receive all documents which are either
    1. adopted by groups
    2. submitted to it for comment or direction;

(b) to consider such documents from the point of view of
    1. their integration into a general plan
    2. their suitability for a Broadsheet
    3. their suitability for limited circulation either to members of PEP or other selected individuals;

(c) to report to the Executive Committee any other matters requiring action by them.

These terms of reference reflect the headache which the persistent problem of co-ordinating a dozen groups and scores of documents

*Israel Sieff*

*Leonard Elmhirst*

had now become. For the same reason it was agreed to find new premises and accordingly we met for the first time on 18 July at 16 Queen Anne's Gate, where later in November the PEP Club was opened.

## Group Working

The method of group working was the key to effective decision making. The climate for determined effort was both an exceptional challenge and exceptionally forbidding; under an Executive concerned with the overall programme and interconnection between its parts and also acting as a pace-maker, the working groups were all-important. We were looking for people who had first-hand experience in industry and administration and who were also capable of seeing their own specialisation in a wider context. Secondly, we wanted members who would themselves be capable of contributing to group discussions and willing to devote much of their spare time to these tasks, without any published attribution which would have precluded the assistance of many experts who occupied official positions. It was not easy to find men and women who combined objective and constructive thinking with a background of practical experience, and who were also ready to find time outside working hours for an arduous task and to derive satisfaction from working with like-minded people in a group effort.

The groups were composed of a judicious mixture of laymen and experts, plus consultants called in as needed. The chairmen and drafting secretaries were usually appointed by the Executive.

As Lawrence Neal pointed out to me in 1932, the chairman needed also to have qualities of leadership. For example, the Industries Group went ahead largely because of the personal inspiration and drive of its chairman Israel Sieff and the ability of its secretary Oliver Roskill, with his remarkable gifts for fact-finding, technical understanding and constructive analysis, and produced a valuable series of industry reports. After all, our main resources and capital were our active members and the quality of their work. The total budget of PEP in the eight years before the war was only about £60,000: yet PEP published 156 Broadsheets and 14 Reports.

## First Steps to Influence Key People

The first need had been to build up our resources without any publicity. After this busy seed-time came the harvest, richer than anyone expected. Operating from our new premises in Queen Anne's Gate we were able to issue the first of what has become over 600 Broadsheets and to produce longer Reports in book form on, for example, Iron and Steel, Cotton, and Coal followed by others on Housing, Gas and the Location of Industry – all between 1933 and 1939. These Reports and the groups who worked on them brought us in touch with key people in industry and the Civil Service.

We referred to these people as 'consultants'. They gave their time freely and became friends as well as advisers. Many people, as Israel Sieff said at the time, were groping for new methods of studying complicated problems and they found in PEP signposts, direct lines of approach and in some cases acceptable conclusions. This was due to a growing conviction that PEP work was thorough and well thought out, and I remember him saying, at the end of a long working day in the new premises, how satisfied he was that PEP was fulfilling a growing need.

As our influence grew we were asked by citizens of other countries, including India (see p. 113), the USA and later Israel, how they should proceed in starting an equivalent of PEP in their own contexts. It would have been useless to send them a constitution setting out objectives. Sir Alexander Carr-Saunders wrote to me many years later about such requests and suggested

> a public history to convey the idea of PEP, its procedure, its internal and external relations. All these aspects of PEP are unusual, perhaps even unique – certainly unique when conceived together. To convey it will need subtlety; it would emerge best from a treatment which had all these characteristics of PEP in mind and sought to make them come to light in the course of a narrative rather than by direct exposition.[1]

It took some years to create a common outlook, a workable administration; but two other internal aids proved invaluable. First there were the Internal Bulletins which conveyed domestic information about our group meetings and our personnel and about the external impact of PEP itself. Reading back through over 100 of them I can see how it reminded members that PEP was not merely a machine for setting up unrelated groups to discuss important and particular topics. I can see how the Bulletins and the Club at 16 Queen Anne's Gate created an esprit de corps. Perhaps the Club,

[1] June 1961, PEP Archive, LSE.

so charmingly managed by May Hosken and her collaborators, was the biggest factor in making possible more group discussions, working dinner meetings, press conferences and regular lunch talks by chairmen of groups, Members of Parliament, trade unionists and eminent men and women from all walks of life. PEP had contact with over 300 leading personalities in the 1930s; the Club had 150 members and the Broadsheet circulation averaged over 2000.

Our object was to influence key people and to rely on the Press to carry the message further. This method worked very much to our advantage in the years 1933–39. It was unusual not to have leading articles in the main newspapers following publication of Broadsheets and Reports.

Another method of 'going public' was the large-scale formal dinner of which there were two, one as early as 29 March 1933, and the second after the publication of the 100th Broadsheet on 1 June 1937. Among those present at the first dinner were the Lords Balfour of Burleigh, De La Warr, Linlithgow, Melchett and Eustace Percy, Sir Edward Grigg, R. S. Hudson MP, Harold Macmillan MP, Lionel Montagu, Sir Wyndham Portal, Major Oliver Stanley MP, A. W. Street, Sir Stephen Tallents, Sir Raymond Unwin and Sir Horace Wilson, not to mention those linked with PEP. Israel Sieff and I spoke on behalf of PEP and the Rt. Hon. Oliver Stanley replied. Needless to say, the speeches were prepared after intimate consultation with members of the Directorate. In the first speech the insets read as follows:

Origin of PEP
The Meaning of Planning
The Human Element
The Profit Motive
Sharing the Surplus
Self-government for Industry
Purchasing Power and Lower Costs
The Chartered Corporation
Labour and Management
Marketing Sets the Pace
Parliament and Industry
Building and Agriculture
Land
Finance

The second speech covered:

A National Employment Policy
Basis for the Social Services and their Integration
Local Government and Community Services
Democracy and Government
Planning and Information
National Projection

At the second dinner the speakers included Sir Herbert Samuel, Tom Williams, Sir Thomas Barlow, Sir Richard Gregory, Dr J. J. Mallon, Warden of Toynbee Hall, and Max Nicholson, by then the General Secretary. Ronald Cartland MP, who was present, was the first Member of Parliament to be killed in the war; and Sir Arnold Wilson MP, an older man who made a monumental study for us of Industrial Assurance, insisted on active service in the RAF and was also killed while on duty as a tail gunner in a bombing raid. As the storm gathered in that last period before the war, some of the Working Members of PEP became occupied with emergency activities, but PEP itself continued with much of its normal work.

None of the developments with PEP happened by accident; they were the result of cut-and-thrust discussion and practical experience. PEP might have developed in other ways; it might have broken down and nearly did more than once; it might have been side-tracked into propaganda or politics or into the fatal mistake of issuing 'manifestoes'. PEP also avoided another and more subtle danger, which too often besets such a body: that of developing into a self-centred coterie. It was determined not to become remote from political tensions and the economic struggle. It must be remembered that in 1931 not only were there over two million unemployed; local Boards of Guardians still existed; there was no national Supplementary Benefit, old age pensions were derisory and social and health services fragmented; the school-leaving age was only 14. There was an absence of international bodies, except a listless League of Nations. A body like PEP therefore met a real need, but it faced considerable criticism at its birth. Criticisms by Conservatives, Liberals and Socialists have already been mentioned; indeed, the word 'planning' was not popular with any political party.

Most members of PEP were either non-political or anti-party. When in 1933 the Prime Minister invited me to fight a by-election on behalf of the National Government at Kilmarnock I was naturally worried, because I was Secretary of a non-party organisation. Friendly correspondence took place between Israel Sieff and Ramsay MacDonald and it was agreed that I should be released from my immediate daily work in PEP.

Over the years PEP has had to define its relations with government and parliament. Before 1931 there was little experience on which to base such a relationship, except in the case of Lloyd George, whose Garden Suburb secretariat, composed of influential political and academic personnel, served his wishes especially from 1918–22. It had in fact long been my conviction and dream that the House of Commons could only work efficiently if Members were supplied with much better factual information from some impartial source. The following chapters give instances of PEP's pre-war publications which are known to have had widespread influence on public discussion, and this influence has grown in the post-war period. In recent years PEP has gone further towards realising my dream by producing invaluable reports on the machinery of government, on the committee system and on the need for better facilities for Members of Parliament (see p. 155).

**The Influence of Reports**
It is always difficult to estimate the influence of research work on practical activity or to measure results. PEP had no formal relations with the government of the day in 1931–39, though members of all parties, including Ministers, were friendly and attended our private and public functions. But it can be shown how some of our publications and decisions influenced government policy.

One example was the work on regional development and the location of industry. From the second Broadsheet in May 1933 on Town and Country Planning, and succeeding ones on Employment Policy, Agriculture, Population etc., a new approach on these subjects was emerging, until *Planning* No. 52 (4 June 1935) announced:

> This week a preliminary meeting is being held to which people who have given special thought to these questions (of regional development) are coming from Scotland, South Wales, Merseyside, Tyneside, Devon, and other parts of the country ... PEP will try to serve as a clearing-house for information and suggestions and will be able to put a certain amount of resources

and a technique of work at the disposal of those interested.

By this time I represented in Parliament a section of a Depressed Area, and I discussed the problem with George Douglas-Hamilton (later Lord Selkirk), who became the Commissioner for Special Areas in Scotland. I doubt whether any other body could have assembled the group which began to work on this problem. A memorandum on Trading Estates was circulated within PEP; a member of the group, none other than Max Nicholson, contributed on 8 July 1935 an article to *The Times*. The Editor, Geoffrey Dawson, gave his influential support to it. On 3 December the Prime Minister announced in the House of Commons the Government's intention to proceed with Trading Estates and in 1936 the Special Areas Reconstruction Act was passed.

PEP had been similarly pioneering studies in the location of industry, for example with the Broadsheet under that title of December 1936, which was followed in July 1937 by the setting up of the Royal Commission on the geographical distribution of the industrial population with Sir Montague Barlow as Chairman. We had been constantly in touch with him before his appointment and steps were taken to keep the Commission informed of PEP work that might be of interest to them. Our work had certainly been of influence even before we published our main Report on *The Location of Industry in Great Britain* in 1939.

Another example concerns the publication of the Press Report in 1938. The group which prepared it consisted of 12 members, ten of whom served for the full period. Practically all the members, who included Gerald Barry, Geoffrey Crowther, S. C. Leslie, Hilda Matheson and L. P. Scott of the *Manchester Guardian*, belonged or had belonged to the Press so that for PEP standards the group was a little too expert; it was also composed of very busy people. I well remember many luncheon meetings when the journalists were hard pressed for time. However, over 80 meetings were held. The Report, which advocated among other things the establishment of a Press Council, sold 500 copies in ten days. When the House of Commons debated the subject of the Press in 1948 I saw many copies of the Report in the House. Even the many critics of PEP acknowledged its relevance, including Kingsley Martin of the *New Statesman*, who wrote: 'This is the result of an elaborate piece of cooperative investigation in which a number of men with good practical knowledge of Fleet Street have cooperated. It is sensible and honest.'[1]

A large international interest in PEP was awakened by a series of Broadsheets on international trade starting with *Inquest on Ottawa* (June 1936) and finishing with a massive *International Trade Report* (May 1937). It was not easy in the 1930s to stand up against the growing forces of nationalism. It was due to Israel Sieff, Sir Arthur Salter and Leonard Elmhirst, fortified by leading bankers and economists and scores of specialists working on a voluntary basis in our groups, that PEP saw the essential links between domestic and foreign policy.

Such concrete examples can explain more clearly than pages of generalisations how PEP made its contribution to current problems. *The British Health Services* and *The British Social Services* were also published in 1937, as well as *The British Press* in 1938. These Reports anticipated the National Health Service, the Beveridge Plan and the Press Council. All of them sold thousands of copies. The Health Services Report became a sort of Bible at the Ministry of Health, according to Sir William Jameson, the Chief Medical Officer, who used it as a basis for designing the National Health Service; and by 1939 a Pelican edition had run into 25,000 copies.

**Post-experience of PEP Members**

One or two examples will show how PEP became a training ground for the wider activities of its members.

Lawrence Neal was a member of the Sea-Fish Commission from 1933–36 and assisted considerably in the drafting of its two Reports on the Herring and White Fish Industries. During the war he was Deputy-Secretary of the first Town and Country Planning Ministry and later Vice-Chairman of the Crawley New Town Corporation.

John Dower, who had responsibility for Town Planning in PEP, later, when working within the Town and Country Planning Ministry, produced a Report which led to the establishment of National Parks.

Early in the war Sir Arthur Salter and others persuaded Max Nicholson to join the Ministry of Shipping, where, as Head of Allocation of Tonnage, he was involved in the high-level strategic Conferences at Cairo, Quebec and elsewhere down to Potsdam.

[1] PEP Archive, LSE.

After the war Herbert Morrison, as Deputy Prime Minister with responsibility for economic planning, secured his services for a further period before, through Julian Huxley's persuasion, he moved across to environmental conservation as Director-General of the Nature Conservancy.

For four years Michael Young was Secretary of PEP, where he developed some original ideas on active democracy in local government and the importance of the consumer. After being Head of the Labour Party's Research Department and Secretary of its Policy Committee from 1945 to 1951, he carried these ideas further when he created such enterprises as *Which* and *Where*, and drafted the constitution of the Open University. He is now Lord Young of Dartington.

My own later experience lay in Parliament and European studies. As Civil Lord of the Admiralty from 1935–37 and Parliamentary Secretary to the Board of Education from 1937–40 I had opportunities to carry forward some ideas originating in PEP, particularly in starting the Youth Service and the Council for Education in Music and the Arts, which led to the establishment of the Arts Council. As a Minister in the later 1930s I was pleased to see Members of Parliament frequenting PEP premises, and to observe them using our material for their speeches, with the original copy, as it were, under the desk. Later elected as independent for a university seat, I am now the only surviving MP elected by proportional representation.

### The Climate Outside

There is an unending sequence of books about the 1930s, in my view too often coloured by the political slant of the authors. Most writers exaggerate the importance of Communists and Fascists, who were far fewer here than on the Continent. Mosley had a minimum of influence in the Labour Party and elsewhere. The Communist Party soon ceased to influence public opinion. Some books such as *The Thirties*[1] by Malcolm Muggeridge were caricatures of a decade. The scholarly classic, *Britain between the Wars*[2] by Professor Mowat, has for long been the most reliable history of the period; but there is now also a group of younger historians, including Paul Addison,

[1] *The Thirties: 1930–40 in Great Britain*, London, Collins, 1967.
[2] *Britain between the Wars: 1918–1940*, London, Methuen, 1955.

Gillian Peele and Chris Cook, who are restoring the balance and looking at the whole period in a wider perspective. A book called *The Slump*, referring to the many discussions which took place at the time, finds that

> these inquiries played a vital part in the emergence of what has been called 'a consensus on social responsibility' in the years leading up to the Second World War. Many of the recommendations on social policy underlying the Welfare State were derived from the investigations and social thought of the thirties. Articulated through the social literature and given form in reports from professional bodies and groups such as PEP, they were already finding limited acceptance in government circles in the years before the war.[1]

Many of us at PEP were closely in touch with public opinion and aware of the facts of unemployment. My own constituency in Kilmarnock was hard hit, though far better off in 1935 than in 1933, and my election majority was doubled between those two years, when unemployment was halved. Archbishop Temple of York was among those deeply concerned with unemployment and wished to engage PEP in an inquiry financed by the Pilgrim Trust. It was decided to release David Owen, Secretary of our Civic Division, to direct the survey, which resulted in the book *Men without Work*.[2] Others who had connections with PEP in the 1930s were engaged on constructive work with the unemployed, for example John Newsom (later Director of Education in Hertfordshire) in Durham and Henry Brooke (later Home Secretary) in South Wales. PEP was anxious to listen to any constructive ideas. I remember an experiment tried out at the PEP Club on 4 March 1936. The notice for an evening meeting read:

> Mr. Tom Harrisson, who after his study of cannibal tribes in the New Hebrides, has been applying similar methods of research to a social survey of Bolton, linked with the Mass Observation movement, will give an account of the surprising discoveries made there on public house life, class distinctions in cemeteries, and the working of religions and political institutions. He will suggest various

---

[1] Stevenson, John and Cook, Chris, *The Slump: Society and Politics during the Depression*, p. 29, London, Cape, 1977.
[2] Cambridge, CUP, 1938.

points of contact between his work at the consumer end and PEP work on the social and economic structure. Mr. Sieff will be in the chair.

Tom Harrisson switched to work in South East Asia for a long time before returning to Sussex University, but one of his associates, Charles Madge, an active worker at PEP, and others like Mark Abrams, later Chairman of PEP, and Michael Young developed new uses for the social survey.

Some movements, popular in their time, had their day and then ceased to be. The Peace Ballot attracted 11 million adherents, but by 1938–39 the people were demanding bullets rather than ballots. The membership of the Left Book Club, associated with the names of Victor Gollancz, Michael Foot and John Strachey, grew into thousands but was frowned on by Herbert Morrison and Ernest Bevin and petered out. Other movements, especially the Next Five Years Group, overlapped to some extent with our personnel; it was run by Lord Allen of Hurtwood and Captain Harold Macmillan MP, and we remained on friendly terms. But we were essentially a research group; they issued political manifestos. In fact they became a sort of unofficial opposition. Cabinet Ministers with whom we were in touch, like Walter Elliot, Oliver Stanley and others from all parties, never found a base strong enough to challenge the 'old guard' in the House of Commons until Winston Churchill became the popular choice of all parties in 1940.

The Fabian Research Department was of course Socialist, but G. D. H. Cole was able to write to us that 'PEP does not represent my own point of view, since I am definitely a Socialist; but ... I have found the PEP reports of very great value'.[1] Lloyd George, who had been busy with his Yellow Books, was impressed by the quality of our consultants and wrote to me asking how much they cost us. He was staggered to discover that the bulk of the research came voluntarily from members who drew on their own experience and assessed it with others in group discussions.

Chatham House (the Royal Institute of International Affairs) was a different proposition. It was then beginning to expand its study groups under the supervision of Commander King-Hall, a colleague in the House of Commons and the founder of the Hansard Society.

---

[1] *Planning* No. 100, 1 June 1937, p. 12.

At the time we were more concerned with economic and social questions, but Lionel Curtis wrote to me in 1934:

> I am always deeply interested to hear from Harold Macmillan about the progress of your enquiries; at Chatham House we are constantly finding that international questions can only be understood by studying our own national domestic questions. You, no doubt, find that in studying domestic problems they constantly broaden out into the international theme. And that is why I should like to see our twin Institutes next door to each other with a hole in the wall between them.[1]

In fact, several years later John Pinder, as Director of PEP, worked very closely with Chatham House and the two Institutes produced a series of distinguished joint publications on Europe (see p. 156).

**The Future**

The fact that PEP was founded in 1931 when the country was in the grip of a grave depression might suggest that a similar initiative is needed today. In fact PEP has continued its existence, since 1978 through PSI, and the present Chairman, Sir Montague Finniston, can look back with pride to his predecessors who include Sir Basil Blackett, Lord Sieff, Leonard Elmhirst, Lord Holford and Lord Roll. The annual budget has risen from £2000 in the first year to over £1 million. Lord Roll, now Joint President, has stressed in his Introduction to this volume that PEP, and now PSI, has through this half-century been guided by the principles of relevance, scholarship, independence and impartiality.

Many of us would like to see particular changes in the political machine, but is there a will to agree about more fundamental underlying problems? Can a mixed economy work without some political consensus? Can we retain in Britain radio and television free from government or purely commercial interests? Can we retain an independent Civil Service and police force? How is it that political remedies too often become stale slogans and therefore result in sterile confrontations? Political parties too often become, as Whitehead once said, 'vehicles for inert ideas'. But at least we are still an open society and PSI, the successor to PEP, if it retains its courage, remains poised to continue its influence on events.

[1] PEP Archive, LSE.

# 2

# PEP through the 1930s: Growth, Thinking, Performance

## Max Nicholson

As Kenneth Lindsay has explained, the spring and summer months of 1931 were devoted to bringing together a varied gathering of volunteers from different professions and vocations, and trying to sort them out coherently as effective participants in a series of study groups intended to review, and to advance from, the initial platform provided by the National Plan. After the original recruitment in March the most important wave of newcomers joined in June, including the future Chairman, Israel Sieff, Oliver Roskill, Professor A. M. Carr-Saunders, Sir Henry Bunbury, Harold Howitt, Dr C. P. Blacker, John Dower and others representing in the highest degree the qualities which PEP sought to focus, and to be focused by.

The Inaugural General Meeting on 29 June at the Royal Society of Arts (see p. 13) may be taken as the point from which preliminary contacts and debates began to give way to a going concern. In the Chairman's statement it was explained that for the ensuing two years small study groups dealing with particular aspects of national life would work without publicity, in concert with a co-ordinating Directorate, towards the production of a general plan to be completed within three years. This seemingly innocuous programme was soon to give rise to serious conflicts of view. My assumption had been that in order to clarify the framework of the plan it was most urgent to make progress with Machinery of Government and the Technique of Planning. On the first topic a preliminary meeting at Sir Basil Blackett's house on 27 March had rapidly become bogged down over its terms of reference, and the subject afterwards became almost taboo. On 30 April a preliminary meeting had been held on

Technique of Planning, attended by J. C. Pritchard (who became Chairman of the group we called TEC PLAN), J. W. Lawrence, A. E. Blake, P. Hutchison, P. Skelton and myself. This group viewed its function as being 'to form an advance guard which should try to discover and deal with the various unsolved and actually undefined problems likely to arise at the stage when PEP has analysed the troubles to be faced, outlined means of tackling them, and is ready by summer 1933 to integrate them into a plan'. It was envisaged that the group would have to advise by what principles and techniques discrepancies between parts of the plan could be averted or corrected, and how to safeguard against failures of timing or overloading of critical points. By the second meeting, on 12 May, papers had already been prepared for discussion on planning in the USA, Germany (pre-Hitler) and the USSR. The group later agreed on a need for rapid intensive work, involving each member in not less than six hours weekly on its behalf, backed by a series of exacting weekend meetings, as well as others during the evening in London. TEC PLAN accordingly soon became the most advanced group not only in its concept of planning but in the volume of work accomplished.

**Early Efforts and Latent Conflicts**
As other groups got into their somewhat more deliberate stride it gradually emerged that while all were committed to reviewing objectively their chosen fields, and to submitting to some kind of eventual co-ordination, none shared TEC PLAN's enthusiasm for embracing planning as a new and vital professional technique and discipline leading to a more effective and comparable handling of complex issues, at the stages both of preparation and of action. This divergence, which will be further discussed later, first came to a head between TEC PLAN and the powerful and confident Industries Group, whose different approach is described in the following chapter.

In October, PEP's first office at 10 Gray's Inn Place became operative. It is worth noting here that PEP assembled itself out of the air and started working actively without waiting for such mundane appurtenances as an office, a budget, or a formal constitution. It did however set great store by communication. There were more than 60 members at the Second General Meeting at University College on 28 January 1932, notable among them Sir

Arthur Salter and Thomas Barlow. Reports were made by the Chairmen of nine groups: Industry, Agriculture, Public Utilities, Finance, Social Structure, Land Planning, Education, TEC PLAN and Government. The meeting led to a request to each group to send in, by 25 March, a brief answer to three questions:

1. What are the ideal conditions which you visualise as ultimately obtainable within your field?
2. What is the utmost practicable long-term objective, say 25 years?
3. What should be the immediate short-term programme 1933–37?

These questions illustrate an ambitious time-scale of work which it proved impossible to sustain in the face of the chronic British addiction to 'muddling through'. The growing urgency of international political and economic problems, and the need for more intensive information and education of the public about planning, added to the pressures confronting the Directorate as PEP entered its second year. The manpower, funds and other resources available were grossly insufficient for its enormous self-imposed task, even given the dedicated efforts of over a hundred Working Members and their wealth of influential contacts. The attainment of credibility was becoming urgent. Internal demands were intensifying for early action to achieve it by modifications of the programme, which would also relieve latent conflicts within. The latest and most serious of these centred around the inclination of the Chairman, Sir Basil Blackett, to look at the outside world in terms of a British Imperial mission. This was not acceptable to the majority view, whose spokesman was Sir Arthur Salter, for an unequivocally world outlook, as had indeed been strongly urged in the original National Plan. The divergence over this, and other differences between Blackett and the majority of the Directorate, resulted in his departure from the Chairmanship, as Kenneth Lindsay has recounted (pp. 16–17).

This most traumatic episode in PEP's early history fortunately passed without publicity or serious recriminations, and with a minimum of resignations. It confirmed the cohesion and resolution of the majority of the membership, but in doing so it virtually put an end to the strained but constructive dialogue between the Technique of Planning Group and the others tackling specific subject areas. TEC PLAN ploughed an increasingly lonely furrow, taking on itself the thorough working over and reformulation of the original National Plan, and the testing of its underlying principles and methods. When its work was completed the rift had become so wide that the Directorate was no longer thinking seriously in terms of producing any comprehensive and co-ordinated plan. TEC PLAN accordingly published its definitive conclusions independently, in December 1933, under the modest title *A View on Planning*. In its two dozen pages it covered much the same broad field as the National Plan, with revisions and explanations reflecting two years of intensive group work. Except in so far as I myself formed a common link it was not however pursued further within PEP. The regrettable fact was that not only the nation and its leaders but even the main body of PEP members were not really interested in planning as a process and a discipline. The very word eventually became unpalatable to some.

Returning, however, to the summer of 1932, much else was happening in PEP. A quest was in progress for a sound and acceptable fresh definition of planning, bringing out the distinction between 'Communist Planning' and 'Capitalist Planning', and reconciling the theoretical with the practical. It was found necessary to identify different functional categories of members, fulfilling complementary roles, and to arrive at a more effective decentralised structure, linking kindred groups within an Economic and a Civic Division, capable of undertaking a good deal of initial co-ordination on their own. Growing importance was attached to pursuing 'all and every method for securing acceptance of a plan for Great Britain',[1] especially through a well-timed and well-conceived programme of publications.

These pressing problems siphoned off a good deal of energy but did little to relieve growing tensions. In this confused period I felt compelled on 26 July to put in my resignation from the Directorate, and maintained it in face of persuasion to the contrary; I relented however to the extent of agreeing to help on specific tasks related to the badly-needed persuasion and publicity programme. I was, indeed, torn between my primary concern to develop and apply genuine national planning and a growing awareness that the resistance was proving too great, both within and outside PEP. The question was whether the attainable half-loaf of comprehensive,

[1] Directorate meeting 7 July 1932, quoted in agenda, PEP Archive, LSE.

factual, constructive review of the entire range of national activities and policies was better than no bread, and what hope it might hold of winning the other half later. Israel Sieff, taking over as Chairman at the New Year of 1933, brought fresh inspiration and rapid action. We differed greatly in background and ways of thinking, but he soon won me over. I have never met anyone I have more deeply valued and admired. A close understanding developed between us, and although we by no means always agreed I cannot remember ever entering into serious conflict with him. His wisdom and empathy were a perpetual strength.

**PEP Goes Public**
During the next few weeks things happened fast. The four-man Executive of Sieff, Elmhirst, Whiskard and Lindsay, in which I participated soon after its establishment, was more businesslike than the Directorate it replaced (see p. 19). The budget was expanded to the dizzy level of £3835. Working Members were recognised and the rest classed as Associates. On the Publicity Committee, which was now my special care, I had the pleasure of working closely again with Gerald Barry. On 29 March we took our first step towards going public with a large-scale formal dinner at the Savoy attended by a hundred members and guests and addressed by Israel Sieff and Kenneth Lindsay, whose speeches were to form PEP's earliest publication. The guest list (see p. 23) demonstrated both Kenneth Lindsay's thorough penetration of the more thoughtful circles supporting the then National Government and of the moderate activists in public affairs, but also PEP's failure to win support from trade union leaders, the politically-minded Left, and the organised employers and managers then forming two distinct groups. The main speech by Israel Sieff, which expounded PEP's basic thinking in concrete terms and lasted forty-five minutes, makes impressive reading. (The headings of its various sections are listed on p. 23). Unfortunately Oliver Stanley's reply for the government is not included in the currently available record; it was sympathetic, but following events were to conspire to divert attention at the highest political levels from the fundamental changes in principle and practice which PEP sought. Among these contemporary events were Hitler's appointment as Chancellor of Germany and the ensuing suppression of opposition elements there, which had immediate repercussions here due to the influence of well-informed refugees.

Hindsight suggests that the greatest chance of setting the United Kingdom on a fresh long-term course had been missed. Most of the next 20 years were to be pre-empted by preparation for, conduct of, and recovery from World War II. Even had this been recognised, however, it might well have been argued that the new PEP programme made sense, concentrating as it did on immediate measures of reconstruction, industry by industry and service by service.

The dinner was rated a success in that it put PEP on the map, assembled a wide and influential group of informed supporters, and prepared the way for the launching next month of the first of hundreds of regular Broadsheets in the series which we entitled *Planning*. This dealt not with generalities but with the reconstruction of the Iron and Steel Industry. It was followed at fortnightly intervals by others on Town and Country Planning, Britain and World Trade, Employment Policy, the Public Concern, and Planning in America, demonstrating the breadth as well as the depth of PEP's scope.

It should be explained at this point that after two years of postponing any form of publication PEP had reluctantly brought itself to take the plunge, but had characteristically chosen a low-key and unobtrusive medium. The inspiration for this came from Israel Sieff, who had been impressed by the successes gained in promoting Zionism through the private circulation of a series of well thought-out 'broadsheets' to leading opinion-formers. By following such a pattern circulation could be concentrated in areas where it appeared most important; anonymity could be preserved; and a certain club atmosphere could be created among readers who would feel privileged and linked together by the regular receipt of material which often gave a preview of forthcoming Reports and of incipient policies. To sustain this fortnightly flow at a high standard presupposed that enough working groups would be producing enough suitably digested material which they could be persuaded to release for the necessary rewriting in the lively yet disciplined house style adopted for *Planning*. In fact it did prove possible to maintain the regular schedule. As to the selected design it can now be disclosed that this was shamelessly plagiarised from a then current avant-garde literary periodical entitled, if memory serves, *New Verse*. It proved a convenient and attractive format for carrying PEP's message over the years, and its length, with plenty of bold side-headings, enabled even busy readers to absorb its contents when other heavier offerings repelled them.

The Reports, on the other hand, were addressed to readers with the necessary focus of interest and background of training and experience to be prepared to tackle much more solid and if need be semi-technical material. Those lacking such qualifications could usually rest assured that what they most needed to know in the Reports was already available in the more readable and compact form of the Broadsheets. The process of linkage was reinforced from time to time by reproducing in a Broadsheet comments by leading industrialists and others on a Report, and by summarising its reception, especially in the technical press.

Shortly after the Savoy dinner PEP moved into its spacious and convenient new headquarters at 16 Queen Anne's Gate, overlooking St James's Park, and the full Iron and Steel Report (see p. 56), first of a long line, was published in July. Messages published in the Broadsheets from leading personalities in their fields demonstrated a warm and appreciative reception for the new initiatives.

### The Principle of Anonymity

Incidentally, however, some embarrassment arose over reconciling PEP's prized tradition of anonymity with its excursions into the public arena. The core of this anonymity was the non-disclosure of names of group members, which was a practical necessity in order to enable civil servants and managers in large organisations to participate in discussing critical aspects and policy issues which, if they had been named, would have aroused speculation concerning the intentions and attitudes of their parent bodies, and perhaps led to friction with less intellectually adventurous colleagues. As much of the drafting in this period was actually done by group members it was also impracticable to name a particular author for a Report or Broadsheet. These limitations were, however, gradually mitigated by holding press conferences at the launching of Reports, at which trusted journalists were allowed to meet and question members of the group on a basis of confidentiality.

It was quite plain that the existence and general aims and nature of PEP itself could not remain confidential, and indeed must be fully explained, subject to the anonymity of Working Members. This was done regularly in the *Planning* Broadsheets, and was largely successful, although in certain quarters suspicion persisted that PEP was a subversive secret society aiming to spring upon the nation a fully-fledged conspiracy for a Communist or Fascist State. On one occasion this was pressed so strongly upon the Metropolitan Police that I had a visit from an embarrassed officer of the Special Branch, to whom I showed a list of Working Members revealing just who these dangerous revolutionaries were.

The only practical issue which gave some difficulty was the publication of a list of members of the governing body. After the original Directorate lapsed during 1933, management had passed to the small Executive, which met some 80 times during the decade. In 1936 it was found desirable to create a new senior Council. It was felt by members, however, that no Council names could fairly and comprehensively represent the wide range of expertise, affiliations and attitudes combined within PEP, and the difference was only settled after a long wait for a consensus.

Another matter of embarrassment was the very low proportion of women among the Working Members. Although a number were on the list only a handful took an active part, including Elizabeth Denby, Eva Hubback, Hilda Matheson, Dr Innes Pearse of the Peckham Pioneer Health Centre and Jacqueline Tyrwhitt. We were always in theory looking for women, but our poor success, for whatever reason, occasioned some adverse comment.

Within the first two years of Broadsheet publication 48 had appeared, accompanied by two more full Reports, on *The British Cotton Industry* and *Housing England*, together with a Self-Government for Industry Bill. The PEP Club, which had opened for Working Members and supporters at 16 Queen Anne's Gate, greatly assisted in holding group meetings over meals, and in running an influential series of lunch talks with picked speakers. Working Members' Meetings were held three times, yielding an acceptable voice in the running of PEP to those who were contributing most effort to it, and replacing General Meetings which had threatened to become dominated by others less involved.

### Heart-searching and Self-criticism

Nevertheless heart-searching and self-criticism continued, and was strongly reflected even at the Executive weekend meeting in March 1935. Far from congratulating itself on such rapid progress, the Executive meditated gloomily on the absence to date of a general design into which the admirable pieces of work already produced, and future pieces should fit. How could 'the shapes of the design ... be forced to emerge from the bringing together of the results and proposals built up by individual Groups from their factual investigations . . .'? Could not something be achieved by a reformulation of PEP faith, giving renewed driving power and momentum? The Chairman lamented that surveys before the meeting showed not only large gaps in the general picture but so much more gap than picture that it was difficult to see any picture. Even where the most thorough work had been done, extremely important aspects of the subject had been neglected. There was no clear view of philosophic principles. PEP's work constituted a great advance, but it must be illuminated if it was to be really fruitful. The Chairman concluded that the time had come to go back to original sources and redefine aims and objectives, and thereby to secure a meaning for the terms 'plan' and 'planning'. 'Just as Nature in her planning had created a machine with powers of adaptation, so human planning should try to plan a mechanism that would enable society to adapt itself to changes.' In recalling this *cri de coeur* even those who were not present can perhaps hear the inspiring tones of Israel Sieff's voice as he deplored 'the over-stressing of the mechanistic aspect and the neglect of the essential human factors in industry.

Others felt that PEP had gone a long way, but there was a lack of a focal point. PEP should declare itself for as much liberty to the individual as was consistent with a high standard of living (not necessarily in a material sense), ruling out communism and all forms of despotism but working out an industrial structure as free as was consistent with preventing its encroachment on the rights of the individual. How was enthusiasm to be re-infused? The younger people were not being drawn in. Was it right that the Executive should be an unchanging body?

A long discussion then took place of PEP organisation, leading on to the inability of the existing group pattern to tackle various overlapping problems such as siting of industry and co-partnership.

It was agreed that there should be no static society; PEP was engaged in a crusade for continuous change, using planning to enable the best standard of living to be achieved in every changed situation. Working Members of PEP needed to be intellectually and emotionally persuaded of this, and a Working Members' Meeting to tackle the issue was fixed for the end of the month. Discussion continued on the desirability of bringing the various aspects into focus in terms of one locality such as Oldham, and on the other hand giving higher priority to the big contemporary social and economic problems which cut across particular industries and services. (The first of these ideas was never put into practice, but the second brought about a substantial change in future programming priorities.)

Finally the discussion moved on to persuasion and implementation, expressed by Kenneth Lindsay in the question 'Do we affect the times in which we live?' He commented on the misapplication of sound ideas in badly drawn legislation, and on the importance of what would now be called monitoring and feedback. Account must be taken of outside criticism and counter proposals. The PEP approach had made great headway among thinking people, and was reflected in broader lines of criticism in public affairs, and more attention to balance. The Chairman observed that the father of change was the inspiration of the best minds thinking in advance, and the mother was the pressure upwards from the common sense of the mass of the public. It was agreed, however, to be out of the question for PEP itself to undertake publicity directly to the public at large. PEP should also steer clear of any party political commitments; its work should be equally at the disposal of government and opposition. This last point was especially relevant since Kenneth Lindsay's election to Parliament as National Labour Member for Kilmarnock in November 1933, and his special relation to the Prime Minister, which led in 1935 to his appointment as Civil Lord of the Admiralty, and to his progressive relinquishment of his PEP responsibilities, which it fell to me to take up.

### PEP Settles Down to Work

This particular Executive discussion in March 1935 has been selected for fairly full treatment because it seems to mark most clearly the transition from the early experimental stage to settled and established working, and also because it so plainly illustrates the odd and fruitful blend of confident presumption over PEP's capacities and lofty role with an appetite for agonising reappraisal of its failings and limitations. After 1932 the central burden of guidance fell on an inner group composed of Israel Sieff, Leonard Elmhirst, Geoffrey Whiskard (until his move to Australia at the end of 1935), Lawrence Neal, Kenneth Lindsay and myself. It was in such prolonged and spirited exchanges that we hammered out, from our diverse backgrounds and approaches, a PEP line which could be successfully followed through while keeping our even more motley band of Working Members together.

That band had now grown to around 140, active in an average of some 15 separate groups, spanning a range of subjects ranging from such long-familiar problems as steel, cotton, coal, housing and agriculture to newly emerging ones such as the national organisation of health and social services, town and country planning, fuel policy, the state of the Press, the use of statistics, consumer protection and government public relations, the last two being subjects almost unheard of when PEP first reviewed them in 1933 and 1934. In addition PEP kept track of relevant developments both at home and abroad, and made a series of broader essays on underlying issues. During 1935 Working Members had to read, note and criticise about 50 million words of duplicated memoranda, drafts and minutes, involving more than 8000 recorded items through the mail, and often three or four redrafts before appearing in the form of published Reports or Broadsheets, which had already exceeded a million words within the first three years. With a full-time staff of only six persons this level and quality of production called for not only sustained effort but a high degree of co-ordination and mutual understanding. The absence of formal membership, the anonymity of Working Members, the refusal to engage in mass propaganda or in political action, the absence of branches outside London and in fact the whole policy of PEP were dictated by the need for maintaining the necessary conditions for a large and steady output of constructive thought and of factual studies with the voluntary help of a large number of people having many other responsibilities and commitments. Stated in these terms the novel working methods of PEP must be judged to have succeeded, and indeed for sheer cost-effectiveness in money and manpower it might well prove difficult to match their performance, either before or since, when the broad scope and diversity of the programme are taken into account.

Such a pace of output might well have been used as the conventional lazy mind's excuse for 'not having time to think'. It is all the more remarkable, therefore, that 1935 saw a thorough reappraisal of the programme in the light of fresh experience of PEP's earlier prescriptions in practice, and of changing trends in the home and world economies. In a well-reasoned critique of Industries Group policy Noel Hall pointed out that owing to devaluation of the pound and the stringency of working capital imposed on our competitors by their levels of inflation there was less urgency than four years earlier to restructure British industry by concentrating output in the most efficient units, while success in avoiding price increases, and even in lowering them, had released consumers' incomes for the satisfaction of new individual wants, leading to some expansion and diversification of the British economy. This pointed to the need for shifting emphasis to wholesale and retail distribution and to Britain's role in world trade.

Similar thoughts had already led to a marked shift in focus from narrower and more conventional subjects to broader and more fundamental ones. For example PEP was a pioneer in charting problems of industrial location and regional development. The social services and the fuel industries were viewed as a whole, and fresh light was thrown on the supply and distribution of foodstuffs, not forgetting agricultural research. Here, under the slogan 'Eat More Science', it was pointed out that while both farmers and research workers were underpaid the contribution of the latter was presented in forms which were unpalatable and unintelligible to the working farmer with his minimal education and poor opportunities for broadening it.

**Resistance to National Planning**
On the strength of fuller feedback it was now possible to define and answer the main criticisms of planning voiced in Parliamentary debates and public discussion. No less than 14 were listed and answered:

1. planning is against human nature (or against British traditions);

2. planning inevitably means centralisation and bureaucracy, or more State interference;

3. planning means more and more large organisations which stifle the individual;

4. planning requires supermen who do not exist, or when they occur usually turn out to be frauds;

5. planning will supersede healthy competition and bankruptcy, which alone make for the survival of the fittest and therefore for progress;

6. planning will take away the consumer's freedom of choice;

7. planning may be a success so long as it is only partial, but will

prove entirely different in its effects as it widens its scope and is no longer operating against a background of competitive costs and competitive habits of mind. Moreover, once you start planning you cannot stop halfway, and whole-hog planning means tyranny;

8. planning leads to Socialism (or Fascism, as the case may be);

9. planning is bolstering up Capitalism;

10. planning is International Bolshevism;

11. planning must be international or it will lead to war;

12. planning will be an instrument for lowering the status of labour;

13. planning means restriction;

14. planning is only a passing fashion and will soon lead to a reaction against itself.

Unfortunately space does not permit giving the answers provided to these questions. At the time we regarded them as convincing, although we conceded the need to be specially vigilant about 2 and 7. History however shows that 14 was the most valid objection, and our comment 'This may be so, but all the signs point in the opposite direction' may well have been true at the time, but was neutralised by wartime and post-war reactions. Like it or not, it is an obvious fact that the British Establishment is as far from wanting or understanding planning in national affairs as it was 40 years ago, and that the various so-called planning initiatives undertaken meanwhile have done nothing to reawaken national interest in the whole approach. PEP in the thirties, while itself working in the direction of a more comprehensive, balanced and co-ordinated handling of national affairs, could do no more than shift pragmatically from an industry-by-industry type of treatment to focusing on more widely ramifying issues and trends indicating the need for fuller integration and longer-term policies and programmes. Thus far public opinion proved amenable, although even here the strength of sectional vested interests and the lack of training and drive in following through agreed lines on a broad front was apt to lead to disappointing results, expecially when action occurred at such a snail's pace that the context was drastically changed and the plan was overtaken by other events.

**The Pre-war Peak**

While activity continued unabated in 1936 it is to 1937 that we may look as the apotheosis of PEP's pre-war effort. It saw the publication of three major Reports – *International Trade* in May, *The British Social Services* in June and *The British Health Services* in December; and at least the last two of these were to lead to fundamental new developments in the national framework. The *International Trade* Report, although it had no such specific sequel, was notable in establishing a decisive case for dropping the restrictive economic imperialism enshrined in the Ottawa Agreements of 1932. PEP insisted that 'no one part of the world can permanently enjoy a specially insulated private prosperity leaving other parts of the world to stew in their own juice. Prosperity in nations, as in individuals, carries with it social obligations, the price of which is bound to be heavy in the long run. The run may not, in fact, be all that long where wretched and desperate populations live close to our shores ...'[1] Such sentiments are voiced almost ad nauseam in these days; how many other references can be found for them as far back as 44 years ago? The implications in case of a major war were spelt out at the same time, in a Broadsheet preview three years before World War II.

The Report on *The British Health Services* had an extraordinarily favourable reception, being welcomed on publication day by leading articles in 11 national and provincial dailies and given news prominence in 40. More important still, the serious and specialised periodicals treated it with the utmost respect, the *British Medical Journal* mentioning its claim to be 'the first attempt to show how all the health services, preventive, curative, environmental and ancillary, work and fit together, what they have achieved, and where their defects and problems lie', adding simply 'the claim is justified'. *The Lancet* agreed that 'PEP are not pitching their claim too high'. The British Medical Association issued a statement that 'The Report will be welcomed by the medical profession. It represents an amount of patient inquiry and critical thought which only those who have personally examined the complex problems of health organisation can fully appreciate'. The Report on *The British Social Services* was also most favourably received, for example with a *Times* leader and

[1] *Planning* No. 86, 17 November 1936, p. 2.

more than two columns of summary on the morning of publication. In addition to these subjects the Broadsheet programme in 1937 included three Broadsheets on Agriculture and three on Milk, and one on *The Impact of Invention*, which discussed how labour would be displaced by application of photo-electric cells, televox and other automatic registering and controlling devices, anticipating current forecasts on the microchip.

An equally interesting Broadsheet[1] contained an uninhibited discussion of aspects of planning and the confusions to which it gave rise, largely in the form of a review of *Ends and Means*[2] by Aldous Huxley (an original member of PEP) and *Socialism versus Capitalism*[3] by Professor A. C. Pigou, two works which would repay re-reading today. Huxley's emphasis on the consistent identification by free men through the ages of the ideal man as non-attached to bodily sensations, power, possessions, even to science, art and individual persons led him sadly to conclude 'Instead of advancing towards the ideal goal, most of the peoples of the world are rapidly moving away from it ... without progress in charity technological advance is useless. It has merely provided us with more efficient means for going backwards.'[4] After a further 40 years, who can confidently rebut Huxley's finding?

Domestically the high spot of the year was the issue in June of the 100th Broadsheet, with messages from 27 well-known readers, who were asked to criticise but were much more inclined to praise. The Marquess of Lothian (Philip Kerr) observed 'I am not sure that it is possible to make politics scientific, but it is certainly essential that there should be a body of scientific knowledge as the raw material which our intuitive faculties must handle'. Lord Allen of Hurtwood remarked 'You have proved that by far the most powerful technique for inducing people to accept a policy is to show them not so much that something or other must be done as how to do it'. Sir Ernest Gowers feared 'that *Planning* is suffering, even in quarters that ought to know better, from our national habit of forming opinions rather by emotional reaction to labels than by intellectual examination of ideas'. G. R. Mitchison pointed to 'inherent difficulties in examining problems that are essentially political with-

---

[1] *Planning* No. 113, December 1937.
[2] Chatto and Windus, London, 1937.
[3] Macmillan, London, 1937.
[4] Quoted in *Planning* No. 113, 28 December 1937, p. 3.

out adopting a political point of view' and suggested that PEP tended 'to neglect the human factor in politics and in planning'. Oscar Thompson suggested that PEP's emphasis on planning derived from its having started 'when the whole commercial world was falling to pieces' but commended the presentation 'in such form that one may altogether disagree with the conclusions and still find the paper itself interesting – and stimulative of new lines of thought'. G. D. H. Cole characteristically commented 'I have no criticism to make of PEP and its work, except that I should like to see all its members and research workers converted to Socialism'.

In apologising for having inflicted on our readers some three-quarters of a million words I promised to try to refrain from any that would not help 'either by stating compactly what previously had to be read in wordy or largely irrelevant documents, or by bringing to light misunderstandings and disposing of arguments at cross-purposes, or by making available principles and patterns of thought which help in clearing a path through the jungle'. We saw ourselves as doing a new kind of job 'in between the social and economic organism, on the one hand, and Parliament or the Press on the other', applying a fraction of the knowledge, expertise and goodwill which would otherwise run to waste towards the solution of national problems. In addition to particular contributions we hoped that our example would spread more widely the fact-finding, constructive evolutionary approach towards social and economic problems.

### The Shadow of Impending War
The ensuing phase in 1938 and the first two-thirds of 1939 was to see the end of the inter-war period. Only one Report of first-class significance was published – that on *The British Press* in April 1938 (see p. 26). An abortive attempt was made to launch a Scottish PEP group. More solid gains were the approval of a Trust Deed finally giving PEP formal status as an educational charity and the purchase of a long lease for 16 Queen Anne's Gate, which provided a sheet anchor through the troubled period to come.

Already during the earlier months of 1939 several of us were enrolled in shadow posts in anticipation of the coming of European war. In those weeks of impending doom we became more and more troubled, not least by contact with Ministers, that the government would be caught without any coherent and credible concept of what we would be fighting for, other than to win. The mental and moral confusion which would result, and the effects upon morale and relations among allies, seemed to be totally unrecognised. We therefore took preliminary steps in July 1939, several weeks before war was declared, to create a Post-War Aims Group, not formally embodied in PEP at the time, but drawing upon PEP's expertise and including some PEP members. At least three documents were drafted during August.

A week after the outset of hostilities, on 8 September, I was able to circulate for comment among those known to be interested in the problem a draft which 'attempts to bring discussion on the problems of war-aims, peace terms and world order to a concrete point' with the intention of eventual circulation among a thinking audience. Less than a month later this had developed into a 40-page statement on *European Order and World Order: What are we fighting for?* (see pp. 83–5), which according to a MS note was drafted by (in addition to myself) Dick Crossman, Denis Routh, Michael Zvegintzov, Julian and Michael Huxley, Professor Egerton, R. S. R. Fitter and Michael Young.

This initiative aroused keen interest and involved us in seeing the Foreign Secretary, Lord Halifax; in a visit to Paris with official facilities in December 1939; and in many further consultations leading to the limited circulation of a revised version early in 1940. The subsequent developments are recounted by Michael Young (see pp. 88–92). Some eventually appeared as wartime PEP broadsheets, but the copious material available would repay working over in detail for a study of what was known, believed and contemplated relating to the post-war world early in World War II.

**What Kind of Body was PEP?**
During the thirties one of the most chronic problems facing those who ran PEP was to explain what kind of body it was. As it became more familiar other organisations were described, on the most super-ficial grounds, as 'a kind of PEP'. In fact PEP had no true precedent or counterpart; as an organism it was unique, and no history would be complete without showing in what way.

First of all PEP was entirely unattached, not just organisationally but intellectually and in spirit. It fitted in no movement, party or interest group, although it had personal links with many. It was also open-ended, not ruling out consideration of any aspect of public affairs, social or economic, national or international or regional.

Minds boggled at the acrobatic virtuosity with which it passed from one flying trapeze to another. It demanded the closest trust and understanding between Working Members who often had little in common and would never have met otherwise. All in turn had to trust the small, dedicated self-perpetuating oligarchy which steered the course and faced the big challenges. Plenty of shrewd observers at the outset gave PEP a life expectation of three years at the utmost, and they had good reason to do so, but almost inexplicably they were proved wrong.

Conscientious and thorough about public affairs, PEP was happy-go-lucky about its own house-keeping. For several years it had no proper constitution or budget, and as an apostle of planning it would have earned low marks for planning itself. On two occasions during the thirties it found itself in an ambiguous relation to breakaway groups – TEC PLAN and Post-War Aims – in both of which I was a founder member and moving spirit, while simultaneously playing a key role in PEP itself. Other bodies, such as Noel Hall's National Institute of Economic and Social Research, set up in 1937, and some of the Dartington-based studies, had a similarly loose and informal connection. It was perhaps this protean capability which saved PEP from bitter schism.

PEP was apt to describe itself as a research group, but such a description could be misleading. The emphasis was always on fact-finding, and during the thirties PEP relied mainly on investigations done by others and on privileged access to the data stores of existing agencies and voluntary bodies in each special field, supplemented by copious interviews and discussions with experts and administrators or managers who were ready to talk. Statistics, often unpublished, were freely drawn upon. It was unusual, especially in the earlier years, for PEP to employ field investigators. The word 'group' also needs explanation. More correctly PEP was a group of groups, some of which were more equal than others, but all of which were under continuous scrutiny regarding their performance and standards, from several angles. PEP was therefore very different from a research institute, for which it was sometimes mistaken. It was strongly action-oriented, to use later jargon, and every word it produced was appraised and verified by people who had long and senior experience of what was done, and why and how, in the field under study. It would never have issued a product of an academic relying entirely on written and interview sources, and unprovided with means for putting them in practical perspective.

This emphasis on action might well have led PEP to become a propaganda body or a pressure group. There was constant debate and concern to ensure that published recommendations were promptly and seriously considered in the appropriate responsible quarter. Subsequent action and inaction were persistently monitored, and no chance was let slip to promote influential follow-up. In that pre-war world, however, such things could be done discreetly and unobtrusively; there was no need to indulge in ungentlemanly tactics or drum-beating. Moreover, the areas of public affairs in which PEP mainly worked were then of little news value beyond the serious press. Even the BBC became interested only infrequently. The carefully handpicked nature of the Working Membership precluded infiltration by ambitious and discordant elements, and also minimised risks of unhelpful leakages, which could easily have breached the assurance of individual anonymity.

It may well be asked what grounds PEP had for being so confident that its findings and recommendations stood a good chance of being implemented, despite its lack of ties with top decision makers, and its self-restraint in regard to the cruder forms of public pressure. This has already been answered, as far as it is possible, in the previous pages. On the one hand the resistance to change of any kind and the tightness of dogmatically united interest groups around the Establishment formed a massive barrier. On the other hand the strength of obvious external pressures to adapt and the leaven of influential and public-spirited people able and willing to carry the message into so many quarters gave the PEP methods a reasonable chance to work, at least until after the middle thirties. Comparison of the recommendations of PEP at given dates and the subsequent actions and measures cannot prove a causal relationship, but does reveal a remarkably frequent pattern of events at least partly matching PEP proposals (for examples see pp. 25–7).

This record shows that the early struggles of PEP reflected a fundamental dualism which was at once a strength and a weakness. A great part of the effort went into fact-finding studies on a consensus basis, calculated to command the support and respect of most professionals and of all but the more extremist and dogmatic of the informed public. But PEP was not interested in facts for their own sake. It held that disciplined regard for the facts would best promote agreement on policy and cohesion in carrying it out, and would thus bring about the orderly and more rapid change which the group held dear. Thus far the consensus was clear and robust, but from the circumstances of its foundation PEP could not stop there without compunction. Above its matter-of-fact landscape its sky was brightly but mysteriously illuminated by the elusive star or meteor of planning. Some saw it as the one true lodestar which would lead to a stable, prosperous and civilised future. Others found it disturbingly confusing, and some roundly pronounced it to be simply a will-o-the-wisp. As time went on fewer and fewer were prepared to join in the chorus of 'Lead Kindly Light', or to dedicate themselves to the quest for the Holy Grail. At one time there seemed to be a threat of an outbreak of a religious feud on the matter but in the end the PEP conviction of trusting the fact-finding approach proved stronger than the act of faith which was required in order to put planning first. I personally still believe that had PEP been ready to stand up unflinchingly for planning, and had it been possible to convince leaders of public opinion and the Establishment to tread that path, many of the blunders and miseries of the past few decades could have been avoided. As at the moment an historian, however, I must sadly adopt the view that neither of these 'ifs' could at the time have been satisfied, and that PEP followed the only course consistent with maintaining its credibility and avoiding a split. By this view I am condemned to perpetual nostalgia and to a certain sense of guilt at having gone along the less virtuous path of realism.

**Planning in Hindsight**
The standard bearer of the planning concept within PEP from the earliest days was the Technique of Planning Group – TEC PLAN as it modishly called itself. Its title proclaimed its distinctive approach – planning was not to be treated as a political gimmick, or an excuse for bureaucracy and despotism, but as a more sophisticated discipline for surveying and evaluating resources and for using them flexibly but skilfully as a whole over unusually long time-scales and with unusual emphasis upon relations between ends and means. It was believed that Britain had much to learn in order to understand planning, let alone to use it, and that there was a need to examine the positive and negative experience of other countries, as well as to study the subject intensively at home, both in theory and in practice.

In retrospect it is clear that those who, like myself, entered the fray with a simple concept of a choice whether to plan or not to plan were partly right but largely mistaken in terms of the state of the art and the technical as well as the political problems involved. We lumped together three quite distinct planes of thought, attitude and action. The first, on which we may claim to have been right, was that it was possible, desirable and indeed essential to supersede piecemeal treatment of the various elements of public policy by co-ordinated treatment, and action based upon rule-of-thumb and hunch by fact-based and research-based programmes. From that then novel but sound and now widely conceded position, however, we rushed on to assume that accurate and comprehensive forecasting over a decade or more could rapidly be developed as a basis for reliable decision-making. Now, sadder and wiser, we have to admit that, even with the help of greatly improved computer and other aids and an embryonic science of futurology, we are still at least decades from achieving a standard of economic and social forecasting which will adequately support comprehensive medium-range let alone long-range planning in public affairs. Model-making techniques, so much in vogue a decade or so ago, have proved of very restricted utility in practice, as also in the field of ecology, where I was concerned with them in the International Biological Pro-gramme of the International Council of Scientific Unions.

The third plane is the political, and it recalls the impulsively selected title Political and Economic Planning. We are perhaps en-titled to some credit, at a time when so many alert minds were being beguiled by the specious doctrines of Communism and Fascism, that we never for a moment deviated from the paramountcy of democratic principles, and indeed their extended application through wider participation and greater devolution of power. We grossly under-estimated, however, the inbuilt resistance to change in the face even of the clearest and most persuasive demonstrations of its neces-sity and advantageousness. The chronic and unshakeable bone-headedness of major elements in British society, and their inability and unwillingness to adapt to contemporary needs, have far sur-passed anything which we ever anticipated in our gloomiest moments. The combination of the second and third planes has set a currently insurmountable limit to the evolution of national planning as we envisaged it. On the other hand the potential on the first plane is relatively unobstructed and has been enlarged by technological advances, although even here political and administrative inhibitions and deficiencies have slowed and reduced progress far below what it might and should have been.

Even on this first plane, however, the filling in during the ensuing half-century of many of the gaps in the administrative and social structure which had been correctly identified has not brought the full benefits which we thought could be assumed. Smooth and concerted functioning have been to a surprising extent disrupted by growing party politicisation at the operating level, by bureaucracy and institutional jealousies and empire-building and by lower standards of responsibility and public spirit than it seemed reasonable to expect 50 years ago. While many admirable advances have been made the wealth, happiness and even the health and welfare of the nation fall disappointingly short of what the various measures advocated and eventually adopted might have been counted upon to bring about.

Personally, as I have argued in *The System*,[1] I attribute much of this shortfall to the poor professional capability of administrators in central and local government, whose training and management have, with some shining exceptions, proved quite unequal to the national need. This shortfall becomes more conspicuous as technological and other improvements in media coverage make manifest to all problems and sufferings which 50 years ago were familiar to relatively few.

Had the knowledge been vouchsafed to me, when I joined in launching PEP, that it would fall to me to look back on the record five decades later, I would have been eager for a preview of the outcome of all our efforts. Standing now on these distant shores of the 1980s I must confess to some bafflement. If you ask me now 'Was it worth it?' I am inclined to respond uncertainly 'You tell me'. No doubt, however, that, like any other response, is highly subjective.

---

[1] Nicholson, Max, *The System: The Misgovernment of Modern Britain*, London, Hodder and Stoughton, 1967.

# 3
# PEP Through the 1930s: The Industries Group

## ——Oliver Roskill——

The main contributions of the Industries Group in the early 1930s were the following beliefs – all extraordinarily *vieux jeu* only 50 years later, but at that time to some extent, anyway, original:

1. that forward planning is necessary for an industry as a whole as well as for individual companies and cannot be done without access to facts and figures, which were hardly ever available at that time – long before Central Statistical Office, *Monthly Digest of Statistics* etc. existed;

2. that forward planning must take into account problems of technological advance as well as economics and industrial structure. At that time employment of technical staff was still the exception rather than the rule in industry. The number of technically qualified graduates (or equivalent) as a proportion of the total work force was far smaller than today. The kind of technical problems exercising us at that time were the displacement of mule by ring spindles in the cotton industry, Bessemer converters versus open hearth furnaces in steel, use of blast-furnace gas for heating coke-ovens, use of surplus coke-oven gas for public supply, line assembly versus batch production and the scope for automation in some branches of engineering;

3. that industrial problems can often be approached advantageously from the 'consumer end'. This was at a time when modern marketing techniques were almost unknown and the idea that the consumer – normally through the retailer – should be the

arbiter of his requirements was original. Moreover in industries involving a chain of processes – at that time commonly carried out by separate companies – it was of only limited use for the consumer to make his requirement clear to the last manufacturer in the chain; the process might often have to be carried through a succession of stages right back to the raw material. This in turn tended to lead to the concept of 'vertical integration' and was both one reason for the phenomenal success of **Marks & Spencer** and a reason why Israel Sieff's ideas had such an enormous influence in the early days of the Industries Group of PEP;

4. that 'profit must come from increased throughput' (to quote from the first document of the Industries Group).[1] This, too, we owed to Israel Sieff, and the fact that it now looks obvious is an indication of the change which has taken place – for example the abolition of retail price maintenance and the 'fair trading' and monopolies legislation. The normal reaction in industry for some time after the Great Depression was to try to fix prices through cartels and trade associations. The idea that if capacity exceeded demand, the latter should be increased by reducing costs right the way back from finished product to raw material, and then, through improved marketing and distribution, reducing prices was new. It was viewed with scepticism by all but a handful of businessmen;

5. the importance of promoting good human relations in industry had been established in the Mond–Turner dialogues in the 1920s. The 1926 General Strike and the Great Depression left bitterness in their wake, but widespread sympathy for the enormous numbers of unemployed had led to few constructive ideas beyond paying them 'the dole', or embarking on a great programme of public works which was firmly opposed by the Treasury and many people in the City. Israel Sieff brought in the fresh standpoint that industry itself should meet the challenge. The fundamental need, in his view, as in that of Roosevelt a little later, was to 'overcome fear', and to adopt principles which he and Simon Marks were successfully applying through **Marks & Spencer**. Milne-Bailey at Transport House was a strong supporter of PEP, and contributed much in his quiet scholarly way, both

---

[1] 1st Industries Report, 29 October 1931 (A1), PEP Archive, LSE.

generally and to the work on individual industries, although he had only very limited influence on their trade unions.

**Method of Working**

I had established one of the first firms of industrial (or management) consultants in this country in 1929 and was employed by the Executive Committee of PEP to draft the factual material and to put forward some suggested conclusions which followed from the facts for discussion by the Industries Group. This group normally invited distinguished leaders from the industry under discussion to join it either as members or in a consultative capacity. I thus had the advantages of meeting a number of important industrialists and drawing a small remuneration which helped to get my firm established.

The range of industries covered was wide. The factual material of the first Report, on iron and steel, I drafted myself in the evenings when I was working in Birmingham for the Copper and Brass trade associations in connection with the problems of the Ottawa Agreement. As an entirely incidental result of this activity I happened to meet a number of the steel re-rollers in the Midlands who occupied a more important position in the steel industry than is the case today. Men like Sir William Larke of the former Federation of British Iron and Steel Manufacturers were at first cautious and sceptical of the ability of any outside body without practical experience of iron and steel manufacture to make any useful contribution. But he introduced iron masters, still of the old school of the Bells and the Bolckows, such as McDiarmid of Stewarts & Lloyds and Charles Mitchell of Dorman Long, who, rather to their surprise, found some sense in the drafts of the Group and the discussions to which they led. I was lucky in that my maternal great uncle was at that time chairman of Consett Iron, and although already in poor health and quite unable to believe that anyone outside the steel industry could have the slightest understanding of its problems, was generous with his time in talking about them. On technical matters the Group had the benefit of much advice from F. W. Harbord whose firm (Riley, Harbord & Law) was then one of the leading consultants to the iron and steel industry – before the days when turn-key projects by contractors became common. When published, the Report was looked on with scepticism by the industry but received widespread and favourable comment in the Press, including the technical and trade journals of the industry which probably enlarged its readership, especially in the ranks of management, and enhanced its reputation. Industrial economics was at that time a less important branch of the 'dismal science' than it later became, but the report attracted the attention of economists such as Professor Sargent Florence. (I found many years later that it was still on the list of recommended reading for the Economics Tripos at Cambridge.)

## Use Made of the Reports

It is almost impossible to assess the contribution such a report makes to events in an industry. At that time the gist and the conclusions of the Industries Group Reports, (which most of my non-technical fellow-members of the Group found rather hard reading), were brilliantly summarised by Max Nicholson in the form of Broadsheets of perhaps 10,000 words. These undoubtedly commanded a far wider readership, much of it outside the industry concerned and, along with reviews in the trade and technical journals, probably induced a considerable number of younger men in the industry to read the Report itself.

Many of the ideas in the Report were not themselves original but were not yet generally accepted by the leaders of the industry (many of them older men who had carried on after the war when otherwise they might have been superseded by the 'missing generation'). For example the bigger blast furnaces in the early 1930s had a capacity of about 600 tons a day, perhaps one-tenth of the giants of today, and the report rightly drew attention to the economies of scale. Pig iron was still widely cast, and hot metal transfer to steel furnaces was rare. Fuel economy (for example firing coke-ovens with blast furnace gas) received only scant attention. The cost advantages of the basic Bessemer process were recognised, but the British industry hung on too long to its open-hearth furnace traditions and cheap imports of basic Bessemer steel from the Continent were a thorn in the side of the British steel companies, whose criticisms that they contained frequent inclusions of slag were not always fully justified. Change in British industry was slow enough anyway, but at the very least the Industries Group Reports helped to accelerate change if only by getting it talked about and thus gradually accepted.

The second Report was on the cotton industry and the leading personality who fathered this was Sir Thomas Barlow, chairman of

Barlow & Jones ('Osman' brand towels, etc.). I have several happy recollections of being entertained to dinner by him to discuss drafts at the Trocadero Restaurant, which might be thought a surprising choice by anyone who did not know that Tommy Barlow considered it had the best hock cellar in London, a matter on which he was able to pronounce with no less authority than on Dürer drawings – or even cotton. He co-operated wholeheartedly in the work while protesting at intervals (perhaps because of the influence of the 'Manchester School') that he was 'not a planner' – an attitude with which (despite my work for PEP) I had a good deal of sympathy. Another important contributor was John Ryan, then managing director of the ill-starred Lancashire Cotton Corporation and one of the fathers of what must have been one of the earliest 'redundancy schemes' (to buy up and destroy surplus spindles). Ryan later became vice-chairman of the Metal Box Co. but always remained a loyal supporter of PEP.

In the case of the two first Industries Group Reports, PEP had a friendly rival – the Bankers Industrial Development Co., for whose work Professor Clay was responsible. Like PEP, this organisation resulted from intense public concern about industrial unemployment, partly attributable to lack of investment in modernisation. Unlike PEP, however, it was sponsored by the Bank of England.

The Industries Group comprised busy men who gave up not only many evenings to meetings but also much spare time to reading and commenting on drafts. Israel Sieff was not only the source of many of the ideas which gave rise to a common approach to industrial problems by men of very different academic background and practical experience; he was also very frequently a generous host whose excellent cellar and fine pictures made as big a contribution to the high level of regular attendance as the interest of the discussions and a high-minded determination to do something to help lift Britain out of the depression of the early 1930s. The group often met at 21 Sussex Place in one of the beautiful Georgian terraces round Regent's Park, then at his penthouse on top of Brook House, Park Lane, and then at 39 Hyde Park Gate, even after PEP had acquired the lease of 16 Queen Anne's Gate, where many of the larger meetings were held.

**Choice of Subjects**
Considerable discussion was given to the choice of subjects for study.

At one stage some members felt that as the Group so frequently found itself discussing financial problems, there should perhaps be a separate Finance Group. This was indeed tried and one or two meetings of possible members were held; but Israel had always been sceptical about the idea. He often used the phrase which now sounds rather quaint – almost Biblical – that finance should be 'the hand-maid of industry'. Problems of industrial organisation and structure, labour relations, technology, distribution and so on must be resolved first; finance would follow. On labour relations he always tried to get trade union leaders interested and involved in the work of the Group. A successful example was Richard Coppock in the case of the building industry and Arthur Pugh was also helpful in connection with iron and steel. The building industry had been chosen for study partly because the housing shortage was much more serious then than now and partly because immobility of labour was an obvious obstacle to the reduction of unemployment. The main reason was because the Group took the view that house-building created demand for the products of so many industries, not only obvious ones such as bricks, cement and timber but also appreciably affected others such as brass castings, lead (and later copper) pipe and sheet, paint and so on. It was thus very much in line with Sieff's conviction that in order to reduce the price to the consumer, it was necessary to get all the materials and services involved to improve their efficiency and cut their costs in order to benefit from increased sales.

The work on building and housing was one factor which led to a very ambitious project: to prepare reports on all the fuel industries (coal, gas and electricity) to be followed – though this did not happen until much later, by which time they had all been nationalised – by one on national fuel policy, one of the earliest attempts to tackle a subject which is still as 'live' as it was in the inter-war period, with the added complications introduced by nuclear power, North Sea oil and gas and the growth in concern for the environment.

Work on the electricity Report proceeded simultaneously with that of the McGowan Committee (to which PEP gave evidence). This and the Montague Barlow Commission (see pp. 26 and 64) were, I think, the only cases where PEP worked in parallel with, though quite independently of, an officially appointed body. As the numerous and favourable reviews in the technical and daily press pointed out, the two Reports reached broadly similar conclusions.[1] This was at a time when there were numerous municipally-owned electricity undertakings supplying relatively dense urban areas, and large companies often supplying surrounding rural areas, with, therefore, wide differences in cost which (quite apart from municipal pride and unwillingness to surrender one of their profitable activities) made the evolution of a logical structure particularly difficult.

Though the work of PEP on industry was suspended during the war, production of the Broadsheets continued and when the tide had turned and victory appeared more or less certain, the Government started to look at the problem of post-war industrial reconstruction, and in particular, the changes in industry involved in reverting from swords to ploughshares. The Board of Trade made a grant to PEP (later supplemented by a grant from the Ministry of Supply) to prepare a Report on all branches of the engineering industries, which had an influence on the subsequent enormous expansion of the motor vehicle and the domestic appliance industries (see pp. 102–3).

I use the word 'influence' with caution as I have often been asked 'what did all these Reports really achieve?' It is a difficult question to answer, though in view of the greatly increased demands of my firm on my time I would not have continued to be associated with the work for about three decades unless I had been convinced that it was well worth while. It is an easier question to answer in the case of the Civic Division of PEP whose original work on the social services undoubtedly exercised a big influence on the Beveridge Report and also on the Health Service. Individual industrialists did not thumb through the recommendations of the industry Reports and set about implementing them in their own businesses. The Reports were, however, widely read and discussed throughout the industries concerned and, to put it at its lowest, were much used as sources of information when few such sources existed. It would not be an excessive claim that many of the 'Little Neddy' reports are the grand-children of those produced by PEP. Moreover the very idea of bringing together a group of public-spirited people from an industry (employers, managers and employees) along with some well-qualified 'outsiders' in order to discuss an industry's problems owes some-

[1] See for example *The Electrician*, 4 December 1936; *The Times* (main leader) 5 December 1936; *Electrical Industries*, 9 December 1936; *Electrical Times*, 10 December 1936.

thing, at least, to the Industries Group. I do not think it had ever been done before, though I have already mentioned the two BID Co. Reports which appeared at about the same time.

Another example of the gradual adoption of ideas put forward many years ago is the reported policy of 'enlightened use of public purchasing' said to be favoured by Sir Keith Joseph. The Civil Aviation Authority, for example, is currently expected to spend a very large sum on re-equipping airports with Dutch radar. Under the proposed new policy it would be expected to have informed British suppliers, say, five years in advance of its requirements and to have encouraged them to carry out research and development needed to meet them. The equipment would in due course be open to international tender, but the British suppliers should by then be in a strong competitive position. (This of course is common practice on the part of several of our major competitors such as the USA and France.) It has been reported that the idea was submitted by Sir Derek Rayner, a director of Marks & Spencer on secondment to the Government. Whether or not this is so, it closely resembles the views which originated with Israel Sieff and were discussed by the Industries Group in connection with the Buy British campaign in the 1930s. Sieff believed that exhortation to Buy British was not enough: it was essential for buyers not only to make their requirements known but to help British manufacturers to supply them. The point was discussed for example in connection with purchase of mining machinery by the coal industry.

**Anonymity Rule**

Credit is, as often as not wrongly, attached to individuals and anonymity was a firm principle in the early days of PEP. As both Kenneth Lindsay and Max Nicholson have pointed out (see pp. 21 and 38), a number of senior civil servants were members of groups and they would probably have been stopped if it had attracted personal publicity. Sir Henry Bunbury (of the Post Office), for example, made important contributions to the work on the public utility industries. PEP had also always included members of all main political parties (and of none), and its ideas and recommendations were open to the use of any party which favoured them – without acknowledgement and without being associated with any particular person. The anonymity rule was, however, abandoned during the post-war period, as Richard Bailey records (p. 120). A reason which led to the decision to make this important change was the necessity to recruit – normally at that time with the approval of the professor concerned – young research workers to undertake work on particular projects. It was difficult to obtain people of high calibre unless they were allowed to put their names on the reports produced.

The quest for fame will probably always remain a spur to those with ambition. However young they are when they first hear the Brahms (or any other) Requiem, the emotional reaction to which it is likely to give rise will be stronger than the realisation of the truth of the message. To the end of their life even when the grass has begun to wither there will probably be a further objective unattained.

Unfortunately the ideas underlying the original spur suffer from senescence and the demands of an active life make it increasingly difficult to amend or replace them. While many people want to join a cause which provides ideas as a prefabricated dogma, the ambitious generally want to give their ideas the imprint of their own personality. They are generally willing to adopt them from an anonymous source, but less willing if the source is itself a competitor for fame. For this reason and others, I have always thought the abandonment of anonymity by PEP was a mistake.

The following is a list of Industry Reports for the preparation of the factual material for which my firm was responsible:

| | | | |
|---|---|---|---|
| Report on the British Iron and Steel Industry | July 1933 | Foolscap | 80pp |
| Report on the British Cotton Industry | June 1934 | Foolscap | 147pp |
| Housing England | Dec. 1934 | Foolscap | 158pp |
| Report on the British Coal Industry | Feb. 1936 | Foolscap | 214pp |
| Report on the Supply of Electricity in Great Britain | Dec. 1936 | Octavo | 171pp |
| Report on the Location of Industry in Great Britain | March 1939 | Octavo | 314pp |
| Report on the Gas Industry in Great Britain | March 1939 | Octavo | 213pp |

| The British Fuel and Power | | | |
|---|---|---|---|
| Industries | Oct. 1947 | Octavo | 406pp |

In addition there was one Report (in which we were not involved) on a rather special 'industry' – the Press, which was the result of a particularly strong and well-informed group (see p. 26). There were also a number of Reports published in the inter-war period dealing with subjects where there were both social and industrial implications. Most of these were 'fathered' by Ronald Davison and much of the work was done by David Owen. *The Entrance to Industry* and *The Exit from Industry* were two which made a big impact. My firm, and in particular my partner Oliver L. Lawrence CBE, assisted in the preparation of the Report on *International Trade*. I should also mention another partner, the late John R. G. Lamb who was specially concerned with the work on Gas, Electricity and the Fuel and Power Industries. The Gas Group was fortunate in having the assistance of one of the leading figures in the industry, Dr E. W. Smith of Woodall-Duckham, who had, as well as a most kindly nature, a keen mind wide open to ideas on innovation and reform; of C. A. Masterman of the Gas Light and Coke Co., well known, among other reasons, for his pioneer work on underground gasification of coal – now a very 'live' subject in the USA; and of E. J. Fottrell and George Evetts. The Electricity Group under the chairmanship of Henry Nimmo similarly benefited from the help of Graeme Haldane, one of the original founder members of PEP and a partner in Merz & Maclellan, one of the leading firms of electrical consulting engineers. Another member of colourful personality and forceful views was Hugh Quigley of the old Central Electricity Board. A. P. Young was an industrialist of unusual background, having been in charge of the (then British-run) Kailan Mining Administration in China, together with its associated power station – a very low cost undertaking.

**Studies of Subjects Affecting Many Industries**
In the early post-war period the Industries Group ceased to function as a group and the study of individual industries was abandoned. Much of the time of the Executive Committee was devoted to selecting for study subjects which affected all (or many) industries and which were likely to come to the forefront after, say, a year or whatever other period was thought necessary to undertake the

study and publish the Report. This may be illustrated by listing some of the industrial subjects on which Reports were published in the 1970s. These are: *Wage Determination in Industry*; *Industry in the Development Areas*; *Training Adults for Skilled Jobs*; *The Impact of Employment Protection Laws*; *Creating New Jobs*. One which received very widespread attention was on *Thrusters and Sleepers*, published in 1965.

The change from the study of individual industries was not so abrupt as might appear. Already before the war PEP had pioneered the study of Regional Development and through its *Report on the Location of Industry* might with justice claim to have had a significant influence on the commission under the chairmanship of Sir Montague Barlow, on government policy in what were then called the Special Areas, and in particular on the location, design and management of the new Trading Estates such as Treforest and Team Valley (see p. 26). A leading member of the PEP Executive Committee, Bill Holford, was closely associated in a professional capacity with the latter; and later, in a somewhat similar way, my firm were commissioned to prepare 'An Industrial Plan for West Cumberland'.

The original Industries Group put up a number of hares but – fortunately – abandoned the chase of some. At the time when the idea of the Corporate State was beginning to attract attention, despite its association with Italian fascism, I remember we had a meeting at which one of the guests was Captain Harold Macmillan, then member for Stockton-on-Tees, and later a leading member of the Next Five Years Group which, through Kenneth Lindsay, had close contacts with PEP. This particular meeting discussed among other things an Enabling Bill which would deal with 'self-government in industry' and the relationship between individual companies and the industry in which they operated. The discussion covered also the related question of reform of the House of Lords (to which PEP returned in the 1970s – see p. 154).

Although there was always a strong sense of common purpose to which Israel Sieff probably made the biggest contribution, the Industries Group was never in danger of becoming a mutual admiration society. The difference of background, occupation and experience of the members often led to arguments which – if not heated – were conducted between persons of high intellectual stature, so that ideas and draft documents were generally subjected to searching and perhaps caustic criticism.

PEP has always called itself non-political (meaning that it was not to be constrained by the standpoints of party politics). It certainly included people who probably voted for each of the three main political parties. To the 'politically-conscious', 'non-political' has tended to become identified with Conservative but PEP was certainly not Conservative either in the party-political or in the traditionalist sense. It questioned the status quo rather than supporting it. On the other hand those members who probably would have voted Labour were not 'Clause Four' men. I can recollect no-one advocating public ownership of the means of production, distribution and exchange; we were, after all, a Group which believed in private enterprise. The furthest the Industries Group would have gone would have been to accept that in some cases, for example where monopoly appears to be in the public interest (for example the London General Omnibus Co. versus 'pirate' buses), public ownership should follow – the point of view generally associated with Herbert Morrison.

**Relations with the Establishment**
Being 'non-political', PEP was not, at least for the first two or three decades, a body readily accepted by the 'Establishment', and in particular by the 'Industrial Establishment'. Though agreeing that there is an 'Establishment', few people agree on any definition of the term. For the purpose of trying to describe what was *not* the outlook of those who joined or assisted the Industries Group, I offer, as a partial definition of the Establishment, people who accept the ethos and customs of those in authority and climb the established ladders of advancement in whatever occupation they follow. An organisation which sets out to question current assumptions, to assemble and study the facts and see in what direction they point, is unlikely to find immediate favour with those responsible for keeping the machine running. And it is probably unnecessary to remind anybody that in the first half (or more) of the 1930s, the machinery of industry was not running smoothly. It is necessary to add that even in the early days there were a few Establishment figures in PEP (e.g. some very senior civil servants) but, in general, they did not concern themselves very much with the work of the Industries Group.

This resulted in difficulty in recruiting the tougher-minded industrialists and managers to the Industries Group with its rather radical approach and willingness to look at unconventional ways of dealing with current problems. This was never wholly solved, and though I personally would have liked to see a stronger representation of industrialists of standing on the Industries Group, the tendency became to function more like a very modest select committee of the House of Commons and to invite leading industrialists to come to meetings, give their views and answer questions. Few refused to do this and on the whole the method worked well. The fact that Lawrence Neal, vice-chairman of the Industries Group, was like Israel Sieff also a retailer might be thought to have given the retail point of view too much weight. As his book *Retailing and the Public*[1] published in the early days of PEP shows, however, he represented more what is sometimes called the 'Greats' type of mind – a Socratic acuteness of questioning, thesis and reasoned argument rather than a view representing his own particular trade.

In later years PEP has tended to become increasingly a member of the Establishment – as can be seen by looking at the membership of Council in the last two or three decades and at the reception given to its publications by newspapers and magazines read by 'top people'. Notwithstanding this, it has managed to retain both its non-political balance and its radical approach to problems – a tight-rope walk for which the present members of the permanent staff must be given much credit.

**Freedom and Planning**

There were many arguments about the compatibility of freedom and planning. This is a subject much broader than the problems it poses for companies, but it is relevant to say here that anything which might seem to point towards centralised planning (e.g. on Russian Gosplan lines, involving the fixing by a central bureaucracy of output figures for individual factories or companies) was anathema to most industrialists and managers who gave help to PEP. It was also, of course, a very long way from Israel Sieff's ideas on rapid response to consumer choice by industry (through all stages of production right back to the raw material). Despite this, in the minds of many people in industry and commerce in the 1930s, the association of the idea of planning with the Russian five-year plans was probably one of the factors which gave rise to difficulties in enlarging the circle of supporters of PEP among those who earned their living in industry.

[1] London, George Allen & Unwin, 1932.

Nor did hard-headed businessmen find themselves at ease either with the idealistic attitudes of many of the younger members or with the academic economists.

Connected with this was the problem of secrecy. Secrecy about commercial as well as technological matters was much more widely accepted as the norm in Britain (though not in the USA) at that time, and planning – even if not imposed by a central bureaucracy – involved discussion and thus disclosure of firms' plans. It also involved a very high degree of flexibility in order to be successful. This was another example of a way in which PEP Industries Group was ahead of its time. It is now accepted in some cases at any rate, that if, say, there is room for one new ethylene plant in the country, if the minimum economic capacity of such a plant is, say, 500,000 tons a year, and if half a dozen companies, British or foreign, are all contemplating building such a plant, discussion of plans and possibly some degree of intervention by central government is necessary if waste of capital resources and redundant capacity is to be avoided. This was by no means accepted in the 1930s, and we have suffered from prolonged redundancy of machines and men in many industries as a result.

There is also the question of who is to determine whether there is room for one such plant or two, or none at all. Industrial market research was almost unknown at that time, and partly as a result of our discussions in the Industries Group, soon became an important aspect of my firm's activities as well as of the various 'industry' Reports issued by PEP. A good example was the pioneering work in attempting estimates of the future demand for housing of all types and sizes (and hence of the capacity of the building materials industries).

There is a long time-lag between the planning of a new housing development and the day the first occupant moves in. In designing and building a turbo-generator the time-lag is longer still. We hardly yet know what it is in the case of newly designed nuclear power stations. Hence the importance of combining the need to plan ahead with provision for maximum flexibility of plans in the face of changed circumstances, some of which could not have been foreseen at the time the plans were made. It is very difficult to make accurate estimates of demand for anything five years ahead and, I believe, impossible ten years ahead. We were very conscious in the 1930s of the structural rigidities in British industry and the need to relax them. Fifty years later many of these same rigidities remain – which is less a measure of the lack of success of the work of the Industries Group than of the slow pace of change in British industry.

**Availability of Statistics; Quality Control of Consumer Goods**
One active member of the original Industries Group should be mentioned for two reasons. R. H. S. Spicer, scholar of Eton and King's who served in the Coldstream Guards during the war, had a varied career. He worked for the Engineering Employers Federation (at which time he wrote what was then the standard textbook on engineering wages) and the Retail Distributors Association. He combined an original mind with wide practical knowledge of business and great foresight. Quite outside the programme of study of individual industries already described, he submitted two papers. The first was 'A proposed clearing house for Civil Intelligence and Statistics' in May 1932, many years before the Central Statistical Office existed. This was at a time when hardly any statisticians were employed in government departments, compared with 292 in central government alone in 1980, and a total in all government organisations of 562[1] which Sir Derek Rayner is said to be trying hard to reduce – such are the extremes to which the pendulum of fashion may swing.

The second paper, with which F. R. Cowell and a number of others were also closely associated, was on the need for testing and approval of a wide range of consumer goods so that consumers should be better informed about value for money. Robert Spicer was far from being a Ralph Nader. His attitude was that producers of first quality goods were often tarred with the brush of those producing shoddy goods, and that Israel Sieff's emphasis on consumers' choice being quickly reflected back to manufacturers would be aided if consumers were better informed, particularly since durable consumer goods were becoming increasingly technical. The relation of these ideas to those of the Retail Trading Standards Association, with which he was also associated through his work as director of the Retail Distributors Association, will be obvious. PEP took legal advice about the scheme and on the basis of this decided that it was too hot to handle on account of the dangers of libel actions.

It was not until 1957, about 25 years later, that Michael Young (see Chapter 4) and Ray Goodman (see Chapter 5), the latter

[1] *The Times*, 6 February 1980.

stimulated by the experience of his American wife in setting up house in England, consulted Gerald Gardiner (later Lord Chancellor), who thought that with certain reservations the type of report issued by Consumers Union in the US could be published in the UK. Ray Goodman and others arranged to get the President of Consumers Union to come and talk to a meeting at the House of Commons arranged by John Edwards, as a result of which the infant Consumers Association was born and soon thrived under the guidance of Michael Young. These (RTSA and Consumers Association) are two examples of PEP's broad and constructive influence on affairs even though it was probably Consumers Union which had the biggest direct influence on the formation of the Consumers Association.

### Relations with the Press; Broadsheets and Addresses
PEP never sought to hide its light and the person responsible for the wide dissemination of its ideas and the results of its group studies was Max Nicholson, who for many years was almost the sole author of the fortnightly Broadsheets which, as I have already indicated, reached a far wider public than the Reports themselves.

Although the work on industry came earlier, PEP has probably had greater influence on social and civic affairs than on individual industries. At intervals, for example in the 100th broadsheet, Max would take a critical look at what PEP had achieved and at reactions to the ideas it advanced, and anyone interested in depth in PEP's history should read these periodic assessments. Nearly all the Broadsheets were reviewed, often at length, both in the daily press (especially *The Times*) and in the trade, professional and general weeklies and monthlies. Some showed special and regular interest. One of these was *Nature* – somewhat unexpectedly to me because PEP was not a favourite home of scientists (Julian Huxley was one of the relatively few of distinction). I like to think that this was due to PEP's factual, almost Baconian approach to problems then (as now) normally treated in a partisan way. Another, quite different example, was the *Colliery Guardian* which gave very favourable reviews to the Reports on coal (and later on the public utility industries) even though the Reports were not as favourably received in some sections of the coal industry.

Apart from the Broadsheets, nearly every member of the Industries Group contributed each according to his own field of activity and his contacts in media or among learned societies, by press articles, broadcasts and addresses. The most important of these in putting PEP 'on the map' in the early stages was a broadcast by Israel Sieff. He was then little known to the public (Marks & Spencer did not occupy the position it does today) and in the BBC series 'Whither Britain' in February 1934 the previous speakers had been H. G. Wells, Winston Churchill and George Bernard Shaw. The *Morning Post* reported the talk at length under the banner headline 'The Unknown Voice on the Ether: An inspiring broadcast'. Many of the ideas he talked about were those mulled over by the Industries Group. The broadcast led to a series of five articles in the *Morning Post* in April, the first of which was entitled 'A policy for prosperity'.

My contribution was a minor one compared with the impact of those broadcasts and articles and if I mention two or three addresses I gave to learned societies it is because I have records of these and do not have them of similar addresses by other members of the Industries Group. One was to the Institute of Fuel in February 1936 entitled 'The Co-ordination of National Fuel and Power Supplies'. Another was to the Royal Institute of British Architects in December 1938 on 'Economics of the Building Industry' to the discussion on which Richard Coppock contributed at length. I also addressed the Marshall Society in Cambridge and the Cotton Board annual conference on several occasions after the war.

As Kenneth Lindsay records (see pp. 26 and 28), the PEP Broadsheets were often seen in the hands of Members in the House of Commons and he did much to encourage their use in this way and to promote contact between MPs – both government and opposition – and members of PEP by arranging dinners at 16 Queen Anne's Gate and other informal meetings.

**Suggestions for New Technology**
The methods by which PEP has influenced industry (and for that matter other fields of activity such as politics) raise the interesting question of how ideas get into circulation and are finally put into action. PEP was never a pressure group in the sense in which these are now known, and have proliferated to cover such a vast range of subjects: abortion, blood sports, child care, dog licensing, and so on through the alphabet. It sought to encourage planning, but has always been a research and fact-finding organisation. Conclusions and recommendations followed from the facts assembled but did not preclude other conclusions being reached from

the same evidence. But the rate at which ideas are adopted and put into action in industry is slow in Britain – probably slower than in most industrialised countries, which is one reason why we have tended to fall behind them. Looking back over the early PEP Reports, dozens of examples come to mind. In May 1980, with considerable publicity much of which gave the impression that this was an entirely new development, a small combined heat and power (CHP) station was started up at Hereford, the first public supply power station selling waste heat to private industry (e.g. a cider factory and a poultry farm). It was pointed out that in factories owning their own generating plant it was not uncommon for exhaust steam to be used for process or space heating. A conventional power station at Hereford would have wasted 67 per cent of the fuel burnt, whereas the new power station, it was claimed, will waste 24 per cent. A working party under the chairmanship of Mr Walter Marshall, deputy chairman of the Atomic Energy Authority, is further considering the contribution CHP could make towards saving of fuel in Britain. Chapter 5 of the PEP Report on the *British Fuel and Power Industries* published 33 years earlier is headed 'Secondary Resources: Exhaust Heat from Power Stations', and after reviewing schemes in operation in other countries and considering the high cost of laying mains for domestic district heating schemes in built-up areas, concludes that the best opportunities exist in new towns where supplies of waste heat may be offered both to domestic and industrial users. Many other examples could be given where the technology and economics of new methods are discussed in the PEP Industry Reports and are still being discussed today.

Even if history never repeats itself it has been fascinating to skim through these 40 to 50 year-old PEP reports for the purpose of writing this chapter. Here again in 1980 not only much of the British textile industry but also of the European textile industry is in serious trouble. The average size of company has increased enormously in 50 years. Cotton, along with some rayon in the 1930s, has been replaced by synthetics (together with a modest relative revival in wood-based rayon owing to the huge increase in the cost of petro-chemical feedstocks), with cotton holding a relatively minor position. But the problem of over-capacity and the difficulty of justifying new capital investment which faces the big companies – Courtaulds, ICI, Tootals, Carrington-Viyella and so on (even some of the names are still the same) – has an eerily familiar ring. Indian competition gave way to Japanese competition and the Japanese are now feeling the draught from Hong Kong, South Korea, Taiwan and more recently Singapore. Textile production (and, increasingly, making-up) moves around the world to the low-wage countries, aided by the decline in the importance of traditional skills and the vast progress in mechanisation and automation. Who in the 1930s foresaw that Japan would be a world leader in, for example, cameras and motor cycles? The most we could claim is that we foresaw the continued acceleration in technological change, and were deeply concerned that Britain seemed even then to be falling behind in the race – propping up old industries and failing to get quickly enough into new ones.

In our Report on cotton we had to start by looking at a post-war level of unemployment ranging from 11 to 50 per cent in the British cotton industry; at a huge redundancy problem of, perhaps, 14 million spindles and 150,000 looms; at the technical weakness of such mills as were financially sound; and at the financial weaknesses caused by 're-financing' – which meant 'getting out' by many mill-owners while the going was good and, when the depression came, leaving the mills, in effect, in the hands of the banks, which had very little experience and still fewer ideas of how to deal with the situation. We also had to look at the great difficulty of getting the unions to agree to what would now be called increased productivity, but was then known by such phrases as 'more looms per weaver'; and at the virtual impossibility of getting voluntary agreement on measures to deal with these onerous difficulties even from any organisation, such as the Joint Committee of Cotton Trade Organisations, which covered a major part of an industry split up rather rigidly into sub-industries (raw cotton purchase, fine spinning, coarse-count spinning, weaving, finishing, merchanting and so on). We had enough on our plate to try to formulate proposals for the British cotton industry: one has only to look at the fate of, for example, the huge Boussac empire to see the present problems in a much wider geographical context.

**Industrial History; Unforeseen Problems?**
Economic history is a long-established academic discipline. Industrial history is, unfortunately, rarely taught and therefore rarely studied. What can be learned by comparing the problems of the textile industry today with those of 50 years ago? First, perhaps,

the dangers of over-expansion during boom times. Yet from the point of view of the individual company, to fail to expand to meet demand is to risk a dangerous reduction in market share. Forecasting based on industrial market research can help but only to a limited degree, not only because the best-conducted forecasting (i.e. *not* based on extrapolation of past trends) does not always prove accurate, but also because of the time-lag in so many industries involved in bringing new capacity into production. Hitherto redundant capacity has generally been tackled – if at all – when it is clearly long overdue. However, developers of gravel workings now have to provide for the restoration of the land for agriculture, forestry or amenity use before a shovelful can be removed. Should we have considered the possible establishment of redundancy funds before expansion of capacity is authorised? Would this involve a degree of state interference which would be unacceptable to the private sector? The cost implications have, so far as I know, never been worked out for any industry and would involve, among other problems, the complexities of inflation accounting, but probably the main objection would be the attraction of the lower cost now and 'after me the deluge'.

Should we have laid greater stress on the importance of speeding up technical innovation – not so much innovation itself as the rapid practical application of innovations? This, as Israel Sieff saw 50 years ago, is a problem of human relations, but we remain a Luddite-minded society compared, for example, with the USA or Japan. How can people be persuaded to relinquish jobs which involve making something in an unnecessarily costly way? This problem soon leads into that of happiness at work, of pride in controlling the most modern machinery and of the elimination, so far as possible, of fear of redundancy without admitting that a worker with a particular job has a right to retain that same job over the whole span of his working life – thus leading back again to prevention of redundant capacity and speeding up of technical innovation.

I have used the cotton industry only as an example; others among the PEP industry Reports (apart from iron and steel) were less concerned with redundancy but there seem to be some interesting – and far from academic – lessons to be learned by comparing the position of the industry now with that 40 or 50 years ago.

I started listing the beliefs of the Industries Group which I thought had made a major contribution to the ideas of the early 1930s. It would be only right to put down also my thoughts about where we went wrong. Israel Sieff was very keen on the structure of organisations. If you got the structure right, other things would follow. This is a view held by many businessmen and one which, in later years, I have come to doubt. It is probably more important to try to get people to share the same objectives and to look at obstacles and problems from the same viewpoint. Sometimes this can be done by persuasion; at other times, unfortunately, it is necessary to use force of circumstances to get a minority to co-operate (if too much force is used it will obviously be self-defeating). But given shared objectives the right structure is generally not too difficult to design. Israel, the fount of so many of the ideas of the Industries Group, was very keen on Marketing Corporations and Industry Councils. In the case of the steel industry, for example, the PEP report proposed the establishment of a Marketing Corporation for each of the 11 main groups of finished product, citing the already existing British Steelworks Association (which dealt mainly with plates, sections and joists) as the type of organisation envisaged. (Each Marketing Corporation was to be divided into two sections, one for home trade and one for exports.) The PEP Group was probably influenced by the ideas of Walter Elliot and the Agricultural Marketing Boards. Kenneth Lindsay (who had been responsible for bringing together, through his own personal friendships and contacts, so many of the diverse types of people who joined PEP Groups) was, I believe, responsible for this connection, and Lawrence Neal had experience of the subject at about the same time through his very active membership of the Sea-Fish Commission. The Marketing Corporations were to take over staff from producers and from the merchant firms, who were then relatively more important than now. This concept was probably somewhat unrealistic, though in the atmosphere of the time less so than may appear in retrospect (the Milk Marketing Board has, for example, withstood the test of time very well). Producers Associations already existed, were to be encouraged and would be responsible for 'the fate of the redundant and the inefficient'. (In another part of the report special commendation was given to Stewarts' and Lloyds' 'great new enterprise' in building at Corby the first basic Bessemer plant in the UK and the first integrated iron and steelworks!)

The Industry Council would be established to provide close and continuous co-operation between Marketing Corporations and Producers Associations and to promote re-equipment and technical integration in the industry, as well as being responsible for many other activities such as research and development which cannot be briefly summarised here.

### Over-emphasised Proposals?

Another way in which, in retrospect, I think we went wrong was succinctly described by Professor Austin Robinson[1] as 'micro-phobia'. We did not anticipate E. F. Schumacher in recognising that there are many times and places where Small is Beautiful. Professor Robinson could scarcely have opened his review of the PEP Coal Report more generously: 'The Industries Group of PEP has once again placed all economists in its debt' (so that already by 1936 PEP had established its reputation among some economists of the first rank). But he criticised, justly I now think, our emphasis on the efficient overall organisation of marketing by pointing out that we underrated the importance of the small entrepreneur in the distribution network. If, as we suggested, many with very small capital and only one lorry (sometimes hired) gave short weight and sold unsuitable coal with a high slate or dust content, 'by all means let them be licensed and if necessary suspended'; but big organisations tend to have big overheads and if the small man can beat them (honestly), good luck to him and good for the consumer. In practice, as often happens, things have worked out rather differently from what either we or Professor Robinson foresaw. The very big organisations in most of the distributive trades have the lowest overheads and generally offer the lowest prices, but in the grocery trade, for example, the proportion of national turnover held by small shops, after falling dramatically for many years, has in the last few years levelled out. Their market share is being maintained even if their prices are higher.

Things have also worked out differently as regards 'bigness' in industry and commerce in general. Since the war, this has resulted mainly from expansion through acquisition, often with little regard to the suitability and compatibility of the companies merged or acquired. Our early concept of the Chartered Corporation which aimed, among other objectives, to promote vertical integration, to permit the elimination of surplus capacity to be brought about as painlessly as possible, and to provide a sound basis for expansion

---

[1] *Economic Journal*, Sept. 1936 XLVI, p. 183.

of the most efficient units, has fallen before the forces of tax advantage and, often, plain megalomania.

One further much-discussed matter of policy about which I have since had doubts (though I think I accepted it at the time) was the stress laid on 'self-government for industry' as a solution to conflict between employers and unions. The general idea was that there should be less government interference in industry (surprisingly in line with the policy of the present Conservative Government), but that great stress should be placed on the social responsibility of industry and on closer co-operation between individual companies involved in the Chartered Corporations already mentioned. Hindsight points to the fact that we did not sufficiently recognise the possible conflict with the maintenance of competition, especially since we were broadly anti-monopoly in outlook, save under the conditions outlined at the time by Herbert Morrison. Social responsibility in industry has increased in recent decades but half a dozen robber barons can do more harm to the attitude of the public towards industry in general than hundreds of 'goodies'. Moreover the legal problems of the responsibilities of directors towards shareholders, towards employers, towards customers and in relation to other considerations (e.g. the environment) still remain unclear.

In a relatively brief survey such as this, there is an almost insoluble problem about mentioning names. If history is the biography of people then by the omission of names much of the colour of the picture is lost. If they are included, it is impossible to mention all who merit mentioning. If I have caused offence by omissions I hope I shall be forgiven.

## Coda

It is difficult to write about the past without looking at the changes which have created the present and speculating about the future (which is dealt with in Sir Charles Carter's Epilogue). So I have persuaded the editor to let me add a coda (which, according to the infallible Groves, 'has to a certain extent an independent existence, and though not always absolutely necessary, cannot often be easily dispensed with').

It is striking to observe, in looking back at the 1930s, that during the last 50 years the number of bodies engaged in economic and social research in Britain and elsewhere has greatly increased. On the one hand, a number of these are pressure groups like Friends of the Earth who (apart from other activities of widespread appeal, such as the protection of whales) have, in their campaign against nuclear power, assembled a large amount of valuable information and arguments which cannot simply be brushed aside. On the other hand there are organisations which have features of pressure groups in that their membership includes a high proportion of people who have fairly clear and common ideas about the kind of society they wish to live in. Yet they would probably hotly deny that their publications, some of which reach a high standard, lack the factual approach which has been the keynote of PEP work. Examples are the Economic Research Council and the Fabian Society. I am using the term pressure group in the sense of a body whose publications start with a policy and assemble facts and arguments in support of it, often omitting those to the contrary. This is the point of view of the advocate–lawyer whereas PEP has tried to put Francis Bacon's philosophical principles into practice – the point of view of the natural scientist, though even less easy to achieve in the social sciences (including economics) owing to the complexity and unpredictability of the human factors involved.

Although, of course, even those who are not on the lunatic fringe frequently fail in their objectives, it is on the whole easier for pressure groups to claim success in getting their views implemented than it is for PEP. Yet PEP built up its early influence not only by factual reports but also by drawing conclusions based on the facts, with Max's persuasive pen putting into broadsheet (abbreviated) form recommendations which might otherwise have been much less widely read. We had less academic respectability than PEP and now PSI have since achieved, but perhaps no less influence on the world of affairs, particularly if our much smaller budget is taken into account. This raises the whole question of how far it is possible to influence attitudes which are often based on deep emotional feelings by arguments based on facts. On the whole, partly owing to the difficulty of giving satisfactory factual accounts of complex issues on television, public opinions have, over the last 50 years, tended in my view to be increasingly based on emotional attitudes.

Several paradoxes are involved in any consideration of a policy which tries to influence people in key positions. On the one hand the course of events is often influenced mainly by individuals with strongly-held views and the corresponding determination to see them implemented – in recent history, for example, Palmerston, Lloyd George and Milner, none of whom would probably have wanted to see a clear statement of all the facts affecting any problem with which they were currently faced. On the other hand, the increasing number of diaries kept by politicians (such as Crossman and Castle) show clearly how difficult it is for individual politicians to make any changes at all, whether based on a factual report or on their personal convictions. Moreover the Civil Service, many individual members of which have played a very big part over the years in the work of PEP, does not in general look kindly on outside advice, though several departments in the last decade or so have com-missioned studies by PEP and PSI.

The implementation of conclusions from the earlier PEP Reports was, as Max Nicholson has stressed (pp. 49–50), greatly facilitated because they involved the work not just of a single author (or team of two) but of a group, meeting to discuss and criticise both the factual material and the conclusions – with this being made clear in the format of the publications. I regard it as essential, too, that such groups should include a minority of people who are not knowledgeable about the subject under discussion, as well as those engaged in different aspects of it. The only qualifications required by the former are a high level of intelligence, an inquiring and critical mind and willingness to give time for the public good. I do not under-estimate the difficulty of finding such people and the extra administrative work involved in organising group meetings with a high attendance. But individuals who are not necessarily 'establish-ment minded' may be less keen to participate if there is too much aura of academic respectability.

In the earlier industrial work every effort was made to cover both technical and economic aspects of the subject as well as social aspects where relevant. In general, technological research organisations have become increasingly distanced from economic and social research organisations. Economic aspects of technical problems tend to be handled, if at all, by the technological research organisation. PEP's recent co-operation with Chatham House has been very fruitful. Would it be possible to establish similar links and joint ventures with learned societies in the field of technology when PSI is studying subjects involving technical problems?

Consumer survey techniques, which had scarcely started in the 1930s, have been increasingly used during the last decade. Looking back, I feel that PEP should have staked a rather higher proportion of its money on a different horse.

I have already mentioned the birth and death of basic bessemer steel at Corby, well within my working lifetime. There have also been five other changes in the steel industry over the same period. The first three could well be described as revolutionary – replacement of sinter furnaces by pellet plants; basic oxygen furnaces; and continuous casting of steel – and the other two will become so – direct reduction (with elimination of the vast capital cost and labour vulnerability of huge modern blast furnaces); and 'mini-steel works' (already proliferating around the world).

Could we have foreseen any of these? I think probably not, which further emphasises the importance of quick reaction to technological change. I think PEP was probably right not to enter the field of 'futurology'; most of those technological visionaries I have had the good fortune to know are doing well if they are right one in ten times. The other nine forecasts are often quite silly, and the visionaries need a well informed private guard against their own bad ideas. On the other hand the man who gets one really important forecast right is the prototype businessman of the future (a rather different type from the businessman of the past who was often driving 'by the seat of his pants', though he also needs many of the same qualities). This is what I have in mind in suggesting that the PEP Industries Group might have gone a little further in trying to bring about cooperation with the professional societies in the applied sciences and technologies.

One function of a body such as PEP has changed little in the last 50 years. One of the weaknesses of Britain is that we remain a 'split society'. A powerful argument for the critical assembly of relevant facts, for which PEP has stood from the beginning, is that it promotes a more unified outlook and reduces party-political differences on policy. Several people[1] have noted that a major reason for the extraordinary rise of Japan to top position in the world measured by many economic and social yardsticks is the intense concern of the Japanese to collect all relevant facts before reaching decisions on policy; and that these facts should, so far as possible, be made known to and discussed by those likely to be affected by the policies

---

[1] See for example Vogel, Ezra F., *Japan as Number One: Lessons for America*, Cambridge, Mass., Harvard University Press, 1979.

concerned – whether a government department (e.g. foreign trade negotiations), the general public (e.g. transport facilities), or a small local community (e.g. refuse disposal and environmental pollution). PEP, and now PSI, is one of the bodies best placed to further such a process in Britain.

# 4

# The Second World War

## Michael Young

Max Nicholson has described earlier how even before war was declared PEP had created a Post-War Aims Group. Within a week of its outbreak he circulated a draft on war aims and peace terms. This set the tone for PEP over the next five years. During the war which Britain so nearly lost the work of PEP was based throughout on the one premise, that we were going to win.

There was no pretence that, when first adopted, it was popular to talk about war aims. The government of Mr Chamberlain was not one of the most distinguished in Britain's history. Its members did not, during the period of the 'phoney war', show any marked resolution in the prosecution of the war, let alone any concern for what might be done in the unlikely event of their efforts being adequate. *Planning* No. 157, published a few months after Hitler's invasion of Poland, with the typically downbeat title of *Reconstruction, 1916–19*, expressed the general mood of PEP when it said that:

> From some standpoints it will seem premature, at the start of what may be a long war, to begin thinking about post-war reconstruction. Those whose mental horizon is never far in front of their noses will react against such a suggestion in precisely the same way that they reacted against, for example, tackling the gold standard and international payments questions before the collapse of 1931, or against facing rearmament when the Nazis began their bid for world domination. Others will urge with more justification that, important as post-war reconstruction is, every hour devoted to it is an hour taken away from winning the war, which has the prior claim on all our resources. Others again will point to the enormous social and economic changes which must be impending,

and will maintain that until the general trend of these changes has emerged any plans for the future can only be building on sand. Yet others are fearful that controversies arising from discussions on reconstruction may impair national unity, or unity between allies.

There were two main reasons for brooking unpopularity. The first was that the war, cataclysmic as it was no doubt to be, was also an immediate opportunity for PEP. It had been calling for national policies to cure unemployment and generally pull the country out of the despond of the 1930s, and now here (if in a rather flimsy shape) was a government which had at last responded if not to Max Nicholson then to Adolph Hitler. Unemployment disappeared; a grip was taken on the economy. PEP had also been calling for a sense of national purpose, not just as leader writers did and do when they can think of nothing better for their daily stint, but backed up by a wealth of detail about the steps that were needed. The national purpose (including steps already recommended) was even more necessary now that the long-expected war had broken out. A new cutting edge was given to what had been said, and implied, before. Planning was vital now if people were to believe (as many of them did not at first) that the war was worth fighting. 'Men are moved by ideas', and PEP was ready to state what moved the men (and the few women) of PEP. In that same declamatory broadsheet from which I have just quoted, the point was put in this way:

Again, it is incontestable that winning the war must come first, but this argument overlooks the great part which planning for subsequent reconstruction can play even in the immediate task of achieving military victory. Men are moved by ideas, and no dictator has yet produced, or is likely to produce, a secret weapon in any way comparable with the military power of a compelling idea compellingly stated. It is astonishing that in the countries where Cromwell's Ironsides and the armies of the French Revolution once swept all before them because they knew what they were fighting for, it should be necessary seriously to assert the need for stating what we stand for, at home and abroad, in terms which will satisfy both the idealism and the many-sided practical interests of contemporary men and women. It is because people today no longer respond to old catchwords, and are rightly suspicious of fine phrases unaccompanied by acceptable proposals for putting them into practice, that thought on post-war reconstruction must be regarded as an essential element in British and French war effort. Indeed, Nazi leaders are credibly reported to have risked the war only because of their confidence in the superior strength of the democracies being nullified by confusion of values and lack of clear thinking on the issues. The Nazis have never made the mistake of neglecting to plan ahead or of underrating the force of ideas, and it is these qualities, rather than any material advantages, that have enabled them to seize the initiative from military powers controlling a far larger share of the world's human and material resources.

## The Essential Element

The 'essential element' PEP proceeded to supply, in good measure, long before the War Cabinet had begun to think that any such element was needed at all. By November 1939, even before the broadsheet I have just quoted from, which expressed the general stance of the organisation, another broadsheet entitled *European Order and World Order*, largely written by Max, sailed with consummate confidence into a rather large subject: the kind of world – world, not just Britain – that needed to come out of the war. 'Despite its immense achievements, Western civilisation now finds itself left without a dynamic and simple faith.' Western civilisation did not include Queen Anne's Gate.

Though the context was international the broadsheet devoted much space to Europe and Britain's relations with it. This could be done without too many qualms being expressed about the contrary pull of the British Commonwealth. PEP had early in its life declared itself to be on the side of the internationalism of a Sir Arthur Salter rather than the imperialism of a Sir Basil Blackett. Even so, the argument was as bold as bold could be. Two world wars had started from conflicts between the nations of Europe. This must not be allowed to happen again, which meant recognising that within Europe nationalism was so dangerous a force that it must be replaced by an approach to federalism – though Max saw federalism as an aim to be achieved eventually, rather than in one great leap as was advocated by the then very active Federal Union movement. 'There seems no escaping the conclusion that the final objective of any new political institutions must be some form of federalism.' A federal Europe would have to be 'based on the full participation of Great Britain, on the finding for Germany of a role which will fully absorb German constructive energies and will prove permanently acceptable to the German people, on the giving of security to France and to all other nations which have felt threatened by German aggression, and on adequate recognition and provision for the interests in Europe of the USA and the USSR'.

The nucleus for a European government would be promoted by a standing European Council of Premiers and a general European assembly, with representation weighted according to population. The assembly would be an embryo Parliament of Europe. Under the European Council would come a common policing agency for Europe. All member states (including Britain) would be prohibited from having heavy artillery, heavy tanks and military aircraft, these being reserved for the common force. 'A main difficulty here would be the problem of Russia, which could hardly be included in a European group, but would have to be in close treaty relations with it if wholesale reduction of armaments was to be attained.'

The second agency to come under the European Council would be an economic one financed by a percentage levy, say of 2·5 per cent on each country's budget, committed to European development as a whole. 'There are many functions such as the improvement of communications, of credit facilities, health services, education and research which could more effectively be promoted by a European agency than by a host of national agencies.' Common funds should also be provided for the poorer countries of the world. 'Part of the resources of the more advanced countries should be jointly made available for assisting the less developed territories to realise their potential productivity. International public works should be undertaken where scientific and market surveys show possibilities.'

The broadsheet did not go quite unnoticed. It was thought that a European federation would have some special appeal in France, which had been attacked twice by Germany within a quarter of a century; anything that could be done to raise morale in France was worth doing. (The broadsheet immediately preceding that, on *The Home Front*, in October, 1939, which I wrote, hailed the new Supreme War Council partly because it consisted of two British and two French representatives and was near to an effective organ of international control.) *European Order and World Order* was translated into French and quite widely circulated across the Channel. Churchill's historic offer to France on the eve of its defeat in 1940 was in accord with the sentiments of the broadsheets. But after that official baton-raising, though broadsheets kept strumming the same tune throughout the war, there was never so much interest again. If only it had been sustained and government policy moved forward on the lines of Salter rather than Blackett; if only Bevin had not been so much a British Commonwealth man; if Churchill had been less an English-speaking union man and had taken that 1939 broadsheet as his brief when he returned to power 12 years later in 1951, then Britain would have been the acknowledged leader of Europe and architect of a more generous Common Market. But PEP history, like that of many other organisations which are concerned with government though not of it, is made up of a chronology of 'if onlys'. Perhaps more strangely, it is a part of PEP history which PEP itself barely seemed to be aware of when, much later, it mounted a large research programme on the Common Market. One of the broadsheets on the European Parliament (No. 478) published in 1964 ended with the melancholy sentence, 'Finally, one can only hope that, if and when the United Kingdom joins the Communities, it will do all it can to strengthen the position of the European Parliament'.

## Large Ambitions, Small Resources

The pace was fast in the first three months because the war had been anticipated, and with it the need for war aims more appealing than unconditional surrender. The more attractive the post-war prospect could be made, the stronger our will to win and the weaker the German resolve. Planning for war implied planning for post-war. On these cardinal points of principle there was no faltering. But unfortunately, though the aspirations could hardly be higher, the resources with which they might be realised were not adequate to the task. 'Slender' is the most obvious word to use. The war halved the staff and doubled the ambitions. Max himself, though he was in the building at Queen Anne's Gate almost every day for lunch or one of the seemingly endless meetings which are the thread running through the life of PEP, left the staff for the newly-created Ministry of Information, along with Archer Lindsey, Miss Beatrice Lawrence, Kate Harris, H. T. Maling and Miss Vera Handcock. The fraternal office run by Oliver Roskill was taken over by the Ministry of Economic Warfare to which he, together with his partners Oliver Lawrence and John Lamb, both of whom had done much drafting for PEP, and the whole staff of O. W. Roskill Industrial Consultants were transferred. Max returned in November 1939 (with Miss Harris), only to leave again in April 1940 for the Ministry of Shipping where he rose to eminence at the sort of dizzy speed which is possible only in wartime.

Richard Fitter, Richard Terrell and François Lafitte – the latter an absolutely key member of the staff – stayed on, for a time. But they would not have been able to manage without an influx of volunteers, headed by Leonard Elmhirst who became more than spare-time Chairman in October 1939. Two retired civil servants, Sir Henry Bunbury and Sir Ronald Davison, also almost joined the staff. Henry did a lot of the administration and managed the finances throughout the war years, and we were hardly ever short of money. In 1945, with the help of a Rockefeller grant and the usual support from Dartington and from Israel Sieff, we were up to an expenditure of £9000 a year, and coasting. Theodor Prager, an Austrian economist who joined the staff during the war, wrote about Henry to me from Vienna in one of the countries that was supposed to be in PEP's new Federal Europe:

> There was Sir Henry, as gentle and kind a man as I ever knew. He had a thing about 'costs', or was it overhead costs, and we were rather inclined to smile at ourselves when the subject came up, not realizing for a while how much good horse sense, combined with idealism and commitment, rare these days, there was in the man; but even before we did he had our affection in a way which only very good, and elderly, people, draw out in one. I would wish his daughters, whom unfortunately we never had the good fortune to meet, to know what a lovable person he was to all of us.

During the first year of the war I was the only full-time person moving the opposite way from the others, inwards. I was appointed personal assistant to Max a few days before the war, in August 1939. Having been a pupil at Dartington Hall School, I already knew about PEP through Leonard Elmhirst. Immediately after Munich I was so sure war was coming, so keen to do something to prepare for it and so disillusioned with my studies at the London School of Economics that I asked Max if he would give me a job planning for the war whose imminence so few people were taking seriously. Max said no – I must finish my studies – but I could write a broadsheet for him, on a subject he had already in mind: what manpower policy should be in the war when it did come. I was extremely lucky. I was able to write the most influential paper I have ever published, perhaps the only one – *Planning* No. 133 of 1 November 1938 – only because I found in the LSE library as if by magic a book by Humbert Wolfe on labour supply in 1914–18. The book wrote the broadsheet for me. So much had evidently gone wrong in that previous war because the government relied on volunteers, many of whom had skilled jobs in industry upon which the forces depended for their supplies. It was obvious that all volunteering for the armed forces should be banned, conscription introduced and a list of essential or reserved occupations drawn up which people should be required to remain in, however much they wanted to 'fight' instead of manufacture planes, grow food or design radar. In a total war of the kind we were going to get, everyone, soldier and worker alike, had to be subject to conscription. This was planning all right, of a far-reaching kind, recommended in a broadsheet written in one evening. The failure of the French government (or the German, for that matter) to go the same way was noted in a broadsheet published early in 1940, *Economic Priorities in War*. The earlier broadsheet secured me the offer of a job in the tiny part of the civil service actually preparing for war and also in PEP when I had finished my studies. PEP it turned out to be. I stayed as a research assistant from August 1939 until June 1941, when I went into a munitions factory, and then came back in March 1942 to act as Secretary when David Owen resigned to become personal assistant to Sir Stafford Cripps and, later, Deputy Executive Secretary of the Preparatory Commission of the United Nations. Presumably I was made *acting* Secretary to begin with partly because, although I was 26, I looked about 18.

Work went ahead and publications likewise until May 1940, when the second broadsheet on *The Home Front* appeared to underline the obvious, this always being one of PEP's characteristics, presumably responsible for its survival. On this occasion it announced what all the world knew: 'With the Nazi invasion of the Low Countries the War has entered an entirely new phase.' The War (which had acquired a capital letter) led to a further dispersal of staff and, for a few months, to a suspension of publication. The building only closed on one day while an unexploded bomb was defused next door. The PEP Club was open for lunch throughout the Battle of Britain and the subsequent night-bombing of London.

In the Elmhirst correspondence at Dartington there is a letter from Dorothy to Leonard of 19 January 1941; it is about one of her visits

to PEP at that time. I was known as Youngster, to distinguish me
from her son, Michael.

> PEP has had to substitute boards for windows and I found David
> working by electric light and the back windows of the dining room
> being bricked in. Lunch takes place in the lower front room, and
> there I had a gay meal with Youngster. His report on London
> has at last been released by Max and now there is hope of publish-
> ing it. Max's reluctance to issuing broadsheets is probably due
> to his fear that standards of research and writing will deteriorate
> and damage the ultimate reputation of PEP – but there are doubt-
> less other reasons too.

The report mentioned by Dorothy was boiled down to a broadsheet, the first to appear when regular publication was resumed in
February 1941. It was a strain to link description with the main
concern with the future which had become PEP's hallmark. Against
the background of 'the drone of bomber engines, the barrage reaching
blindly upwards, the bombs tearing the sky, and the final explosion'
the prosaic fact was noted that the richer boroughs had excelled
with their ARP ... 'Westminster and Kensington, for example, have
been noteworthy for the high standard of their civil defence arrangements, while Stepney has been as noteworthy for its failures'. But
it was rather over-hopeful to believe that this would lead, long-term,
to a much greater ironing out of disposable revenue between the
different parts of London. So it was to imagine that London government might be simplified by making the nine wartime ARP groups
into the nine electoral districts of a London Regional Council. Likewise, even to hint that there might, to relieve transport congestion,
be a peacetime equivalent of the 'Help your neighbour' scheme for
motorists and drivers of motor-cycle combinations living within a
20-mile radius of London. Drivers received extra petrol coupons if
they regularly carried passengers to and from the centre of London.
But to try and imagine how things might be in a future without
bombs was too deeply ingrained in the belief and practice of wartime
PEP to be ignored. Perhaps it was just the right note for the Ministry
of Information which immediately ordered 2000 extra copies of the
broadsheet. If I remember rightly, our paper ration was increased.

**Archbishop of York**
The same habit certainly persisted in the further work that was done

on the new international order. It was given a fillip by the first signs of official interest. The blitzkrieg had converted many more people, even in the government, to the cause, as it became, of planning for the post-war period than many thousands of broadsheets could have done. In November 1940 Lord Halifax and R. A. Butler invited a group from PEP to talk with them at the Foreign Office. Max, David Owen and Julian Huxley were accompanied by the Archbishop of York. The Cabinet by this time had set up a Sub-Committee on Reconstruction. At the instance of Lord Halifax PEP was asked to submit reports on reconstruction problems and, on the special and typically businesslike request of Mr Attlee who was a member of the Sub-Committee, the government set aside a reasonably safe shelter for PEP where meetings could be held and members of study groups sleep overnight. I slept there often.[1] The appearance of Mr Attlee was significant. The Labour Ministers in the coalition government were much keener than the Conservatives on post-war planning. They were more worried that the dole queues would form up again. PEP outside the government became one of Labour's informal allies. In June 1941, the Labour Minister, Arthur Greenwood, asked PEP to prepare evidence for the Beveridge Committee on social insurance.

The Post-War Reconstruction Group, which was to begin as not quite a recognised PEP group, eventually became the International Group. Between them they produced the response to the invitation from Lord Halifax and the Cabinet Sub-Committee. The first fruit was a broadsheet (No. 171) on *America and Britain*, in June 1941, before Pearl Harbour, but after the Lease-Lend Act. It was not as novel or as controversial as the earlier one on Europe. After showing how much the two countries had in common in their past and in the way their war economies were shaping up, the broadsheet expressed confidence that the one country under a President of West European descent and the other under a Prime Minister of partly American descent would draw closer and closer together. 'The important thing is to multiply the threads which bind us, and to create an irresistible vested interest among the people of both nations in the continuous strengthening of those ties.' There was no reference

[1] But wartime work at PEP was not always so safe. Michael Young modestly omits to cite the part of Teddy Prager's note to him (see p. 86) which recalls Michael's unshakeable concentration on the details of an editorial session while the bombs fell closer and closer. (Editor)

to any possible conflict between a special relationship with America and the leading role PEP was projecting for Britain in Europe.

**Future of Europe**

The possibility of such a conflict was admitted, no more. The future of Europe was from the beginning of the war the great topic for PEP. The ardent hope was that the United States would see Britain as the agent of Anglo–Saxondom in Europe and the nations of the British Commonwealth be happy to act as supporters for the mother country of democracy in the rest of the world in its new role as mother of a united democratic Europe. Britain's success with its commonwealth meant that the British peoples had a principle of international organisation to offer as a pattern for a commonwealth of Europe.

*Britain and Europe*, published at the end of 1941, was no doubt sent straight to Lord Halifax at the Foreign Office. He cannot have had many such dazzling visions presented to him. The issue was starkly presented:

> It is in Europe that the old power-system has most manifestly broken down, and the lessons of Hitlerism emerge most clearly. To Hitler, indeed, Europe will owe, as it owed to Napoleon, a number of achievements of permanent value. Above all, he has succeeded in recreating the basis of European unity, although on lines very different from his aims. Much of what he has done in building up economic and administrative unity in Europe, and in breaking down barriers, it will be neither desirable nor possible to undo. The issue is no longer whether Europe should remain united, but in what form and by what leadership.

Even if Germany lost the war it might, without a British initiative, emerge again as the leader of Europe. 'If a victorious Britain were once again to contract out of Europe and the USSR were too weakened by the war to take its place, then slowly but surely, as Germany recovered, the leadership of an impoverished and disunited Europe would pass again to Germany.'

Then followed the case for British leadership, mind you with the full backing of the Dominions and the USA, and in close working agreement with the USSR:

> In her island position at the extremity of Europe and as the metropolis of a world-wide commonwealth based on the oceans,

Great Britain is the natural bridge between Europe and America
and between Europe and the world at large – between Europe and
the universal economic commonwealth. This is a function
which is vital to the future well-being of Europe. It is one which,
if only because of their geographical position, neither the USSR
nor Germany can fulfil, whatever the ideology or form of government.

By receiving on their shores the governments or leading
representatives of the oppressed nations, including Germans themselves, in the fight against Hitlerism, the British people have in
fact already accepted the moral leadership of Europe in war. It
would be an act of renunciation amounting almost to betrayal
to throw it aside in the peace.

The same theme was illustrated in other broadsheets on the future
of Germany and the future of France and, again in a more general
vein, in one called *The New Pattern*. This argued for a more
complete democracy than there had ever been in any European
or other country in peacetime. War had encouraged participation.
A new neighbourliness had been shown to such marvellous effect
in London while it was being bombed. The broadsheet therefore
called for peacetime equivalents of the air-raid wardens, fire-
watchers, social workers and users of meal and rest centres who
would between them re-invigorate democracy throughout Europe.
Education too was to play a new part in making Britain fit for
its new role:

The schools' contribution towards the ideal of learning together
is limited by the fatal class cleavage in the public education system,
the higher social and income groups being forced out of the
national structure by convention instead of being forced into it.
Moreover, learning together stops just at the age when it could
be most fruitful: in some form it might extend to all age groups
who might together learn, for instance, how to swim, sail a boat,
argue logically, use maps, dance, draw, paint, play and listen to
music, act, do first aid, fly, drive different sorts of vehicles, climb,
cook, keep fit, speak in public, take the chair at meetings, arrange
colours, camp, remember things, ride, overcome personal defects,
cut down trees, make and build things, grow things, keep animals,
stand upright, judge character, understand economics, write
English, eat intelligently, navigate by the stars, know the law,
breathe, talk foreign languages, recognise animals and plants,
distinguish between facts and opinions, use statistics or shoot.

The new breed of intellectuals on horseback would have deserved to lead Europe, even the world.

In this series of broadsheets PEP was playing for high stakes. In the 1930s the focus was on the ills of Britain itself. The effect of the war was electric. It made PEP internationalist but with a single focus, the need for a united Continent led by Britain. If the advice had been followed, Max Nicholson, like Jean Monnet, might have been remembered as one of the fathers of the new Europe.

## Beveridge Report

Where the stakes were lower PEP turned out to have a great deal more influence. I have mentioned Arthur Greenwood's invitation to give evidence to the Beveridge Committee. This François Lafitte did in great style. The longest broadsheet so far produced – even longer than *London Under Bombing* – was *Planning for Social Security*, published on 14 July 1942. It was followed in its main recommendations by the Beveridge Report itself, PEP being quite as keen as Beveridge to relieve the insecurity 'whose effects are just as deadening as the effects of unbroken security in a Santa Claus State'. PEP, like Beveridge later, proposed a National Minimum, a financial Plimsoll line, below which no family, whether in work or in distress, should be obliged to sink; universal family allowances; a single Ministry of Social Security to take over the administration of all income–maintenance services; and a National Health Service of the kind that had been foreshadowed in PEP's prescient 1937 report on *The British Health Services*. There was also a great deal of more homely detail – like the proposal that every social security office should have a Citizens' Advice Bureau in it, not controlled by the statutory authorities.

The only important difference – and on this I am sure PEP got it more right than Beveridge – was about how to pay for the new social security. Beveridge plumped for an extension of the insurance contributions to which the British public had become accustomed, PEP for their gradual abolition. The contributions had too many affinities with commercial insurance. If everyone was to be raised above a Plimsoll line it made no sense to make benefits dependent on the right numbers of contributions having been paid. Flat-rate contributions were also regressive – the lower the income, the larger the proportion of it went in contributions. In their place PEP proposed that the full costs of the new comprehensive social security should be borne out of taxes, involving a 'complete overhaul and simplification of taxation machinery and methods'. I remember discussing this by the hour in PEP's nearby pub, *The Two Chairmen*, with François and Teddy Prager and Erwin Rothbarth, a brilliant German refugee who had played hockey with me at LSE and was then Maynard Keynes's assistant before being allowed to break the rules of the wartime manpower policy and volunteer for the Pioneer Corps. He was killed in Holland.

Relations with Keynes were close through most of the war years. Drafts of many broadsheets were sent to him for comment, and all of them when published. He wrote about the Beveridge broadsheet: 'In my opinion it is a particularly good piece of work, one of the best the organisation has ever produced.'[1] Relations with Beveridge were the same. PEP gave evidence to him again for his next report, on full employment.

The broadsheet on *Employment for All*, published in May 1943, contained the guts of that evidence and of what I and Teddy Prager had learnt of the new Keynesianism while we were at the LSE. Doctrine was flavoured with the colour of war:

> Even during a war which for the second time in a century has brought about full, too full, employment, people are fearful of tomorrow. Soldiers travelling on leave, sailors waiting for their ships, munition workers having a lunch-hour game of darts are often, surprisingly often, cynical and shrug-shouldered about the future of the society of which they are a part. They joke grimly about the expected queues outside the Labour Exchanges and even anticipate the day when they, personally, will be thrown on the scrap-heap of unemployment.

Prager and I expanded the broadsheet into a book with the awful title of *There's Work for All*,[2] as I also did with another broadsheet I wrote on the unlikely subject of how to organise post-war civil aviation,[2] not just for Britain but for the world.

These were some of our larger subjects. In addition there were hundreds of smaller ones from consumer research to the journey

[1] PEP Archive, LSE.

[2] Young, Michael and Prager, Theodor, *There's Work for All*, London, Nicholson and Watson, 1945.

[3] *International Air Transport*, 29 June 1943. The book was published under the title *Civil Aviation* by Pilot Press, (Target for Tomorrow series), London, 1944.

to work, some having the benefit (if it was a benefit) of a series of broadsheets to themselves. One such was on government information services. The group on the domestic service was chaired by S. C. Leslie, who was in charge of public relations at the Home Office. It proposed (*Planning* No. 230) that a Central Publicity Unit should be set up after the war; this was done, in the form of the Central Office of Information. The one on overseas services (*Planning* No. 213) proposed that a Publicity Department should be set up inside the Foreign Office and this was also done with another name – not perhaps surprising since one of the members of the group, Alan Dudley, was also an official at the Foreign Office who later became Head of its Information Policy Department.

On this sort of level relations with the civil service were very close. They used us; we used them. I do not remember ever being turned away when I went to any department for help, as I was always doing, along with other members of the staff. We also got on well with the press. Almost all the broadsheets were reviewed and treated as news stories. One little event was the 200th broadsheet in 1943. *The Times* of 25 January said in a leading article:

> The body familiarly known as PEP (Political and Economic Planning) has now published number 200 in its series of reports or 'broadsheets'. In the twelve years that they have been at work PEP have scored a success and earned a reputation of no small significance. They have taken for their field of study, and by their efforts have done much to enlarge, that territory of the social sciences in which wide collaboration is practicable among men and women of different political views. The foundation of their method is derived from the natural and experimental sciences; it consists in a scrupulous attention to fact. But to PEP belongs the credit of founding itself expressly upon this belief and of proving it true that an impartial approach is possible to many large questions in the realm of politics. Both the degree in which consent is attainable among those who are prepared to accept the discipline of inquiry and to follow the argument where it leads and the extent to which the method is applicable in current matters of public concern have had a highly encouraging demonstration in the experience of PEP.

The attentions of the press were one of the reasons for the steady increase in the number of subscribers to *Planning*, from just under 500 in 1942 to 2057 early in 1944. Discussion groups in the services and in industry (I started an Industrial Bureau of Current Affairs as a counterpart to the Army Bureau) were able to subscribe at half price, ten shillings a year. A single copy of each broadsheet was air-mailed to New York where it was reproduced by the *New Republic* for swift despatch to American subscribers. The National Planning Association had been established in Washington on the model of PEP, largely as the result of the effort put in by Leonard Elmhirst, and NPA helped us to raise an American subscription list. We had a special relationship.

### Happiness on £750 a year

There was too much improvisation and we probably tried to do too much, and did not do it well enough. In my final report to the Executive Committee when I resigned as Secretary in 1945 – I was very well satisfied with my salary of £750 a year, that was not the reason – there was not much in it about a united Europe or a regenerated democracy:

> The Secretary has also had to contend with most of the petty administrative matters which are always coming up. Over many years PEP has become a kind of post office for information and hundreds of people make use of it as though it were a combination of a PRO, a Labour Exchange and Selfridge's Information Bureau. We may be asked to suggest the names of authors for a series of articles in Picture Post, or a series of books in the Target for Tomorrow series, speakers for the Reigate Rotary Club or London Co-operative Forum, speakers to talk to RAF units in the Mediterranean, experts to comment on a report on the Pottery Industry, prepared by the Stoke WEA, or a report on the Coal Industry prepared by the Pontypool Social Settlement, or to comment ourselves on a memorandum by Colonel Devereux or by the Reconstruction Director of Bristol Aeroplane Company, or to criticise and to prepare a reading list for Army Education booklets, or to help to start a new magazine or to find a job for someone or to find someone for a job. In the course of a few months literally hundreds of such requests flow into the office by letter, by telephone and, worst, in the shape of a visitor. The simplest response would be to say 'Sorry, we can't help' to all the enquirers. But this would be out of the question. We are our-selves helped in large numbers of ways by many people and we cannot refuse our co-operation in return. And we can never feel content to leave the implementation of PEP ideas to the mere publication of the broadsheet. If PEP members can be helped to find outlets in such books as those published in the New Democracy and Target for Tomorrow series, that is all to the good.

If we can in any way help a local Reconstruction Group in Chatham or a town planner in Glasgow, then that too is worthwhile.

Routine PEP administration is also heavy. There are the printers and publishers to deal with, the proofs of the reports and broadsheets to read. There are the meetings to arrange, bad attenders to follow up, people to invite and people to thank for commenting on any one of the several hundred substantial drafts which leave the office every year. There are newspapers to write to about broadsheets, critics and admirers to appease or congratulate on their good judgment, American and other foreigners to entertain. Again there are hundreds of jobs, but Miss Harris and Miss Nuttall provide the most competent, indispensable assistance.

So the Secretary has tended to become a mere tactician. He has been buried in day to day affairs instead of having time to think about policy and to advise the Executive accordingly. He has had far too little time for what should be his main job, namely mapping out suggestions for policy, assisting drafters and, since he is normally the only person who goes to all group meetings, coordinating the work of the different groups and drafters. These two years have been a breathless struggle. Without Henry Bunbury it would have been quite impossible to avoid drowning.

The conclusions which emerge from this analysis are as follows: firstly and tritely, PEP must employ on its staff only people who can write with reasonable clarity. It is a delusion to think that bad drafters can be trained. Lack of drafting ability seems to be like cancer, incurable except by surgery: two of the worse offenders have left the staff in the last month. There should be a chance to build on surer foundations in the next year. In choosing new staff it should be realised that the only essential qualifications are (1) drafting ability, (2) intelligence.

I was still heady with hope when I took up my new job as Secretary of the Labour Party Policy Committee and Head of the Research Department. *Let Us Face the Future*, as the Labour Party programme for the 1945 General Election was rather ham-handedly called, had packed into it as many ideas from PEP as I could decently get past Herbert Morrison, the manager of the campaign.

# 5

# The First Post-war Decade

## Raymond Goodman

PEP emerged from the war in much the same condition, on a miniature scale, as the country itself: a solid programme for rehabilitating and reshaping society for peacetime, an urgent need to relieve the overworked team that had held things together on the 'Home Front', a great fund of enthusiasm to get on with the job, and a shortage of almost everything else.

The immediate task was to rebuild the groups and recruit new staff. Several of the small band of members and staff who had been able to work with PEP during the war years were absorbed in fulltime jobs elsewhere, although most of them continued to give time to group work, several as chairmen. After Michael Young left early in the spring of 1945 to head the Labour Party's Research Department, Denis Routh and Guy Hunter had in turn taken over as Director, but the latter was anxious to take up an appointment as head of Urchfont College in Wiltshire. A personnel selection committee was appointed by the Executive, and between December 1945 and June of the following year an almost entirely new research staff and a new Director had been recruited; some of us were interviewed while still in uniform. Only one or two had any professional experience before the war, although most had completed their education. As might have been expected, the recruits for the most part had a background in the social sciences – economics, politics, or social administration – although there was an infusion from the humanities in connection with the work on the visual arts and the film industry. The natural sciences, however, were unrepresented. Looking back, it seems regrettable that the remarkable flowering of technological research and application during the war, which continued into peacetime, was largely overlooked in PEP's otherwise broad coverage of important topics. But we were not entirely 'monocultural' as C. P. Snow might later have said. We had scientists like Julian Huxley and Michael Perrin on our governing bodies, and through an occasional speaker at lunches at the PEP Club we kept in touch with the world of science.

The roles of the Executive, the working members and the staff of PEP were altered subtly but significantly by the new post-war conditions. Perhaps the main difference was in the circumstances of leading members of the Executive and the groups. The civil servants, for example, no longer played, like the fountains in Trafalgar Square, from ten to four in offices that Anthony Trollope would not have found totally unfamiliar. In the 1940s and 1950s they had difficulty getting to meetings at lunchtime or dinner meetings as early as seven o'clock. Their counterparts in the universities were faced with a sudden flood of ex-servicemen and women, and the demands of an expanding system of higher education; and in industry with the switch from war production to the needs of the home and export markets. The change from under- to over-employment meant that such drafting as working members were able to do – and some did a surprising amount – had to be fitted into limited leisure hours. Even so, most of the fact-finding and research had to be done by the staff.

Another significant change from before the war was that government management of the economy during wartime had created a need for economists and statisticians; many of the departments afterwards retained or increased staff in these disciplines. Several of the senior ones – notably Alec Cairncross, who was Economic Adviser to the Board of Trade from 1946 to 1949, Philip Chantler who held a similar post at Fuel and Power, and Edward Warner at the Foreign Office – were active members of PEP. They had access to information on a far broader scale than before the war, and were able to discuss economic issues at a level of sophistication that earlier civil servants would have found hard to grasp, if not a little unseemly. Similarly, in the newly nationalised industries, the enlarged social services and even the private sector, economic information, statistics and their interpreters multiplied in malthusian numbers. Social and opinion surveys, which also owed much to the war, had become essential tools of government, as well as the political parties, academic research and the advertising industry. In the universities, departments of sociology, not regarded as a respectable discipline in most of them before the war, began to be established. Research institutes, such as the National Institute of Economic and Social Research, were now working in a field where PEP had not only to be aware of these developments but to stay up with the leaders.

Although these changes meant greater competition for PEP, the political and intellectual climate was friendlier to the kind of ideas that PEP fostered than it had been in the thirties. No longer was planning regarded as an instrument of communism, the corporate state or the devil, depending on one's viewpoint. There were, of course, famous rows between the government and the medical profession over the creation of a National Health Service, and the nationalisation of major industries was scarcely carried out by consensus. But there was no serious challenge to the principal goals of full employment, comprehensive social services and a more positive role for government in economic and social affairs. Differences between the two major parties centred mainly on the proper degree of control over the decisions and actions of private business and the general public. When the Conservatives returned to power in 1951 they celebrated with a 'dash for freedom' and removed many of the controls that survived Harold Wilson's 'bonfire'.

Rationing was not finally abolished until 1954, and exchange control had to wait another 25 years before being lifted by a new Conservative administration. Monetary policy was re-introduced as a tool of government, although not as the centrepiece of economic policy that it became in the present administration. The essential structure of the Welfare State, as it had come to be called, was left unchanged and in some ways improved. Denationalisation was confined to the steel industry and parts of road haulage. This was the era of 'Butskellism', the afterglow of wartime national unity.

The generally amiable atmosphere of the time pervaded Queen Anne's Gate. Several members of the new staff had political ambitions which were more the occasion for teasing than controversy when we met for tea in the library at four o'clock. Angus Maude and James MacColl for the Tories and for Labour, respectively, nursed constituencies and became members of the House of Commons in 1950. Jo Grimond also entered the House in 1950, and became Leader of the Liberal Party in 1956; meanwhile, the portion of his time that he did not spend on PEP work he gave to Liberal politics. Tom McKitterick tilted a lance for Labour in York and was unhorsed. Among the women, Jennifer Jenkins was the wife of a rising young star on the Labour benches, and before joining PEP Lalage Sharp was one of a group of able young women who livened up the proceedings of the Holborn Borough Council.

The staffing 'establishment' in those years was not very formal, but there was an understanding that each major study required one senior and one junior research assistant. Since we planned to have about five major studies going at a time, this meant a nominal strength of some ten research staff to serve the working groups, prepare the reports and write the majority of the broadsheets. Editing and some of the original writing, especially of broadsheets that did not stem from the main studies, fell to me as Director and my editorial assistants (from early 1950, George McRobie who later became a leading disciple of Fritz Schumacher, the messiah of beauty in small things, and is now Chairman of the Intermediate Technology Group). The broadsheets served many purposes: to keep members and subscribers in touch with our work; to comment on topical issues; to foreshadow the results of a major study and on occasion to substitute for one that could not be completed in book form; and to give the groups an outlet for interim studies or work that fell outside the boundaries of their final report. During the first post-war decade we published an average of 14–15 broadsheets a year. When the subject was of general interest, as many of them were, they attracted the notice of the national press, which treated them as news items. The trade and specialised press picked up broadsheets in their fields. The editor of one leading scientific journal regularly used the broadsheets as a quarry for his editorials.

It was assumed that there would be a considerable turnover of the research staff as studies were completed, but that the administrative staff would provide continuity. The latter, headed by Marion Nuttall, known affectionately as 'Matron', Kate Harris (publications and publicity) and Della Matthews (accounts) stayed for many years. This small staff was augmented in the early post-war years by Oliver Roskill's office, which was commissioned to prepare reports on the engineering and fuel and power industries. However, the staff was seldom up to strength. When someone left, or took on a part-time appointment elsewhere (for example, as a member of one of the New Town Corporations), he was not always replaced.

At one time we were down to a single senior and six juniors. Leaving vacancies unfilled was the simplest way of balancing the budget at times of special stringency, but at some cost in delaying work on important studies. Delays could have been more serious, but for the help in drafting given on occasion by members of the Executive and key members of the groups.

### The First Post-war Programme

The programme of work for the immediate post-war period was drawn up at an Executive weekend meeting in May 1945. Reporting in October 1948 on the completion of the programme, the 289th broadsheet remarked:

> Looking ahead three years ago it was not difficult to make an intelligent guess about the nature of the main problems which would beset Britain in the reconstruction period ... First and foremost, there was the deterioration in Britain's international economic situation as the result, among other things, of the sale of overseas investments, the loss of nearly half the merchant fleet and the rapidly rising prices of food and raw materials ... At the same time, a complementary examination was needed of the main elements of domestic economic policy which the task of increasing production for export and the home market made necessary.

The problems may have been easy to discern, but the solutions were less so. War and the demands of reconstruction stood the principal problem on its head. No longer was it a question of bringing idle resources into productive use – to which Keynes had provided the intellectual key – but of meeting vast requirements to re-equip industry and essential services, expand consumer supplies, and sell goods abroad to earn foreign exchange, from resources that were already overstrained. On top of all that the newly elected government, reflecting the general wish, made demands on men and materials for defence, better housing, improved health services, and greater provision for secondary and university education.

Compounding the shortage of resources was the accumulation of large external claims in the form of foreign debt and the sterling balances of Commonwealth countries, which had to be serviced with 'unrequited exports'. There was also a sharp deterioration in Britain's terms of trade. These problems were addressed in the report on *Britain and World Trade* (June 1947), which correctly stressed the urgency of the export drive. The report was the first comprehensive post-war treatment of its subject, and indeed of international trade generally. The quality of the analysis owed much to an experienced group and an able draftsman, Tony Gilpin. The report was well received and distributed widely abroad, especially in the USA. In retrospect the group appears to have been unduly impressed by the efficacy of the new machinery, of which the International Trade Organisation was to have been the centrepiece, in promoting an early return to the free movement of goods and capital, and overly concerned about the likelihood of an American slump. But it was hard to foresee the persistence of discriminatory trade measures caused by the wartime surge of productive capacity in the USA and the slow recovery elsewhere, or the acceptance by the USA under the Marshall Plan of discriminatory policies it had hitherto opposed. Moreover, the group had completed its work before the appalling harvest of 1947 and the fuel crisis of the following winter, and the sterling convertibility crisis was even farther off.

On the industrial front, mention has already been made of the work on the fuel and power and engineering industries. Again the choice was apt. These groups of industries comprised the core of the economy upon which the success of the reconstruction and export effort largely depended. A mass of information was collected which proved of considerable value both to government and to industry itself. But it proved more difficult to draw conclusions for policy from the facts. There was indeed a division of opinion within the Fuel and Power Group and the Executive, some preferring to publish only the factual results of the study (after reducing them to a manageable compass): letting the facts speak for themselves, in a PEP tradition. However, the majority view was that the facts needed interpretation, and a section of conclusions and recommendations was included. It is ironical that publication of this particular report was held up by the fuel crisis in the late winter of 1946–47. Even so, to produce a report of this magnitude as early as 1947 was a creditable effort. One wonders how the group would have reacted if some soothsayer had given them a hint of the potential energy that lay under the North Sea.

In the case of engineering, it had been intended originally to cover 25 separate branches of the industry, but the scope was later narrowed to some of the key sections. Even so, the engineering study was probably the most ambitious PEP had ever undertaken. The resources that Oliver Roskill's office was able to devote to the work were very limited, even with the support of grants from the Board of Trade and the Ministry of Supply. Industry was at first less enthusiastic, one leading industrialist responding to PEP's inquiries with a curt 'impertinent'. There was a memorable evening at which one of the principal car manufacturers, backed by the Second Secretary of the ministry providing part of the funds, attacked the group, not so much in substance as for presuming to investigate the industry's problems. Later we recruited the Director of their trade association, who became an active member of PEP, and with his help produced a report that was well received. In the light of the car industry's continuing problems, we could usefully have repeated the inquiry every few years. Broadsheets, although not full reports, were also published on agricultural and textile machinery, machine tools, bicycles, locomotives and the market for household appliances.

Trade associations themselves were a subject of study on which we collected much material and published a broadsheet, but staffing and other problems prevented our writing a full report. The index of trade associations that was compiled for the study was later turned over to the Federation of British Industries, which did not appear to have one of its own. Contacts developed in the course of these studies, and the reports themselves served to strengthen PEP's ties with industry, of which more later.

We did not neglect the other side of the bargaining table. Earlier chapters have referred to PEP's work on industrial relations before and during the war. From this developed a study of trade unionism, on which a draft report had been prepared during and immediately after the war. My own first task on joining PEP in May 1946 was to complete the work on this report. But it had suffered from the passage of time and the changes of authorship, and I had to advise the Executive that it did not meet PEP's standards as a comprehensive treatment of its subject. Certain aspects of the subject, however, were well covered and could be presented as a collection of studies in trade unionism. With the help of John Edwards, then Parliamentary Secretary to the Board of Trade, and an assistant from Transport House, we put together a volume on *British Trade Unionism* and issued it in July 1948. The response was encouraging, no doubt reflecting the general interest in a movement that had played a key role during the war and which Winston Churchill dubbed an Estate of the Realm. The volume ran through two editions, and a revised edition was issued in the mid-1950s. Nevertheless, it is regrettable that we could not put a larger investment of time and thought into this side of our work, particularly by examining the growth of industrial unionism in the USA, or the then recent experiment in Germany which owed much to the advice of the British TUC. A comparative study of that kind might have helped the trade union movement to remedy some of its structural weaknesses, particularly its fragmentation among a thousand or more unions affiliated to the TUC alone, and the consequent diffusion of responsibility.

The manpower study was also something of a disappointment, in that we were unable to fulfil the original grand design. The wartime experience of directing scarce labour to essential uses and the successful (on the whole) redeployment of five million servicemen and women suggested the need for manpower budgeting as a means of ensuring that key industries and services got the manpower they needed, and of maintaining full employment. The group started well and by the autumn of 1946 had issued its first broadsheet on *Manpower Stocktaking*. Whether manpower budgeting in a free market economy, in the sense of forecasting and then trying to match labour demand and supply, is feasible (or even desirable) except under war conditions, is debatable. In any case the group's attempts at forecasting the manpower requirements of particular industries were thwarted by power cuts and raw material shortages and the other crises that afflicted the economy in the following winter. The lack of essential data on such a broad and amorphous topic was also beyond PEP's resources to remedy. The intention of preparing a full report was therefore abandoned although a short, largely factual report was issued in 1951. Attention was focused more on factors affecting the supply of manpower and improving its quality through better education and training. In this the group was more successful, especially in its work on higher administrative, scientific and technical manpower on which a separate sub-group was formed (known for short as the 'Top-level Manpower' Group). The latter produced a series of interesting broadsheets, and its studies formed a springboard for our later work on the universities.

Manpower embraces womanpower, and PEP can take credit for some early contributions to a subject that did not attract the public eye in a serious way for a decade or more. *Mothers in Jobs* appeared in 1946, *Employment of Women* in 1948, and in 1954 we published *Graduate Wives*, the results of a special inquiry by Elizabeth Layton on the difficulties of university trained women in reconciling the claims of professional and family life.

With the translation into reality of wartime plans for the social services, to which PEP's work had made a notable contribution, there was no immediate need for major studies. It was agreed that PEP should keep a watching brief especially on gaps in the provision, and produce an occasional broadsheet on a special topic. One such topic was the health of mothers and children on which a group was formed in 1945. Meanwhile, there was a race to complete work on the population study before the Royal Commission completed theirs. By a joint effort of the senior staff under Max Nicholson's guidance we beat them by a length and published *Population Policy in Great Britain* in April 1948. This report, the conclusions of which were broadly confirmed by those of the official body, was less a study of demographics than of social policy. It inquired into the attitudes of men and women to parenthood, and how these were affected by changes in material circumstances and personal values, drawing out the implications for education, housing, the social services and taxation. The report thus had direct links with PEP's earlier work on social policy issues, with the current studies of maternal and child health and manpower, and the work on housing policy that was shortly to be taken up. Experience gained in the study of population questions in Britain was later drawn on for a broader inquiry into world population problems published early in PEP's second post-war decade.

Towards the end of the war Michael Young proposed a 'grass-roots' study of political and social institutions and the ordinary citizen. This was to be an important expression of PEP's desire to move on from structural questions to more complex issues affecting the quality of life. A group was formed in 1945 to prepare a report on Active Democracy – the junior research assistant on the study had the engaging habit of answering the telephone with the rousing cry: 'Active Democracy speaking!'. The group decided to concentrate on the local community, and undertook a fair amount of field work. It divided its activities along two parallel lines of inquiry: the inter-action of local authorities and the public, and the role of voluntary associations, which are a feature of 'anglo-saxon' societies. A series of interesting broadsheets were produced on such subjects as local elections, councils and their schools and their tenants, life in new towns, clubs and societies. However, with all its enthusiasm and hard work the group was not able to arrive at a general prescription for making democratic institutions more vital, and no general report was prepared. Here was another case of PEP's reach exceeding its grasp, but as the poet implied, we were right to try.

### Roles of the Executive and Council

Before turning to the next phase of PEP's work, a word should be said about the two bodies responsible for guiding its activities, the Executive Committee and the Council of Management. As noted earlier, the strain on senior people at the time was very heavy. Of the 17 members of the Executive, some were unable to attend meetings at all and others attended only occasionally. The main burden was carried by five or six members, who were also active in group work. In the course of the early post-war years the Executive was strengthened by adding new members, several of whom had long associations with PEP. Sir Charles Colston (Chairman of Hoover), John Edwards MP, M. W. Perrin (Chairman of the Wellcome Foundation), John Lawrence and Geoffrey Wilson all joined in this period; Harry Mance (member and later Chairman of Lloyds) came in as Joint Treasurer and later took over from Sir Henry Bunbury. Angus Maude joined after leaving the staff to head the Conservative Political Centre. Those who could not attend meetings regularly resigned and were invited to join the Council. Leonard Elmhirst, Alec Cairncross and John Edwards took on the chairmanship of the Executive in succession after Max Nicholson resigned the office on his appointment in 1948 as Director-General of the Nature Conservancy (he returned as Chairman in the mid-1950s). To supplement the necessarily brief lunchtime meetings, the Committee agreed to meet once a month over dinner for a more extended discussion. The revival of the annual Executive weekend provided the occasion for an even fuller review of current and future work, as well as financial and administrative matters, based on a detailed report by the Director. Leonard Elmhirst at Dartington Hall, Oliver Roskill at The Priory near Reading, or Israel Sieff at his cottage in Brimpton provided a most agreeable venue and good food and drink.

The Council, which was dormant during the war, sprang to life again during the troubled winter of 1946–47. In the spring of 1947 the Council decided to become a group itself to consider the causes of unrest and low morale in the coalfields and elsewhere in industry, of which the fuel crisis appeared to be symptom. Under Leonard

Elmhirst's chairmanship and strengthened by the addition of Sir George Schuster, they engaged Patricia Elton Mayo – daughter of the man who carried out the Hawthorne experiment – to do the field work. By the spring of the following year, the group had produced an extended broadsheet on *The Human Factor in Industry*, which was the first comprehensive statement in Britain on the subject of human relations in industry. The Council Group considered continuing to work on other aspects of the problem, but decided that, having sounded the main themes, they should await the results of more intensive field work by other bodies, and convene again in two or three years' time.

Both the Council and the Executive from time to time faced the problem of finance. Our staple sources of income held up reasonably well (subscriptions to the broadsheets, sales of reports and covenanted donations) but these were never sufficient to cover much more than overhead costs. Grants from foundations (Elmgrant, Nuffield, Rockefeller) helped to support the research but were usually given for a term of years and in some cases on a declining scale. Funds earmarked for particular studies – the Ministry of Supply grant for the engineering inquiry is an example – were helpful, so long as they did not come with strings attached. But special appeals to business and private supporters were always needed to make ends meet. The nadir of our financial fortunes was reached in 1949 when the Chairman posed the question at the Executive weekend whether we should consider winding up the organisation. The position had been deteriorating for a year or more, and PEP had been able to continue only by drawing on a substantial loan from the Westminster Bank, which of course had to be repaid over a period of a few years. Israel Sieff once again took the initiative and called together a sub-committee of the Council early in 1949 to draw up a statement of PEP's financial needs and launch an appeal for funds. Although this effort fell far short of the target (£10,000) it did secure about £1000 in donations from business, including the large clearing banks, which were valuable because they were offered as annual donations.

It was also decided to hold a dinner at the Savoy Hotel for leading businessmen, which would give us an opportunity of explaining PEP's approach and plans, and broadening our contacts. An earlier dinner at the same hotel (January 1947) had helped to re-establish PEP's links with industry and raised the level of donations modestly over the succeeding months. The second dinner, held in late April

1950 and generously underwritten by Israel Sieff and Leonard and Dorothy Elmhirst, was also a successful occasion both in itself and in its effect on the flow of funds. Although PEP was never comfortable financially (Israel said to me at that time, 'A body like PEP must expect to live dangerously') the crisis passed and thereafter we managed to stay mostly in the black.

However, the building at Queen Anne's Gate chose this time to remind us of the impermanence of human institutions. The elegant drawing room on the first floor, used by the PEP Club as a lounge, was supported by a single 25-foot beam of wood resting on the walls. At least, that was the way it had been constructed; but age or wartime bombing had caused one end to slip off the wall. Unless the floor was immediately strengthened we would have to cease using the room, which would put an end to plans for building up the Club's membership and might mean its demise. The Club was more than a pleasant adjunct of PEP. Its convenient location a few steps from Whitehall made it comparatively easy to arrange meetings over lunch or dinner. Providing a bar and a meal in the evening meant that the groups kept at their task for more than an hour or so before heading home. Lunch in the Club enabled members to keep in touch with one another and the work, and gave group secretaries a chance to discuss a point with their Chairman or a key member. Occasional speaker luncheons were arranged on a special topic or some facet of PEP's work. J. D. Bernal, Harold Wilson and Henry Wallace (*qua* agriculturalist) come to mind as speakers during my period. So the floor was strengthened and the Club survived.

Discussions about PEP's role and its future were a frequent theme of Executive Committee meetings in the late 1940s. It was agreed that there was a continuing need to look back and re-examine the conclusions of earlier studies and assess the progress in carrying out their recommendations. There was also a need for an objective analysis by an independent body like PEP of official policies and official information. But if that were all, PEP would run the risk of becoming stale and losing its distinctive quality. To quote the Director's Report to the 1947 weekend:

If PEP is to maintain its pioneering reputation it must be continuously moving ahead of the rest of the field. The Council Group and the Active Democracy Group offer a lead here. The social science front is beginning to be pushed beyond material problems of structure and organisation to the more intangible problems of human relations and attitudes. Plenty of work still needs to be done on the former, but the emphasis of the new programme should be on the latter.

There were, however, some differences of approach within the Executive between the 'fact-finders' and the 'pioneers', as indeed there had been from the earliest days. PEP still carried in its leaflet the phrase '... facts are apt to speak for themselves, if we find them out, all of them, and weigh them up objectively and honestly'. But it was hardly possible to collect all the facts on a complex issue; decisions were needed on what was likely to be relevant and a degree of selectivity was inevitable. As already noted, some of our major studies would have benefited from an early discussion of objectives and the principal themes to be pursued. Recognising the importance of mapping out in advance the territory to be covered, extensive outlines of future studies were prepared by the staff or by the member sponsoring the proposal, and put on the agenda of the Executive for discussion. But two years after the 1947 weekend meeting we were still debating the nature of PEP's contribution. At the 413th meeting, when the conclusions of the 1949 weekend at Dartington were reviewed, there was a lively exchange between those who felt that we should concentrate our work on a narrower range of topics, penetrating each to a greater depth, and those who argued that PEP's comparative advantage lay in group work – drawing together people with experience of a problem from various angles of vision and throwing out ideas for others to analyse in a more thorough-going way. On the whole the latter view prevailed, but acknowledging that ideas and proposals, to be credible, needed to rest on a solid foundation of research work.

One interesting suggestion put forward at that time by Michael Young was that, in the absence of an official body for the social sciences, PEP should take on some of its functions, acting as a link between men of ideas and practical men of affairs, and publishing an annual review of work in the social sciences. Although this proposal was not adopted, social scientists did look to PEP as a natural (not to say neutral) meeting ground for those working on the practical and theoretical sides of their discipline. A group of sociologists, opinion survey practitioners and others met regularly at

PEP and became the nucleus of the British Sociological Association, founded in 1951. Several working members (Professors Carr-Saunders, Glass, Simey and Titmuss, and myself as Hon. General Secretary) were elected to the first Executive Committee. Others (the Madge brothers, François Lafitte and Michael Young) took up research or teaching posts in sociology or related subjects at the universities. During that period Young and I produced a pair of broadsheets on government aid for the social sciences, and Louis Moss (Director of the Government's Social Survey) and I another pair on the techniques and uses of sample surveys. A group of young economists in government and the universities also met at PEP for a period, organised by a member of the staff, Phillip Hayes. They produced broadsheets on the sterling balances and other topics. However, in economics PEP had more competition from the NIESR and other bodies.

An interesting example of a successful 'look backwards' was provided by the Press Group. In 1948 the Government set up a Royal Commission to inquire into the press, on which PEP had issued its authoritative report in 1938 (see p. 26). Copies of the report were provided to members of the Commission at their request, and a reprint was hastily ordered which was much in demand. Kenneth Lindsay has related how he saw the green-covered volume flourished freely on both sides of the House of Commons during the debate on the subject. In June of that year the Press Group reconvened with Gerald Barry (then Editor of the *News Chronicle*) again in the chair, and Geoffrey Crowther (Editor of *The Economist*) among members present. Gerald Barry and the Director were invited to meet the Commission and spent a couple of hours answering questions on the work of the group and the report. The main outcome of the Commission's inquiry was the setting up of the Press Council, not one of the more effective bodies of our time.

### The Second Phase
The second phase of post-war work comprised three major studies: on the universities, on housing policy and on government and industry. All three had roots in earlier PEP work. As already noted, the study of the future of British universities stemmed from the work on 'top-level manpower' although PEP had not previously tackled the subject of higher education as such. Housing policy was a natural outgrowth of earlier work on the social services, health and popula-

tion policy. Government–industry relations had similar connections with earlier industrial studies and the more recent work of the Council Group. Although these studies had strong groups, only the third eventually produced a full report between hard covers. But all were prolific producers of broadsheets.

The Housing Group discovered an astonishing lack of information on the nature and condition of the nation's stock of houses, and had to spend considerable efforts on fact-gathering. But it also looked into policy questions and had the help of the Economists Group organised by Phillip Hayes in an attack on the economics of housing. Altogether the group produced eight broadsheets on various aspects of its subject, which were studied and widely quoted by the local housing authorities. The absence of a definitive report at the end of the day was not felt to be a serious loss, particularly as government policy for housing was constantly changing and the shorter studies were more easily able to keep abreast of the situation.

The Universities Group was almost too distinguished and knowledgeable about university affairs, and in the best academic tradition members were reluctant to trim their views to arrive at a consensus. Among other differences, there was a split in the group between those who proposed a major expansion of universities along traditional British lines and those who would have preferred to turn the polytechnics into technical universities or 'Grandes Ecoles' on the Continental model. The group produced some useful studies on the selection of students, student awards, the make-up of university courses, and universities and adult education. A report was drafted but the iterative process of checking facts and bringing them up to date took up much time, and the project was eventually abandoned. But PEP's interest in students and the universities continued and led to later work on graduates in industry, women graduates, to which reference has already been made, and colonial students in Britain.

The Government and Industry Group worked to a synopsis that covered the general conditions affecting government–industry relationships in the post-war era; a review of taxation policy, existing controls on investment, building, exports and imports, and foreign exchange dealings; an account of the structure of government departments and agencies dealing with industrial matters; and a corresponding section on the organisation of industry in its relations with government. The group prepared broadsheets on a number of these subjects and its work provided the theme for the annual dinner in 1950. The report on *Government and Industry* was published early in 1952, and although it did not quite fill the canvas originally prepared for it, was nevertheless received as a valuable contribution to an understanding of the economic machinery of government in contemporary Britain.

Two other important themes in PEP's work deserve mention: international studies and relations with groups overseas; and studies in leisure pursuits and the arts. The early work on world trade during this period was to have been complemented by an analysis of post-war problems in Western Europe and the prospects of economic integration. However, staffing and other problems forced us to drop this attempt, and the thread of European integration was not picked up again until PEP's second post-war decade. We did, however, make contact with like-minded bodies in France and published two broad-sheets on economic issues in that country; we also commented on the situation in Germany, then under the control of the Allied Powers.

**International Work**

There was considerable interest at the time in the working of the newly established United Nations and its agencies, certain aspects of which were discussed by the International Trade Group. In 1950 a new group was set up, with Geoffrey Wilson as Chairman, to con-sider the functions and administration of these bodies, and in due course it produced broadsheets on the role of the UN Secretariat, staffing questions, and so on. There was a lively interest too in what is now known as the Third World (then sometimes called, not very felicitously, 'backward areas') for much of which Britain still had responsibility but which was moving towards independence. Studies were done on technical assistance, and on the special problems of South Asia. A seminal broadsheet was written by Max under the title *Prospect of a Decade* in the first month of 1951, which touched on this theme, and was followed soon after by another on *The Strategy of World Development*.

A full report on economic development was planned, but was later focused on world food supply and population under a group chaired initially by Lord Simon of Wythenshawe, who expressed a particular interest in this critical aspect of the subject, and later by John Lawrence. (Geoffrey Wilson had left Britain by that time to take charge of the Colombo Plan Technical Co-operation Bureau in the city of that name, although he remained a member of the Executive on leave of absence, so to speak.) The report, published in 1955 under the title *World Population and Resources* (see p. 123), was one of the earliest attempts at a full treatment of this subject, which became increasingly pressing with the passing of the years.

During the late 1940s and early 1950s we were in touch with friends in India where there was a small but loyal readership of the broadsheets. Dr Lokanathan, then Director General of ECAFE, and Dr Sudhir Sen, Secretary of the Damodar Valley Corporation, were two of them. They were interested in the possibility of joint studies with PEP of Asian problems, and in the formation of an Indian institute with similar objectives. Leonard Elmhirst, with his broad connections on the sub-continent, fostered the latter proposal, and during a visit to India in the winter of 1951–2 canvassed the idea with Indian and British businessmen in Calcutta. The government and civil service were favourably inclined (*sine qua non* in India), and the Indian Institute of Planning, equipped with an impressive list of council members, was on the verge of coming into being. But it never quite did, and PEP was just too far away to give it the final push.

In the conditions of the time it proved difficult to make formal arrangements for joint work with bodies overseas. A proposal by the National Planning Association in Washington for a collaborative study of problems in international development, especially population, was accepted in principle by PEP, as we were then considering a similar project. In the end we went ahead on our own. However, Leonard Elmhirst, Israel Sieff, Henry Bunbury and I, among others, all visited the United States during this period and made contact with NPA, the Twentieth Century Fund and other kindred bodies. We also looked in on the major foundations, with mixed success. David Owen, by then an Under Secretary at the United Nations but remaining a member of the Council, kept us in touch with affairs at the UN and was helpful in our international work. There was also a steady flow of visitors from abroad to PEP, anxious to re-establish contact after the war or seek an independent opinion on some aspect of British social and economic policy, which was of considerable world-wide interest.

### The Arts and Leisure

PEP's connection with the arts first developed as a consequence of the Arts Enquiry launched by Dartington. This in turn was stimulated by the surge of activity in the visual and performing arts during and after the war. PEP had no direct input into the Enquiry, except to help edit the material, but undertook to publish the results as PEP reports. The first of these, on *The Visual Arts*, appeared in 1946; the second, on *The Factual Film*, in 1947; and the third, on *Music*, in 1949. These reports attracted wide attention, and more than one journalistic eyebrow was raised at PEP's venturing into such fields. One consequence was a request in 1950 from the British Film Institute that PEP undertake a study of the film industry. There had been earlier reports on film production (Gater) and distribution and exhibition (Plant) but not on the whole industry. The institute was concerned mainly about the financial condition of the industry, then in one of its redder patches, but accepted PEP's stipulation that the inquiry should use a wider lens, and consider the industry's place in the national economy, its relation to the press, the BBC and other media. A condition on their side, backed by an offer to contribute to the costs, was that the report be completed within 18 months, as they were anxious to put the findings of an independent inquiry before the government and the public as soon as possible. We came within a month of meeting that condition, then a record for a major PEP report.

The following note appears in the Director's report to the Executive for 1952 shortly after publication:

> The *Film Report* ... was undertaken by a group drawn largely from the film world, which is not noted for the gravity of its views, and by a secretary [Duncan Crow] who is by temperament more of an artist than a research worker. They planned a lively essay on their subject, and some of the early synopses read more like film scenarios than blueprints of a PEP report. In the event, the report has turned out to be one of the best pieces of historical and economic analysis so far produced by PEP, but even those who have praised it most have not been able to say that it makes light reading.

The report attracted enormous attention and was well received in the industry itself.

This report, and the earlier work by the Arts Enquiry, led to a suggestion that PEP make a broad study of the arts and sciences, along the lines of a recent Canadian Royal Commission which looked at everything from broadcasting to Indian handicrafts. Had Duncan Crow been able to take on the task, we would probably have found the means to finance it, but his health was not up to another period of rigorous research and drafting. Another suggestion, from Gerald Barry, was that PEP do for television the kind of thorough investigation we had just completed for films. Here is another instance of a subject being proposed for study a year or so before it caught the public's attention. Had we been able to fit a study on television into our programme, and complete it quickly enough, the report would have made a timely contribution to the discussion of the Conservative Government's decision to end the BBC's monopoly and establish a second, commercial, service. But there were always more interesting topics on PEP's list of possible major studies than we were able to tackle.

Shorter studies, however, could be considered for the broadsheet programme. Broadsheets on *The Economics of the Orchestra* and the *Opera in Britain* were a natural outcome of the Arts Enquiry report on music. Their work on the arts, and our own venture into the world of entertainment during the study on the film industry, inspired younger members of the staff to try their hand at investigating other leisure 'industries'. This they regarded as light relief from economic and social studies of the normal type. But they were not done lightly, and served to show that provision for leisure is a major economic activity. In the course of 1951 broadsheets were issued on *The Economics of Bookpublishing* and *The Gramophone Record: Industry and Art* (Phillip Hayes), the latter catching the industry before the great disc boom of the late 1950s and 1960s. An even more enterprising effort by George McRobie and John Brunner resulted in a pair of broadsheets on *The Football Industry* and *Cricket* (which we hardly liked to describe as an 'industry') and later one on *The Economics of Domestic Pets*. The first made suggestions for reforming the structure of Association football, and the relations between owners, managers and players, which had some influence over the years.

Looking back more than 25 years, and from the other side of the Atlantic, I am struck by how much PEP accomplished with so few resources. The enthusiasm of working members and staff to reshape society after a long and exhausting war had much to do with it.

So, perhaps, did the fact that the problems we tackled, intractable as some of them proved to be, were largely problems of how to do what most people agreed should be done. Now it is more difficult even to define the problems. And perhaps it was the last period when the combination of experience and good minds could suggest prescriptions for policy without the use of computers and other newfangled devices.

By 1953 it seemed to me that PEP needed a new head with a fresh angle of vision, and that I should move on. So the baton passed at the end of that year, and after a brief spell in business I left for Washington and the World Bank. PEP's work on population and development sowed the seeds of that decision.

# 6

# The Second Post-war Decade: 1954–64

## Richard Bailey

### A Time of Change

It is already 16 years since I finished my ten-year stint as Director of PEP. Recollections inevitably become selective after such an interval, the less formal events are liable to be given the wrong dates, remarks attributed to the wrong person, and the contents of publications forgotten. Again the recollections of any one individual will be highly subjective, highlighting his own activities and forgetting at least some of those of colleagues. But even if research could establish all these facts, I do not think that a detailed chronicle of PEP's activity, with particulars of every publication, decisions by the Council and Executive Committee, and the activities of the research staff, is quite what is required in a volume of this kind. I feel that we should, rather, address ourselves to such questions as how PEP was organised, who was involved, and why it was remarkable that such a body should have managed to last for nearly 50 years. When I became its Director in January 1954 I knew little about PEP's work except for the Press Report of 1938, which I had found extremely useful, and a handful of broadsheets which had come my way. It was not until I was installed in office with responsibility for its activities that I realised that this was no ordinary institution, but one operating under unwritten rules the application of which brought out the contradictions between objectives and the means available for their realisation.

Although the drafting of a National Plan in the early 1930s had been a major factor in bringing PEP into existence, it had no formal constitution and was presided over by a self-perpetuating oligarchy.

After 25 years it was still very much a private institution bound by no external obligations except the legal requirements regarding libel applicable to PEP publications; and as its programme was not restricted to a specific field, it was free to investigate anything provided it could find the necessary money. In practice this was a very real limitation, as PEP had no adequate regular source of income but depended on the generosity of private individuals, appeals to business firms, and occasional foundation grants for specific studies.

The importance of the ten years from 1954–64 was that they saw the beginning of the transformation of what was largely a private, partly amateur body into the Policy Studies Institute, a professional organisation with less insecure finance, of which PEP now forms a part. This was by no means an easy process, nor was the movement all in one direction, and some of those involved did not realise the fundamental nature of the changes taking place. In the pages that follow I have attempted to describe how PEP operated during this period, the changes that took place and the problems that had to be overcome.

**Basic Operations**
My first act as Director-Designate of PEP was to attend the annual Council weekend meeting held in October 1953. These weekend affairs, which had been held at intervals since the first one at Dartington in April 1931 (see p. 12), were occasions for getting away from London to discuss future plans and research projects. The first item on the formal agenda at this particular meeting was the confirmation of my appointment as Director. This was agreed without dissent. The second item was a discussion on 'the next five years'. After various suggestions had been put forward, Michael Young proposed that as PEP had now carried out the work it had been set up to do it should be disbanded. The proposal was discussed for a while and then rejected on the grounds that some matters in the broad field of PEP's interests still needed attention. The moment had passed. PEP was launched into its second 25 years, and the question of redundancy pay to the newly-appointed Director did not arise.

At that time PEP was still housed in 16 Queen Anne's Gate, a house of great elegance and charm. Unfortunately the finances of the organisation were not sufficient to cover all its needs, and the upkeep of the building had a low priority. The grand rooms overlooking St James's Park were in reasonable condition but as one mounted to the upper floors the decorations became increasingly shabby and the furnishings sparse and decrepit.

These upper reaches were inhabited by the research staff, who were recruited usually for a term of two or three years to carry out a particular project. The hiring of staff for short periods in this way meant that there were frequent comings and goings. Although to the outside world PEP appeared to be an established repository of information and opinion on the social sciences, industrial economics and a number of other matters, the nature and extent of its in-house expertise was constantly changing. However, PEP contrived to be an institution in the sense that it carried out objective research and produced reports acknowledged to be of a high standard. Most of the members of the Council which presided over PEP's efforts had been together since the early 1930s, and the institute gained authority from its association with the working members, who in my time numbered about 150 civil servants, businessmen and academics. The main factor in keeping its name before the public was the series of broadsheets which still appeared under the title *Planning* at roughly monthly intervals. These dealt with a wide variety of subjects only a few of which were derived from the research programme. Many of them were written by outside contributors who did not take kindly to having the record of their enthusiasms, or sometimes their discontents, edited. As a result some very unorthodox views were attributed to PEP from time to time. The broadsheets appeared anonymously, most of the subjects were topical and the treatment was largely non-technical.

### The Steering Groups
The practice which distinguished PEP from many other institutions remained the use of steering groups, the identity of whose members was never published, to supervise the major research projects. When this procedure came into being in the 1930s (see pp. 21, 49) reports were prepared for the groups as spare time tasks either by members of the Council or by individuals invited to write them on an *ad hoc* basis. As PEP's influence grew and it became possible to secure foundation grants for some of its projects, the close connection between the groups and the Council gradually changed. By the 1950s it was not unusual to have groups consisting entirely of outsiders working with the research staff without any representative

from the Council. However, the Council continued to select the group chairmen and vet the lists of members of steering groups. In some cases group membership included a selection of the major authorities on a subject, to the great benefit of the eventual report. The research officers drafted papers which were discussed by the steering group at meetings usually held in the early evening at 16 Queen Anne's Gate. Some groups met regularly at perhaps monthly intervals. Others, where field work was involved, tended to meet several times to agree on the questionnaire and size of the sample and other details and then disperse for a season until the results were ready for inspection. The contribution of steering groups varied considerably, as would be expected.

**Authors Anonymous**

Of the procedures brought forward from the 1930s the least popular with the research staff was the rule that all publications were put out on the authority of PEP as an institution, and were not attributable to individuals. In the days when publications resulted from discussion between a group of people talking in the evenings with one of their number presenting drafts, taking notes and putting what was said into a coherent form, it would clearly have been undesirable to attribute the result to any one of those present.

However, to a research officer who worked for two or three years on a specialised study, and spent six months or more writing up the report ready for publication, the position appeared in quite a different light. While it was true to say that members of the steering group who were chosen because of their knowledge of the subject under study made a useful contribution, the value of the finished work depended on the ability of the research officer to turn a mass of unco-ordinated material into a readable and cogently argued report. If this was not done a great deal of time and money had been spent in vain. As research workers were not in the 1950s paid handsomely, the main reward for their period at PEP was to be able to claim authorship of a report which had probably been well received by the press and by informed opinion on the subject. When I arrived at PEP the fiction of immaculate composition was still maintained. This was eventually changed, not without considerable opposition from the Council, so that the introduction of each report included a statement to the effect that the steering committee appointed to supervise the project by the Council was most grateful to the following named research workers for their hard work etc. etc. throughout the life of the project and skill in the preparation of the report. This was better than nothing, but up to 1967 authors' names did not appear on the covers of reports or broadsheets.

The fact that the Council was not prepared to break with the practices of the 1930s was only one aspect of the upstairs, downstairs situation at 16 Queen Anne's Gate. Most of the research workers never met the Council members at all during the period of their appointment. Some of them would know a particular member of the Council, or of the Executive Committee, who happened to be a member of their steering group, but that was all. The connection between the Council and the research workers was through the Director, the Executive Chairman and the Secretary. The office of Executive Chairman, a paid appointment, was held by John Edwards MP, who had been Financial Secretary to the Treasury in the second Attlee Government. On leaving office in 1951 he gave a great deal of his time to the affairs of PEP and had an office in Queen Anne's Gate. Apart from the authority that comes from holding high ministerial office he was extremely well informed, and adept at opening the right doors. I cannot speak too highly of the helpful and kindly reception which he gave me and the patience with which he saw me through the running-in period in these strangely arcane surroundings.

### The PEP Club

The PEP Club occupied the two best rooms in 16 Queen Anne's Gate up to 1956. The Club members *per se* had no connection with what went on upstairs, although they included working members and others who had a general interest in PEP's research programme and other activities. The research staff, being on the premises already, were ex officio Club members. As time went by the number of Club members declined and although it continued to attract a handful of loyal supporters, most of those who lunched there did so not from any desire to support PEP's work but because it was conveniently situated for their offices, and the food provided by the incomparable Mrs Margaret Newall was both appetising and cheap. The Club lost money steadily over the years and was finally wound up in 1956, partly on the grounds of economy and partly because the rooms it occupied were needed to house the growing research staff. Some of those dislodged resented the closure and there is one prominent MP and former Cabinet Minister who never fails to complain about its departure whenever we meet.

**Finance**
Voluntary bodies never have enough money to do all the things that their members individually and collectively regard as essential for the continuation of civilisation as they know it. That PEP contrived to reach so many of its goals while living from hand to mouth was a constant source of wonder.

In the mid-1950s this operation had two parts. On the financial side expenditure could be divided into essentials, which had to be paid for promptly, and floating items over which greater flexibility prevailed. At the same time the dates on which funds would be coming in were carefully marked on the calendars and in the diaries by Miss Della Matthews the accountant, and a list prepared of the bills which could then be paid. The other side of the operation was heavy dependence on voluntary activity. The broadsheets owed a great deal to help received from civil servants and others who either prepared drafts themselves or guided their production by staff members. Some of the studies at this time benefited from work which was either entirely unpaid or for which nominal fees barely covering expenses were forthcoming.

The study on *Colonial Students in Britain*, which was completed in 1955, is a good example of this technique. It was financed by a number of small grants from the Nuffield Foundation and the Noel Buxton Trust, and periodic appeals to business firms with Commonwealth interests, successfully carried out by Oliver Woods, who was Commonwealth Editor and later Deputy Editor of *The Times* and had been largely responsible for setting the project up. The research officer, Richard Izard, was responsible for the field work and interviews which formed the main part of the report but other sections were contributed by individuals. One of these was Hugh Paget who had specialised knowledge of the arrangements for colonial students from his experience as Warden of the Hans Crescent Hostel in London. Unfortunately he was suddenly transferred to Amsterdam as British Council Representative in the Netherlands before the work was completed. This project was also notable because the field work was actually carried out by colonial students from British universities.

Both the study on *Colonial Students in Britain* and that on *World*

*Population and Resources* were examples of a unique form of activity. Both were undertaken at the instigation of individuals who believed strongly in the importance of the subjects and invited PEP to organise and carry out the studies. Oliver Woods was instrumental in bringing together a number of specialists on Commonwealth education who worked as the steering group for this project over a period of four years. Lord Simon of Wythenshawe, as well as being the originator of the idea for a World Population Study (see pp. 112–13), put up some of the money himself and obtained the rest from the Nuffield Foundation and the Eugenic Society. The members of this group included Dr P. S. R. Blacker, Julian Huxley, Max Nicholson, Baroness (Mary) Stocks, Solly Zuckerman and others.

Servicing a group of such eminence had its difficulties. Jack Gray, the research officer responsible, who himself made a considerable contribution to the work, was liable to be summoned at any time to go to discuss particular points with Lord Simon at his flat in Marsham Court. Apart from the report, which appeared in 1955 and quickly exhausted its print-run, the group also produced two broadsheets, for both of which the text was argued over until the very last moment so that frantic efforts were necessary to secure their publication by the required date. One of them was distributed to delegates at the UN World Population Conference in Rome in 1954.

*World Population and Resources* itself was regarded as one of the major PEP reports of the 1950s. Although it was not the first to relate world population to resources the report, under Simon's relentless and shrewd direction, produced a notably well-informed and far-sighted analysis. This may be illustrated by its treatment of oil reserves, which it pronounced to be 'ample for the needs of the world up to the year 2000' but added 'One reservation must, however, be made. In an increasingly nationalistic world the oil-producing countries may prefer to keep some of their oil resources against the time when they need them themselves rather than to exploit them immediately. It is also possible that as a result of political factors some of the Middle East oil – and it is in this region that the bulk of the world's reserves are situated – may be lost to non-Communist countries.'[1] This judgement, which owed much to the advice of E. F. Schumacher, seems to have escaped the notice of the politicians and their advisers who made the West so precariously dependent on

---

[1] *World Population and Resources*, 1955, p. 73.

cheap oil until their eyes were rudely opened 19 years later in 1974.

## The Broadsheet Programme
The arrangements for producing broadsheets in those days had a simplicity which has long since been eroded by progress. Our printers, Metchim & Co., then had their works in Lewisham Passage at the end of Queen Anne's Gate, about 150 yards from our front door. What we should have done without this territorial advantage it is impossible to say, because whatever its authorship the copy for each and every broadsheet was invariably produced at the last minute. On press days the Editor had not only to cope with questions of house style, the number of words required and similar routine matters, but also with such delicate problems as persuading some outside author that the Council would never stand for a particular passage and that it would have to be altered or omitted. As soon as the bare modicum of agreement on the text had been reached the Editor would tear off to Metchim's where the printers were waiting to start work on it. Proofs were collected the moment that word came on the telephone that they were ready, and generally returned corrected later on the same day. As many of the broadsheets were produced to coincide with particular topical events the co-operation of the long-suffering Metchim's was essential in securing publicity. Publication day was normally a Monday and the broadsheets were released to the press in time for notices to appear in the Sunday papers. Some of the broadsheets attracted considerable publicity in the press and on the radio, and inspired both cartoonists and writers of letters to *The Times*.

Subscribers were supposed to receive 16 copies a year for an annual subscription of £2. There was a reduced rate of £1 'for teachers, students in full-time education, lecturers in adult education and members of HM forces'. As each broadsheet contained from 8–10,000 words subscribers had a very good bargain. The main difficulty in building up the roll of subscribers was the fact that the subjects of the broadsheets ranged widely. In this respect PEP was like Hilaire Belloc who was said to suppose that 'nobody minds, that all his books are of different kinds'.

## Types of Project
From the mid-1950s the more usual type of project was the study designed to attract funds which were known to be available. In 1953

PEP was successful in securing funds for two studies – *Graduates in Industry* (Miss Jane Lidderdale) and *Trade Associations in Britain* (G. McRobie and L. Tivey) – financed by counterpart funds set up to promote research under Marshall Aid arrangements. These studies began early in 1954 and resulted in highly successful reports. *Graduates In Industry*, which was the first field work study of the subject, was particularly successful. Later projects supported by foundation grants were *Family Needs and the Social Services* (Mrs W. Moss) and later a study entitled *Mental Health Facilities in the UK* (G. Rehin) and *Trade Unions in British Industry* (B. Donoughue and K. Hindell). By the early 1960s the usual pattern was for the Council to agree on a number of subjects for study on which applications would be prepared and forwarded to the appropriate foundations. In these cases the Council had less control over the projects and the steering group was in the position of helping to implement specific terms of reference rather than indulging in prolonged argument about what these should be.

This was quite different from earlier projects, some of which had been financed on a somewhat hand to mouth basis. However some of these, notably *Growth in the British Economy* of which the report was published in 1960, made a significant impression. The research officer in charge, Geoffrey Denton, made a considerable contribution to the work of PEP generally, as well as being the author of an important report. This PEP study was one of the first attempts to analyse the factors affecting economic growth. The Chairman of the steering group was Sir Robert Shone, later to become the first Director General of the National Economic Development Office.

## European Studies

*The Beginnings*
The principal departure from recent PEP activities during the 1950s was the decision to examine the situation in Western Europe. John Edwards was a member of the Council of Europe, of which he later became President, and of Western European Union (WEU), so that a steady flow of information on these institutions was available. My own interest in European integration, which went back to the early 1950s, was heightened by a meeting with Jean Monnet in 1955. In that year I visited the headquarters of the European Coal and Steel

Community (ECSC) in Luxembourg after which I wrote a broad-sheet on the subject.[1]

The discussion on the form of British participation in European institutions which was going on at this time had not yet polarised. The Six had agreed at the Messina Conference early in June 1955 that a new stage on the road to European unity should be undertaken and that the next step should be joint action in the development of nuclear energy, followed by the establishment of a general common market. Britain had been invited to participate in these discussions and had been represented at Messina but only by a senior civil servant who was withdrawn at the end of 1955. In April 1956 the Spaak Report appeared containing a comprehensive plan for the joint development of Euratom and a less detailed plan for a Common Market. This was accepted by the Foreign Ministers of the Six as a basis for negotiation of definitive treaties. Meanwhile the Council of the Organisation for European Economic Co-operation (OEEC) decided, in response to a British proposal, to establish a special working party to study possible forms and methods of association between the proposed union of the Six and the other members of the OEEC. In particular the possibility of a Free Trade Area which would include the Common Market of the Six was to be discussed. Reports from the OEEC, White Papers from the British Government and a flurry of other documents appeared during the first half of 1957.

The signing of the Treaty of Rome at the end of March made it clear that the Six were determined to proceed, either by themselves or with other OEEC countries, in establishing a European Common Market. In August 1957 the late Reginald Maudling, then Paymaster-General, was appointed as special co-ordinator within the British Government for Free Trade Area questions. In October 1957 the OEEC Council declared its determination to secure the establishment of a European Free Trade Area comprising all member countries. Prolonged negotiations followed which eventually broke down at the end of 1958.

Before the final breakdown of the OEEC negotiations, industrial leaders from the three Scandinavian countries, Switzerland, Austria and the United Kingdom had discussed the possibility of forming an alternative trading arrangement among themselves if the broader free

---

[1] *The European Coal and Steel Community*, 21 November 1955.

trade area negotiations came to nothing. Soon after the breakdown government officials from these countries and Portugal began discussions of possible arrangements that might be made. This 'little free trade area' with its seven members came into being on 3 May 1960.

I have included this summary of the events of the second half of the 1950s for the benefit of readers who, having no personal recollection of the excitement of those days, have come to associate the EEC with inflation, metrication and harmonisation, not to mention Eurocrats, butter and beef mountains, wine lakes, lamb wars, golden delicious apples, the CAP, and Mrs Thatcher's fight for a sensible UK budget contribution. In 1955 studies of European institutions and policies were being carried out by individuals or not at all. Chatham House, the obvious research body to be examining the subject, had no major European project and when approached the Director General, C. M. Woodhouse, was quite willing for PEP to start work in this field. In the years that followed, PEP's European studies, first *European Organisations* and later on the EEC and EFTA, received international recognition.

## European Organisations

The first European research programme undertaken by PEP was concerned with European organisations. This began in 1956 and was financed by a two-year grant from the Leverhulme Trust. The study analysed and assessed the work of the eight principal European organisations – OEEC, WEU, ECE, NATO, ECSC, Council of Europe, Euratom, and EEC. This was a new departure for PEP and it is an indication of its standing in the world of ideas that it was nevertheless able to attract a number of politicians, civil servants, businessmen and academics to form a formidable steering group. The chairman was Dr Paul Rykens, chairman of Unilever NV, and the members included Geoffrey de Freitas MP, John Edwards MP, Derek Ezra, Frank Figgures, Sir Edmund Hall-Patch, Geoffrey Rippon MP, Eric Roll and Geoffrey Wilson. Between them the group members had had experience at governmental or official level of working with most of the organisations under discussion. The research officers were Dr Ernest Wohlgemuth, who later went on to an academic post, and Michael Palmer, who achieved his ambition of becoming a Eurocrat.

The importance of this project was not simply in providing information on the work of the institutions under study, but in positioning Britain in Europe, and Europe in relation to the rest of the world. By the mid-1950s a divided Europe was faced with the problems of the 'cold war' and the tasks of economic recovery, and the countries of Western Europe were being driven together by common experiences but most of all by common disasters and common fears. Britain was already some way along the road towards granting independence to the Commonwealth countries, but as yet by no means reconciled to the consequent diminution in its importance in the world. When the study began the European Economic Community was still under discussion. By the time the report was published in 1959 the Treaty of Rome had been signed and the EEC and Euratom had come into being alongside the ECSC. The OEEC was about to be replaced by the Organisation for Economic Co-operation and Development (OECD) and the formation of EFTA was imminent.

*European Organisations*, published in 1959, clarified the functions of the regional organisations which had sprung up and their relationship with the world institutions centred on the United Nations. Coming at a time when differences in approach between the Six and the rest of the Western European countries including Britain were emerging, it underlined the decided preference of successive British governments to move towards European unity through intergovernmental action rather than by a federal approach. Britain as the cornerstone of the Commonwealth and a major trading country had difficulty in entering a regional block, while at the same time the need to adjust policies to take account of the emergence of the European Communities clearly created problems for the years ahead. This objective analysis of the origins and work of the European institutions played an important part in establishing PEP as a major contributor to the European debate. The smooth execution of this complicated study and the balanced and fair minded approach of the report owed a great deal to John Edwards, then President of the Council of Europe, who died at Strasbourg a few months after the report appeared.

*The Common Market Project*
While the *European Organisation* project was still in progress preparations began for setting up a study of Britain's relationship to the European Community. The idea for this project had its beginning

in the broadsheet on the *European Coal and Steel Community*, already referred to. The fact that Chatham House had no plans for a study in this field meant that we could sound out the various foundations on the prospects for financial support and also discuss the project with interested individuals.

However it is one thing to have a clear field and quite another to have a viable project. It was known that a Common Market study would be of interest to the Ford Foundation but at that stage we had no contact with them or experience of their working procedures. In April 1957 John Hansard, the Honorary Treasurer of PEP, visited New York and through business colleagues who were involved in the work of the Committee for Economic Development (CED), a private research organisation, received an introduction to Joe Slater and others at the Ford Foundation. From this contact he not only secured information about the format for an application for a Ford grant but also the dates of the forthcoming meetings of the grants committee, and was able to invite Mr Slater to visit Queen Anne's Gate on his next European trip. During the summer an application for funds for a study of Britain and the European Community was prepared and forwarded to the Foundation. During the autumn Joe Slater visited Queen Anne's Gate and met members of the Council and various people who would be involved in the prospective study.

Purely by coincidence I was awarded a Smith–Mundt Fellowship to visit the United States during the first three months of 1958. These Fellowships were awarded to what were described as 'opinion formers' and administered by the State Department. I was given a list of places that it was thought I should see and allowed some discretion as to where else I went. As a result I visited Las Vegas, Dallas, Salt Lake City, the Grand Canyon, New Orleans, San Francisco and points East. In Washington I made contact with Herbert Stein, then Research Director of CED, and discussed possibilities for future co-operation. I did not reach New York until the last two weeks of my visit. There I stayed with Joe Slater in Scarsdale and was told unofficially that PEP was to receive a grant for the Common Market project. The Ford grant was announced in April after my return home and was for $165,000, which was the biggest sum PEP had ever received as a research grant.

Another important event in the early stages of the Common Market operation must be mentioned. Before PEP reached the point of sending in an application to the Ford Foundation we had the good fortune to hear that Miriam Camps, then a research associate of Princeton University, was looking for a base where she could work on a study of the European Economic Community financed by a personal grant from the Ford Foundation. After brief negotiations it was agreed that Mrs Camps should have a room and secretary at Queen Anne's Gate and as well as working on her own book[1] would act as a consultant on the PEP study, if and when it came into being. It was a great advantage to have one of the principal authorities on the Common Market associated with the development of the PEP study. Later on Mrs Camps wrote a number of Occasional Papers in a new series of PEP publications, which attracted widespread interest.

*Occasional Papers*
The staff recruited to work on the Common Market study were in a rather different position from the usual PEP appointments. As the study was very broadly based experts on a number of different aspects of European integration were necessary, so that the research was co-ordinated but did not have a single Director.

This need for expertise was particularly true of agriculture on which PEP was advised by E. M. H. Lloyd. Mr Lloyd was a considerable authority on agricultural administration and politics and had held various important appointments including that of Under-Secretary at the Ministry of Food. He was well acquainted with Sicco Mansholt, the European Commissioner responsible for designing the Common Agricultural Policy (CAP). At intervals Lloyd criticised the proposals put forward from Brussels and a lengthy and highly technical correspondence followed. The results of the Common Market study were published in Occasional Papers which appeared every few weeks. These included papers on the CAP produced by E. M. H. Lloyd and on the negotiations for the European Free Trade Area and the British approach to the Common Market written by Miriam Camps. The rest of the staff working on the study included Denis Clarke, who came from the Information Division of the Treasury and produced two important volumes comparing the Brussels tariff and the British most-favoured-nation tariff. This work

---

[1] This was *Britain and the European Community, 1955–1963*, OUP and Princeton University Press, 1964.

was in great demand as the only source of comparative figures for the various tariffs. Other aspects of the study were dealt with by H. Cowie, Murray Forsyth and for a time Michael Palmer. The study had a small steering group first under the chairmanship of John Edwards, and after his death under Lincoln Steel.

*Impact of the EEC Study*
The impact of the Common Market study both inside and outside PEP was very much wider than that of any other project during my time as Director. Not only did the publications attract a great deal of attention, but as PEP was for a time at any rate the only research institution studying the Common Market problem we received large numbers of visitors from overseas as well as home based civil servants, journalists and academics. The study in fact created a new clientele for PEP publications. These included the United States and European Embassies, trade associations and business firms dealing with Europe and others anxious to discover how trade with other parts of the world would be affected. Members of the staff were in great demand to speak at conferences, attend discussion groups and so on. Invitations came in for PEP to be represented at conferences abroad and several of us became regular attenders at Königswinter. The success of the Common Market study was in large measure due to the fact that traditional methods of work were adapted to suit the new conditions. The steering group exercised a very light control over the activities of the different research officers, and they ranged widely for information and advice. The presence of Miriam Camps on the premises ready to advise at any time was a great advantage.

The interest of the Ford Foundation in the study was evidenced by the frequent visits of Joe Slater and others and also by the setting up, at the Foundation's suggestion, of a joint committee with three foreign research organisations. These were the CED (USA), CEPES (Comité Européen pour le Progrès Economique et Social) which had branches in France, West Germany and Italy, and the SNS (Studieförbundet Näringsliv och Samhälle, of Sweden). This committee met several times a year with the different organisations acting as host. The contact with the CED and its President Dr Alfred C. Neal and Research Director Herbert Stein, who later became Chairman of the Committee of Economic Advisers to President Nixon, was particularly valuable. The friendships made through this joint committee contributed to the wide success of the project.

The interest of the Ford Foundation also resulted in my being asked to join the governing board of a research institute set up with foundation funds in Madrid. Al Neal of CED and Axel Iveroth of SNS also became members.

A project which followed events as closely as the Common Market study inevitably suffers when these take an adverse turn. This was the case when the first British application for membership of the Common Market was vetoed in January 1963. In the period of re-alignment that followed, the study turned to the setting up of EFTA and its possibilities, looked again at the prospects of extending Commonwealth trade, and at the same time observed developments in the European Community. The Common Market project was by no means vetoed by the President's *'Non'* and I was delighted after leaving PEP to hear that it was being continued in association with Chatham House and to see the flow of publications started again (see pp. 155–6).

**Changing Times**

The death of John Edwards had repercussions on both the study programme and PEP's institutional arrangements. His function as Executive Chairman had been to point the members of the Council away from the somewhat theoretical stance which they were apt to adopt, and towards more practical matters such as finance. He also had the distinction of being the only person in the whole organisation who understood the Trust Deed under which the institution had been set up. However there is a limit to what one man can do, especially as in this case his health was far from good. After his death difficulties inevitably arose in the relationships between Council and staff. The administration depended on the dedicated service of a number of highly competent women. Of these Marion Nuttall, who was secretary to the Council over a long period, her successor Joan Wimble and Della Matthews the accountant were outstanding. As PEP moved into the 'swinging sixties' the organisation began to show signs of strain. As well as appointing a Chairman for the Executive Committee the Council decided to advertise for a Director of Studies. As a result John Madge joined PEP. John, who had established a high reputation as a sociologist, settled down quickly in his new surroundings and became a valued colleague. He took charge of all projects except the Common Market study, which remained under my general charge.

Previously when difficulties had arisen there was a straightforward procedure. Problems were talked over with the staff in a joint meeting with John Edwards and myself. The two of us then decided on the line to take with the Executive Committee and we were usually able to get a solution agreed. Without a resident Executive Chairman it was more difficult to secure decisions. The new Chairman of the Executive Committee, Hugh Saunders, was a newcomer to the Council and at first knew little about the way in which PEP managed its internal affairs. While he tended quite naturally to propose the sort of solutions that worked in his own organisation, Unilever, a number of changes were introduced which were important for the administration of PEP. Salary scales were drawn up which were comparable to those paid for research posts in the universities. PEP had had no pension scheme and arrangements were set in hand to enable those who were members of a scheme when they joined the organisation to have their contributions continued by PEP. Discussions were also set in hand to enable PEP staff members to join the universities pension scheme. The building had been redecorated and to some extent refurnished in the later 1950s so that working conditions were now reasonably good. In addition, the large room on the ground floor overlooking Birdcage Walk, which had been the PEP Club dining room, was available as a staff common room.

Some of the new recruits to the staff in the 1960s were not particularly happy with the PEP system. They did not take kindly to the idea of supervision of their work by study groups and regarded themselves as experts hired to produce a report which PEP would eventually have the privilege of publishing. At the same time some members of the staff adopted a much more political approach to their work and this was reflected in their ideas of what PEP's function should be. In particular there were demands for staff participation in drawing up the research programme and for the disbursement of study funds to be the sole responsibility of the research workers concerned. Some members of the Council were aware of the difficulties posed by this changing situation. In particular I received a great deal of help from Bill Holford, then Council Chairman, Israel Sieff and John Hansard.

These kinds of problem were experienced by other voluntary

organisations at that time. The new attitudes were something that older Council members preferred not to recognise. The anonymity rule regarding the signing of publications had been only slightly modified and the legal fiction that all publications were produced by PEP as a whole was still followed. By the second half of my tenth year as Director I began to feel that there must be better ways of spending my time than constantly trying to reconcile the irreconcilable. My decision to move was helped by the fact that the lease on 16 Queen Anne's Gate was nearing its end. It was arranged to sell this and move to new premises in Upper Belgrave Street. As the move was due to take place in December 1963 I decided that ten years was long enough. I became a partner in an important group of civil engineering consultants and at the same time was seconded as a part-time adviser to NEDO. The rest of my story is told by John Pinder in Chapter 7.

On reflection I think too many changes were necessary in too short a time. The benevolent despot approach of earlier days, when the research workers were told what to do, had clearly served its time. On the other hand it was not feasible for the staff to have complete independence in the conduct of projects for which the Council had drawn up terms of reference before their appointment. The foundation grants which paid for the research had been made to PEP on the strength of its reputation, not to individual research workers.

Looking back I think that perhaps the truest statement of PEP's ambivalent position arose from a conversation I had with Dr Hastings Banda, at a meeting organised by Christopher Rowland MP at the offices of the United Africa Company. This was before independence and the African leaders present also included Kenneth Kaunda. At lunch Dr Banda examined my identity label which described me as Director of Political and Economic Planning. 'So you are a politician,' he said. I replied 'No, I am not a politician, I'm the head of a research institute.' 'But it says here "political planning" so you must be a politician.' 'No,' I said, 'we are political in a non-political sense,' meaning of course non party-political. Dr Banda gave me a very old fashioned look and then, digging me heartily in the ribs, began to roar with laughter. 'I'm just the opposite,' he said, 'non-political in a political sense.' The other leaders who were discussing training programmes, irrigation and other important matters were somewhat startled at this interruption.

This story I think does illustrate what PEP was intended to be. It was not affiliated to any particular party and although numerous staff members over the years had been prominent in the main political parties, this was always a spare time activity. What we tried to do was to identify problems of public concern and to report on these in a way that would be helpful to policy makers in government and elsewhere. This was easier in the 1930s when much less research work was done in the universities and few private research bodies existed. In the immediate post-war years there was ample scope for PEP to comment on the working of the new social services, the education system and the organisation of industry. By the 1960s opinions had polarised and the number of organisations and individuals putting out views on all aspects of public affairs had multiplied. For a few years PEP was poised between the outlooks and attitudes of the old and new eras. One has only to consider what has happened to British institutions generally since then to realise that the changes involved at that time for such a body as PEP inevitably created problems which those most closely involved found difficult to surmount. It testifies to the basic strength of the organisation that PEP overcame these problems and is, in the new form of PSI, still flourishing in the 1980s.

# 7

# 1964–1980: From PEP to PSI

## John Pinder

By 1964, PEP had been for more than 30 years a source of useful facts and of proposals that were sometimes strikingly imaginative and influential. Like many other institutes which had by now grown up in Britain and other western countries, it responded to the need for careful study of the problems of complex and rapidly changing societies. One thing that distinguished PEP, however, will be evident to those who have read the earlier chapters of this book: it had been created in a crusading spirit by a remarkable group of people who were deeply committed to further the public good by the intelligent use of facts, rather than submit to dogma or to *laissez faire* and drift.

These founders and the organisation they created had inspired goodwill, respect and affection in a generation of people who by now were leaders in government, business, education and the media. This attractive force was reflected in the kind of people who were associated with PEP. When I joined the staff in 1964, most of the founders who had set their stamp on the organisation, including Israel Sieff, Leonard Elmhirst, Lawrence Neal, Max Nicholson, Kenneth Lindsay and Oliver Roskill, were still more or less closely involved. Hugh Saunders, as Chairman of the Executive Committee, had steered PEP through a difficult period and introduced essential reforms, converting the institute into a charitable company limited by guarantee and ensuring regular rotation of members of the governing body. His description to me of Dick Davies, the Administrative Director, was much along the lines of King Henry V's 'there is much care and valour in this Welshman', and I was to find that Dick's gift for friendship was invaluable in maintaining PEP's goodwill among an amazingly wide range of people. Wise and kindly John Madge brought his international reputation as a sociologist to the institute's research; and the research staff included Murray Forsyth, George Gater, Tim Leggatt and Pauline Morris, who distinguished themselves later in various academic or official capacities.

When the post of Director was advertised, candidates were required to set down on paper their reactions to Max Nicholson's broadsheet on *The Shape of the Sixties* (1963), and the idea of PEP must have tapped a deep spring of energy in me, as I sat up all night writing a long, doubtless too long, essay on the subject. Despite this, I was offered the job and ushered into a new world which has, ever since, been a large and extraordinarily rewarding part of my life.

There was also a problem, which Richard Bailey has described in the last part of Chapter 6. In essence, PEP was suffering some of the growing pains of a modern social science research institute. Not only economics, but several other social sciences were by now professions, with large numbers of graduates becoming employed in research as well as other occupations. A complex kit of research methods had been constructed, involving surveys, case studies, models and the computer-based analysis of statistics. There was a gathering flow of funds for social science research from foundations, government departments and, shortly, the Social Science Research Council. There was a growing demand for studies from departments, universities and the media; and studies which did not meet the new professional standards would not be held of much account.

I do not think there was any incompatibility of principle between good work of the new, professionalised social sciences and of the earlier types done at PEP. The new methods made it possible to improve the data base and to make a more powerful analysis of statistics. But the problem of using the facts to make policy prescriptions remained the same; and PEP's method of involving practitioners in groups to do this was as valid as before. But in practice groups and researchers had not been working well together and PEP had been sapped by the resulting quarrels. Good work was done in the studies of attitudes in British management, mental health services, prisoners' families, and overseas students in Britain, which were nearing completion when I arrived. But the pipeline was devoid of a new flow of studies to follow them.

The researchers left as the studies were completed and there was no money for new studies and researchers to replace them. The institute became a ghost village, with a skeleton population of old-timers from the administrative staff, as well as Dick Davies, John Madge and myself. Without new study grants we could not cover the overheads. The overdraft reached what then seemed the dizzy height of £20,000, and I told John Nash, the Honorary Treasurer, that I was ready to jump rather than wait to be pushed. Always unflappable, he counselled patience; and he was right.

PEP had great underlying strength in the goodwill of people who were in a position to sponsor its research. By 1965 Lord Heyworth, who had earlier been involved in PEP's work, had retired from the chairmanship of Unilever and had completed the Heyworth Report recommending the establishment of the Social Science Research Council. But he was still Chairman of the Leverhulme Trust. He was one of those magnetic characters who quietly commanded attention and drew from people whatever he needed for his purpose. When he came to lunch at PEP, I was innocently unaware that he was drawing from us the impressions which would cause him to decide that the Leverhulme Trust should sponsor studies at PEP on a scale which, it turned out, was to save the institute.

A few days later Lord Murray, who had earlier been active in PEP and was now the Director of the Leverhulme Trust, came to see me at our office, which had been moved in December 1963 to 12 Upper Belgrave Street. He sat down on one side of the great oak table that had graced the club room in Queen Anne's Gate and I sat, some distance away, on the other. He asked whether PEP might agree to make a study of women and their careers. I said that both careers and women were of interest. He asked whether £60,000 would be enough. I said I would put it to the Executive Committee. Quietly, courteously, succinctly, he had said what he came to say. The visit lasted about ten minutes.

I could hardly wait to report this astonishing offer to the next meeting of the Executive Committee. To my amazement, however, Max Nicholson vehemently criticised the inaptness of the proposal compared with PEP's (originally, Max's) existing idea for a great study of land-use planning and how it had controlled the impact of urban growth on the countryside; and he insisted we tell the Leverhulme Trust that they should put their money into this truly important project instead. I saw salvation flying out of the window until some genius for compromise suggested we agree to study

*12 Upper Belgrave Street: PEP's headquarters from 1963–78.*

women and their careers but ask at the same time for a grant to study urban growth.

It was with no small trepidation that I informed Lord Murray we would accept the project on women and their careers but wanted a grant to study urban growth as well. But I reckoned without knowledge of Max's ability to break the rules of ordinary prudent behaviour and win – or of his influence with so many of PEP's network of supporters, including his old friend Keith Murray. Instead of losing the first project, as I had feared, we were awarded a twin grant of £60,000 to study the second as well. PEP was not only saved; it was launched on a new voyage as a thriving research institute.

The next one of PEP's old relationships to bear fruit was that described in Richard Bailey's section on European studies (see p. 129). Joe Slater of the Ford Foundation visited us and the result was a new grant for studies of Britain and the European Community, part of it for PEP's own research and part for joint studies with Chatham House. Then the Social Science Research Council, which was established in 1965 with Michael Young as its first Chairman, awarded grants for studies of MPs' information and of the feasibility of a survey archive, and became responsible for another new study of companies' objectives and responsibilities. In 1966, the Joseph Rowntree Memorial Trust funded a major survey of racial discrimination in England which, as we shall see, had an almost instant impact on legislation as well as among the wider public.

Thus we relaunched a full programme of work. By 1967, we had a staff of 15 researchers and about 30 in all; and Dick Davies organised two glittering public events. Following the impact of the survey of racial discrimination, there was a dinner at which Roy Jenkins, who had just left the Home Office to become Chancellor of the Exchequer, said that the PEP survey had been decisive in the government's decision to go through with the second Race Relations Act. Israel Sieff presided and Edward Boyle and Mark Abrams also spoke. We had Norman St John-Stevas to thank for the other event. His researches on Walter Bagehot had discovered that Bagehot had lived in PEP's elegant new building in Upper Belgrave Street; and he suggested we ask the Greater London Council to erect a commemorative plaque. After a dignified delay they did, and the then Prime Minister, Harold Wilson, unveiled it with a knowledgeable speech.

The next year there was the more intimate and moving occasion of a dinner for Israel (by then Lord) Sieff's 80th birthday, when those who had been devoted to him and to PEP gathered to do him honour. He lived until 1972, and I hope he knew that PEP, in which he and his friends had invested so much work and love, had struck root so as to become a permanent feature of the British scene. For that is what had happened. There was by the early 1970s a group of researchers in the institute who proved able to attract the support needed for continuing their work through that difficult decade, to maintain the relationship with PEP's originators and established supporters, and to make a considerable impact on the national life. They included Bill Daniel, Santosh Mukherjee, Mayer Hillman, Anne Whalley, Isobel Allen, David Smith and Richard Berthoud. Michael Fogarty, David Coombes, Ray Thomas, Mike Thomas, Christopher Layton, Christopher Harlow and Yao-Su Hu made notable contributions for a time, as did John Madge, Charles de Hoghton and Val Schur until their untimely deaths. But PEP had the great fortune to keep a nucleus of gifted researchers through the decade and into the merger with the Centre for Studies in Social Policy in 1978. Much of what follows is the story of their achievements during this period.

### Race Relations and Discrimination Laws

The first event in this story is PEP's first survey of racial discrimination, because it was the first study during the period to have a resounding public impact. In the late summer of 1966 Mark Bonham Carter, then Chairman of the Race Relations Board, asked me if PEP could measure the extent of racial discrimination in Britain within six months. He and the Home Secretary, Roy Jenkins, believed that discrimination was sufficient to justify extending the very limited first Race Relations Act through a second Act which would make discrimination illegal in employment, housing and a number of personal services. But the Cabinet were unsure and powerful interest groups such as the CBI and the TUC insisted that discrimination was too small a nut to justify the sledgehammer of a new Act. The question put to us was simply whether discrimination in these fields was substantial or not.

It seems that a number of authorities had been consulted and advised that a reliable answer could not be obtained in the time available, which was dictated (like so much else in policy research)

by Britain's Procrustean political timetable. Having come to PEP
from a job which involved market research, I thought that field work
could give a good answer, provided that enough surveys were done
to check and double-check on the results. I consulted Mark Abrams,
who had been since July 1964 Chairman of PEP's Executive Committee and was the founder and head of Research Services Limited,
one of the leading survey agencies; and he introduced me to a young
member of the staff called Bill Daniel. We quickly agreed that
surveys of both the ethnic minorities and the white natives would
be required. But what if their versions of what happened should
differ? Only an objective test could demonstrate who was right. Bill
Daniel rapidly developed the idea of a battery of tests, undertaken
by black, brown, white foreign and white British actors in succession
seeking from the same source housing, jobs or services. If all were
refused, the test showed nothing; if the minority actors were accepted,
it showed no discrimination against them; if at some point in the
chain refusal changed to acceptance, discrimination was established.
Several hundred such tests should give an objective statistical
measure of discrimination. The two surveys and the tests together
should eliminate any grounds for doubt by providing a triangulation
on the point in question.

Meanwhile a grant to finance the survey had been offered by the
Joseph Rowntree Memorial Trust and a steering group had been set
up with Mark Bonham Carter as its chairman. Six months of extremely hectic work followed. Surveying the white population on
such an explosive subject was tricky enough; but the survey of the
minorities and the tests were both almost completely uncharted mine-
fields. The relief can be imagined when both the surveys and the
tests gave similar and hence convincing results in each of the six
areas and the three functions studied. All the findings converged to
show that discrimination was substantial though not overwhelming.

The report was published in April 1967 and was, as Roy Jenkins
said, 'decisive' in moving the government to go ahead with the Act.
Seldom can research have had such a direct and immediate effect on
legislation. Since such laws are not very useful if they are not bi-
partisan, it is equally significant that the Opposition did not oppose
the extension of the 1965 Act; we heard that Lord Hailsham, who
was then shadow Home Secretary, read the report and concluded
that its findings were incontrovertible. (Perhaps it was also relevant
that one of the authors of a report on anti-discrimination laws, which

was financed by a grant from Marks & Spencer and published by PEP later in the year, was a young barrister and Conservative called Geoffrey Howe.) Public understanding of the issues is also required if laws of this kind are to be effective; and this must have been helped by the massive press coverage of the report, from a centre spread in the *Daily Mirror* downwards, which the definitive book on race relations of the period described as having 'easily exceeded that given to even the most prestigious Royal Commission'.[1] Bill Daniel also wrote a Penguin version of the report which sold over 70,000 copies.

This event has been described in some detail because it appears, in retrospect, as a classic example of research applied to a policy question which had to be answered by using the tools of empirical social science research. Without the surveys, and indeed without developing the new method of tests in numbers that would produce statistics, the facts required by the policy makers could not have been obtained. Given the facts, the policy makers could take their decision. PEP's view was not sought, however, on the implications of these facts for policy. Once the facts had been made clear, the conclusion that substantial discrimination should be countered by a law was accepted by the main political parties and not resisted by the main interest groups.

It might be asked why PEP, with its tradition of assembling facts as a basis for policy proposals, confined itself in this case to assembling facts. One reason is doubtless that people at PEP implicitly accepted the case for a law. Another is that, despite the consensus on this within the establishment, the issue of race relations was highly fraught among sectors of the public, and we argued that confidence in the reliability of the facts, which is a necessary basis for democratic politics, would be undermined if those who obtained them went on and used them to make a case.

We were again guided by this argument when, six years later, the Home Office asked us to study the general position of the ethnic minorities in British society and measure the gap between their condition and those of the white population in housing, employment and other economic factors. Again, the emphasis was on getting the facts and neither David Smith, who conducted the large and complex set of surveys and case studies, nor the advisory group, chaired

[1] Rose, E. J. B., and associates, *Colour and Citizenship: A Report on British Race Relations*, p. 534, London, OUP, 1969.

by Asa Briggs and including leaders from each important minority, tried to shift the focus to policy prescriptions. Again, the reports received massive publicity, a Penguin was published which sold over 50,000 copies, and the facts obtained were hardly contested from any quarter.

If there were any fears that PEP was abdicating its role as an initiator of ideas for policy, in order to become a sort of office of ethnic statistics, the next developments must have allayed them. For the success of these first two studies led, in the later 1970s, not only to preparations for a third study on similar lines but also to the sponsoring of surveys of the unemployed among the ethnic minorities, of overseas doctors in Britain, of multi-ethnic schools, and of relations between the minorities and the Metropolitan Police, in each of which the policy implications were to feature prominently; and the American Academy of Sciences asked us to make a joint study of policy towards minorities in Britain and the United States. This prompts the conclusion that good work, even if confined at first to finding the facts, can snowball into a programme of research on which policy recommendations are based.

The impact of the study of sex, career and family, which had been initiated by Lord Heyworth and the Leverhulme Trust, was less dramatic. But it too was well timed, since its results in the form of three books and a number of broadsheets were published in the late 1960s and early 1970s, well before the passage of the Sex Discrimination Act of 1975, and were much used through the 1970s when the status of women became a hotly debated issue. The study was led by Michael Fogarty, who left Cardiff to do it after 15 years there as Professor of Industrial Relations, with Robert and Rhona Rapoport. The advisory group, in which high-powered women were a majority, was chaired by Denis Barnes, then Permanent Secretary of the Department of Employment, who was brave enough to say at one meeting that he would refuse to be flown by a woman pilot. Like the studies of race relations, this one used a variety of research methods to construct a comprehensive picture of the subject; and it too was followed, in this case ten years later, by a new look, on behalf of the Equal Opportunities Commission and the SSRC, at the professions and organisations which had been studied in the late 1960s, to find out what change the Sex Discrimination Act had induced. (The answer was 'not much as yet'.)

## Urban Growth and Personal Mobility

The study of urban growth in post-war England, impelled by Max Nicholson and financed by the Leverhulme Trust, produced the most monumental report in PEP's history: so monumental that the publisher took fright at the printing cost and insisted on co-responsibility with PEP instead of a royalty. One reason was the productivity of Peter Hall, who was, from his base as Professor of Geography at Reading University, the editor and principal author. His writing led to some memorable meetings of the advisory group, when Bill Holford and Max Nicholson discussed how the Town and Country Planning Act had worked out in practice, in the light of their personal memories of what Abercrombie and his contemporaries had intended. The other reason was the large output from the other members of the research team, Ray Thomas, Harry Gracey, Roy Drewett and Anne Whalley, who produced compatible results although their different ways of going about it would certainly have shattered any illusion that interdisciplinary research was social science jargon for divine harmony.

The book of the study was notably successful, despite the publisher's fears, and must rank as a landmark in knowledge of the subject. Peter Hall also worked with Resources for the Future in Washington, whom Max had persuaded to make a comparative study in the United States. The close collaboration was helped by a grant from the Ford Foundation, and resulted in a joint book comparing the findings from the two sides of the Atlantic. The other main output of the project was a series of broadsheets by Ray Thomas around the theme of accessibility of work and the extent to which New Towns, by cutting journeys to work, were more self-contained and balanced communities than the historic towns and cities had become. He showed a rare talent for squeezing from the census data drops of precious information which nobody else thought to seek; and this enabled him to pinpoint the difficulties of accessibility and mobility which were confronting those without control of a car, when urban form and transport facilities, in adapting to the convenience of car-owners, were increasingly separating other people from the facilities they need to reach. Before Ray left to go to the Open University he designed a study to explore this problem further, and the Joseph Rowntree Memorial Trust, two of whose Trustees had recently visited Los Angeles and had been shocked by the isolation of non-car-owners there, offered a grant to finance it.

Mayer Hillman, who had left a flourishing architectural practice in order to pursue his interest in urban form, had just completed a doctoral thesis which surveyed accessibility and mobility in a New Town. His external examiner was Bill Holford, who noticed the identity between his interests and what PEP wanted to do. The fit was amazingly close and Mayer came to PEP in 1970 to undertake the study.

He and Anne Whalley surveyed, carefully and in detail, the ways in which access to facilities was denied to non-car-owners in five different types of locality; and a grant from the Department of the Environment enabled them to do the same more extensively for old people and for women with young children in London's Outer Metropolitan Area. In *Personal Mobility and Transport Policy* (1973) they brought home the implications for planning and transport policy, in terms of dispersal of facilities and control over the use of the car. This and subsequent reports in similar vein attracted great publicity and were influential in getting the subject on the political agenda, to the point where their heterodoxy of the early 1970s, when transport policy was dominated by a traffic engineering approach, had become the orthodoxy of the White Paper on *Transport Policy* in 1977. Of course the tides of ecology, small is beautiful and, more mundanely, petrol prices were running in the same direction. But the provision of facts which show in detail the extent and depth of the problem also has its part to play. In the mid-1970s we asked who might be responsible at the Department of the Environment for policy on walking, and were told politely that there was no policy on walking and that such a thing could hardly be conceived. Hillman and Whalley nevertheless made a study which was published in 1979 as *Walking* is *Transport*, and the Minister of Transport announced, at a conference held at PSI in 1980, that a Green Paper on walking would be published later in the year.

Thus social science research in its modern form is not, as some have alleged, just a way of buttressing the preconceived ideas of policy makers. It can help to place social needs on the political agenda and lead policy makers to pay proper attention to them. But the same researchers can also respond to the policy makers' own questions, as Hillman and Whalley did in a report for the Sports Council and the Transport and Road Research Laboratory which demonstrated the merits of easy access to small and local recreational facilities; and in one for the British Railways Board on the social consequences of rail closures.

## Social Policy
In 1969 Dick Crossman, who was then Secretary of State for Social Services, came to lunch at PEP. His diaries confirm that he enjoyed himself,[1] and interspersed with the stream of anecdotes it emerged that he wanted a study to assess the size and rate of growth of the private sector of medical care. John Cornish, the Assistant Secretary dealing with research contracts for the Department, was present and it was left that I would negotiate the terms of reference with him. In this case we were asked for the facts on a subject where there seemed likely to be maximum dissension about their implications for policy, and since the request came from Crossman, I thought it prudent to have the study done by an expert who did not share what I guessed to be Crossman's views. Michael Lee produced a factual report, which clearly satisfied the Department as they asked him to repeat it in subsequent years, and which did not get us into trouble with the Opposition or the doctors, who, according to Crossman, had at first strongly resisted the idea of the study.[2]

This was a small incident in itself, but it had important consequences for PEP, because Cornish was helping Crossman to stimulate growth in the research commissioned by the Department, and his way of doing so had more in common with an older tradition of patronage than with that of the average research council: that is, if he thought your work was worthwhile he would back it without fussing about too many details or what the various professors with an interest in the subject might think. He decided that our work was worthwhile and he supported a series of studies, first on voluntary organisations and then, after he had moved on to other responsibilities which included family planning, on family planning services.

The work on voluntary organisations started with a study on voluntary visiting of old people by Barbara Shenfield and Isobel Allen, continued with several studies that Mike Thomas undertook for other sponsors before becoming a Member of Parliament, and

[1] Crossman, Richard, *The Diaries of a Cabinet Minister*, vol. 3, p. 647, Hamish Hamilton and Jonathan Cape, 1977.
[2] Ibid., p. 749.

has been consolidated by the incorporation in PSI of the Voluntary Organisations Research Unit under Stephen Hatch. On family planning, Isobel Allen in successive studies assessed the effectiveness of various services, and drew conclusions for the development of policy. More generally, the studies which Cornish initiated were the first major manifestation of support for PEP research projects by government departments, which was to become in the 1970s a large element in financing the work of PEP, as of many other institutes.

Although Richard Berthoud, in *The Disadvantages of Inequality*, reviewed the incidence of various aspects of deprivation among different groups of the population, the bulk of our research on social policy was on quite specific subjects, and lacked the scope and ambition of PEP's work in the 1930s, when the reports on the *British Social Services* and the *British Health Services*, both published in 1937, foreshadowed the Beveridge Report and the National Health Service. After the merger with CSSP in 1978, which brought with it such leading experts in different fields as David Eversley, Matilda Goldberg, Leonard Nicholson and Muriel Nissel, the institute was well placed to become more ambitious again and to try to answer some of the many questions about the future of the welfare state; and by 1980 there were signs that, in the 1980s, we would do so.

## Labour Relations, Manpower Policy

In 1968 Monty Finniston joined PEP's Executive Committee. He was then Deputy Chairman of the British Steel Corporation, and was becoming monthly more indignant because an inter-departmental committee, whose job was to consider what action the government might take to provide jobs for redundant steelworkers in Workington, met every month and seemed to do no more than shuffle the paper around. He foresaw that there would be more Workingtons and asked PEP to prepare a report on the provisions required for redundant workers in the event of plant closures and large-scale lay-offs. He put his finger on a subject that was to become central, not only for the steel industry but for the whole British economy; and by doing so he launched PEP on what later became its most important and influential programme of research in the 1970s.

Having experienced Bill Daniel's research on the survey of racial discrimination, I was eager to offer him a job at PEP and as his interests included business education, this became possible when the Department of Education asked us to assess the suitability of the

HND Business Studies course for business needs. He was working on this, again triangulating the issue, with surveys of employers, teachers and former students, when Monty Finniston asked for the report on redevelopment. As an industrial sociologist, Bill was well placed to review the literature and discuss with personnel managers their current practices with respect to redundancy.

At the same time we had to review the agencies that execute the policies of redeployment and industrial location. Santosh Mukherjee, who had recently gone to Oxford after five years as Len Murray's deputy in the TUC's Economic Department and short spells in the Ministry of Labour and the Treasury, had told me just before that he would like to give half his time to research on manpower policy; and this turned out to be a stroke of exceptionally good fortune for PEP. For Santosh went on from this first piece of work for the BSC[1] to produce a series of reports which had a remarkable impact on manpower policy. His comparison of Britain and Sweden, which brought out the role of the Swedish Labour Market Board, was completed when the time was ripe for a major improvement in Britain's labour market institutions, and when the then Prime Minister, Edward Heath, was in need of policies to get on terms with the trade unions; and the report helped to crystallise thinking in favour of the establishment of the Manpower Services Commission. After the MSC was established, it was confronted by the swelling numbers of unemployed. Santosh was asked to study job creation in Canada and his report[2] was a basis for the MSC's Job Creation Scheme. Early in 1976, PEP published his *Unemployment Costs* ..., which showed how heavy a burden was placed on state budgets in European Community countries by the loss of revenue and increase in expenditure due to unemployment. This attracted the attention, among others, of the German federal agency for manpower policy, the IAB at Nuremberg, who asked PEP to make a joint study of alternatives to unemployment, which would spend public money more productively than on the dole. Santosh took charge of this, as well as of a study of British and German trade unions and their approach to manpower use, both financed by the Anglo–German Foundation. In the summer of 1979, when these two large pieces of

[1] Published in Daniel, W. W. *Strategies for Displaced Employees*, PEP, 1970. This also included the results of research by John Allen on the regional policy aspects.

[2] Mukherjee, Santosh, *There's work to be Done: Unemployment and Manpower Policies*, MSC, 1974.

work were nearing completion, he died of heart failure. He had, in his too-short life, accomplished much of value to Britain as well as, through work for the European Community, OECD and ILO, to other countries. Perhaps the best epitaph was coined by Peter Parker, who when Honorary Treasurer of PEP had called him Britain's labour market guru. He was also on the way to fulfilling, through his international work, a similar role for Europe and the world as well.

Bill Daniel, who approached employment problems through the individual worker and the shop floor rather than the agencies of manpower policy, went on from the BSC's redeployment report to study productivity bargaining, not just as a way of negotiating pay but as a means of 'collective bargaining for change'. His *Beyond the Wage-Work Bargain* (1970) showed how such bargains could improve relationships at work and job interest and satisfaction as well as pay and productivity. This work led to *The Right to Manage?* (1972), in which Bill Daniel showed how employee relations could be improved, and in enterprising firms were already being improved, by greater worker involvement. Marcus Sieff initiated the study and, as chairman of the advisory group, brought to it the unique experience of Marks & Spencer in human relations, as his father Israel had done in the earlier, formative years of PEP.

In October 1972, Leonard Elmhirst invited PEP's Executive Committee and senior members of the staff to Dartington for a weekend conference, which turned out to be a seminal meeting, to which we shall return. In particular inflation, then still in single figures, was identified as one of the critical issues for the 1970s, which PEP should study with the focus on attitudes and behaviour of individuals and groups. 'Why,' Max Nicholson asked, 'has man become such an inflationary animal?' Econometrics did not give the answer, and Bill Daniel designed a research programme to investigate attitudes and behaviour and the ways in which they could be converted into inflation through the process of collective bargaining. Before the end of 1973 we had obtained a substantial grant for this study from the Leverhulme Trust. At the same time OPEC quadrupled the price of oil and catapulted Britain's inflation into double figures. It rose rapidly through 1974 and the first half of 1975, by which time government and unions were ready to use incomes policy in order to prevent it from pushing above the annual rate of 30 per cent. Bill Daniel had by then completed surveys which showed that an incomes policy based on a flat rate limit, of the order of £6 a week.

was likely to be widely acceptable. These findings were available at the right moment to help the government judge precisely what they should do in order to bring an extremely dangerous situation under control, and thus to reduce inflation within two years from some 25 per cent to single figures.

In the next year a large and complex survey of collective bargaining at the workplace, based on interviews with three or four people for each establishment, showed that the rate of settlement before the £6 a week limit did not vary with the financial or market position of firms, i.e. that cost push was the dominant force, and confirmed that the £6 a week limit had then been effective. Bill Daniel went on to make proposals for the future development of incomes policy. These had influence in the following phase; but in the reaction against incomes policy in the late 1970s, neither the evidence of cost push nor the proposals for incomes policy were heeded.

By 1972 we also identified unemployment as a growing problem, and Bill Daniel started to prepare a national survey of the unemployed. Officials were not convinced of the need for this, so it was financed from private sources. The findings, published in 1974, showed that the costs of unemployment were high for most of the unemployed, particularly for family men rather than for the young people on whom the spotlight had hitherto been turned. By 1976, the Manpower Services Commission was sponsoring a follow-up survey of those who had been interviewed in 1974, which showed how many of them had since experienced a chequered pattern of employment or ceased to be employed altogether. The MSC based a number of new policy decisions on these findings. By 1980, when unemployment exceeded two million, Bill Daniel was again making a survey for the MSC of a sample specially designed to bring out the experiences of those who are unemployed for shorter spells, while the Department of Employment was sponsoring a survey of the long-term unemployed which was being undertaken by Michael White. With respect to both unemployment and wage determination, the seeds which PEP had planted in the early 1970s without official help had grown into stout trees from which public policy derived a good deal of support.

**Industry**
PEP's main contribution to economic policy in the 1970s was through its work on labour relations, incomes and manpower policy. As

'Oliver Roskill has observed (see pp. 63–4), the focus had moved from industrial sectors (cotton textiles, steel, coal), which had been the subject of his studies in the 1930s, to industrial problems (labour relations, innovation, company law). Yet the first industrial study to be started after I came to PEP was a review of energy policy, for which Oliver himself chaired the group and Jack Hartshorn, then Business Editor of *The Economist*, wrote the report.

The next initiative, however, stimulated by Michael Fogarty when he was still at the University of Wales, was a programme of research on the role of company boards and the reform of company law. Barbara Shenfield and Charles de Hoghton worked with Michael on this, between them writing two books and several broadsheets. Barbara was a strong Tory and we wondered how Jack Jones, who was then only at the start of his transition from fiery rebel to elder statesman, would, as a member of the advisory group, react to her work. Peter Parker was a most adroit chairman, however, and at the only meeting which Jack Jones attended we discussed a draft broadsheet on company fraud, which all were able to agree was a bad thing and ought to be stopped.

After Christopher Layton came to PEP in 1966, to make a study of European co-operation in advanced technology as part of the programme of European studies, innovation became the principal theme in our industrial research. He wrote two books, *European Advanced Technology* (1966) and, based on a report he had produced for the Central Advisory Council for Science and Technology, *Ten Innovations* (1972), as well as a broadsheet presenting the results of research on the probable effects on industrial investment of British membership of the European Community, which was published in 1971 during the debate on prospective British entry. He brought in to work with him Christopher Harlow, who subsequently produced *Innovation and Productivity under Nationalisation* (1977) and Yao-Su Hu, who, on a somewhat different tack, showed in *National Attitudes and the Financing of Industry* (1976) how Britain is short of financial institutions which possess, like the continental and Japanese industrial banks, a deep enough knowledge of industry to be able to judge which investment risks should be backed.

Innovation creates new jobs but it also destroys old ones; and there was one strand missing from PEP's research on redeployment which Monty Finniston had initiated in 1968. Bill Daniel had shown how firms could carry through redundancy programmes in ways that were most conducive to the workers' subsequent re-employment; and Santosh Mukherjee had proposed changes in the institutions of manpower policy from which more effective training and placement would follow. But what if there were no jobs which redundant workers could take up, in places where they might reasonably be expected to seek work? The missing strand was a study on generating jobs in specific places; and Jim Northcott, who had worked for over a decade in consultancy relating to industrial location, agreed to do it. Officials were not keen on more research in this field, as policy was settled for the time being and new ideas might disturb the peace. David Sainsbury was, however, the chairman of a recently established trust, committed to improving industrial performance in Britain's mixed economy, and he agreed to finance the work. Numerous interviews with managers and officials concerned with locating new investments showed that the provision of facilities (c.f. PEP's early work on Trading Estates – see p. 26) and the fixing of arrangements were more decisive than the financial incentives. The officials who had been sceptical at the outset made good use of the report; but happily it had its warmest reception and greatest influence in British Steel (Industries) Ltd., where Monty Finniston's determination to promote new jobs for redundant steelworkers continued to find practical expression, after he had left BSC and his original initiative with PEP had doubtless been forgotten.

When PSI was formed and Charles Carter became Chairman of its Research and Management Committee, the institute had the benefit of guidance from a scholar who was, among other things, one of the pioneers of research on technology diffusion.[1] He launched a programme of research with Jim Northcott into obstacles to the application of microprocessors in British industry, which should ensure that the institute's work on innovation has a greater impact in the 1980s than PEP's useful but more scattered efforts could have in the previous decade.

**General Economic Management**
The programme of European studies when I came to PEP included a project on economic planning in the European Community, which resulted in the book *Economic Planning and Policies in Britain, France and Germany* (1968) by Geoffrey Denton, Murray Forsyth and

[1] See Carter, C. F. and Williams, B. R., *Industry and Technical Progress*, Oxford University Press, 1957; *Investment and Innovation*, 1958; and *Science in Industry*, 1959.

Malcolm MacLennan. This showed that, while the quantitative targets in French planning might not be of much account, the industrial policies in France and Germany (including, in Germany, the competition policy) made a contribution to economic management that was missing in Britain, where microeconomic policies are blown about by the winds of political fashion. This was followed by studies of planning in Yugoslavia, Hungary, the Soviet Union and the Republic of Ireland (the latter a book by Garret FitzGerald, later Foreign Minister and leader of the Fine Gael party), and by a series of broadsheets on the Labour Government's National Plan, including *Inquest on Planning in Britain* (1967) by Samuel Brittan, writing on the rebound from his period as an official in the Department of Economic Affairs. Among other things, he advocated a floating exchange rate. City people on the Executive Committee were alarmed, and this must be the only broadsheet which ever had a disclaimer inserted at the end as well as the beginning. Sam was not exactly amused, but he put up with it.

In the early 1970s PEP's contribution to economic policy was through its work on industrial, manpower and incomes policies. In 1974, however, inflation and unemployment became so severe and political uncertainty so critical that we decided to combine our various streams of research in a report to show how inflation could be brought down, investment raised and the authority of the political institutions restored. The result, *Reshaping Britain*, combined proposals by Bill Daniel for incomes policy, by Santosh Mukherjee for a stronger Manpower Services Commission, by Yao-Su Hu for a revival of industrial investment, and by John Mackintosh (returning to a question raised by PEP in the 1930s – see p. 64) for a reform of the House of Lords, to accommodate the representatives of trade unions and employers.

Eric Roll chaired a powerful advisory group and the report was received enthusiastically by some politicians, industrialists, and Peter Jay in *The Times*. But although the incomes policy was applied and inflation did come down, the idea of systematically combining industrial and manpower policies within a concept of general economic policy lost ground, as the decade wore on, in favour of apparently simple, global levers such as monetary or import control. Perhaps the general idea was not worked out and presented clearly enough; in any case, it has had no better luck as yet than the concept of industrial self-government which PEP developed in the 1930s.

## Politics; Europe

In 1964, PEP provided facilities for the Study of Parliament Group, which resulted in a broadsheet on *Reforming the Commons* (1965), written by members of the group. From this followed studies undertaken in co-operation with the Study of Parliament Group and financed by the SSRC, which led to *The Member of Parliament and his Information* (1970), by Tony Barker and Michael Rush, and John Griffith's *Parliamentary Scrutiny of Government Bills* (1974), as well as to a number of other reports on select committees, services and facilities for MPs, and the implications for parliament of entry into the European Community. Peter Richards, later Chairman of the SPG, also wrote a book for PEP entitled *The Local Government Act 1972: Problems of Implementation* (1975).

The source of our other stream of research on politics during the period was the programme of European studies, which produced *European Political Parties* (1970), edited by Stanley Henig and myself, and brought David Coombes to PEP to study the Commission of the European Community. In *Politics and Bureaucracy in the European Community* (1970) he put his finger on the ambivalence between the Commission's political and administrative roles, and on the danger of imagining that you can escape from politics by calling it technocracy. He then made a study of the control of nationalised industries, in which his *State Enterprise: Business or Politics?* (1971) analysed another case of tension between politics and technocracy. During a spell in the new Chair of European Studies at Loughborough University he edited a PEP book *The Power of the Purse: The Role of European Parliaments in Budgetary Decisions* (1976); and in 1978 he returned to PEP to make a study of *The Future of the European Parliament*, which was published in 1979 during the first European election campaign. This he followed, at PSI's new Centre for European Political Studies, with a programme of research on the relationship between industrial interest groups and politics.

The flow of publications surely helped to enlighten the discussion about political reforms in Britain and in the European Community. But it is hard to point to particular institutional reforms in which PEP's reports played a major part. There can be little doubt, though, that PEP's European studies, foreshadowed by Max Nicholson's war-time advocacy of European union (see pp. 83–5 and 90–92) and started as a major research programme under John Edwards and Richard Bailey in 1956 (see pp. 127–32), influenced Britain's entry into the European Community. Not that British membership was always advocated, even implicitly; but the scores of reports on European matters that PEP issued from the late 1950s to the early 1970s must have heightened consciousness of the importance of the European Community to Britain and certainly helped the formation of opinion by providing a mass of food for rational thought.

A number of particular economic and political studies on European issues have already been mentioned. In addition, there was the European Series of papers produced jointly by PEP and Chatham House. In countries where marriages are arranged by the parents it is claimed that they usually turn out happily. This union was arranged by Joe Slater, who made plain that the Ford Foundation would not be likely to support two institutes in London on one subject unless they were willing to work together; and the arrangements indeed turned out to be happy, and to last longer than many contemporary marriages. Between 1967 and 1976, 27 joint papers were published, on subjects ranging from agriculture to tax and from regional policy to the European Council; there was also a joint Fontana paperback, edited by Richard Mayne and called *Europe Tomorrow: Sixteen Europeans Look Ahead* (1972), which figured in a national list of best-selling paperbacks. Although the two institutes were not, as Lionel Curtis had hoped, 'next door to each other with a hole in the wall between them' (see p. 31), such close co-operation in planning, commissioning authors, organising advisory groups, editing and publishing must be unusual in relations between institutes. Each had something to offer in a subject where the domestic and the international converged. Doubtless it also helped that those involved on both sides – Andrew Shonfield, Miriam Camps and Roger Morgan at Chatham House and myself at PEP – got on particularly well together.

After British entry the European Community became a dimension in studies of subjects such as unemployment, manpower policies and parliamentary reform, but PEP's European studies could only be sporadic in the absence of a regular source of funds for them. The same had been the case with the political studies. In 1977, however, Frans Alting von Geusau and Raymond Georis of the European Cultural Foundation consulted me about the establishment in London of a centre to study the political problems of pluralist democracies, and agreed that this would best be done as a part of

PEP. When PSI was formed in 1978, the European Centre for Political Studies was established as part of the merged institute, with a core grant from the European Cultural Foundation. Roger Morgan joined the institute as head of the Centre and David Coombes continued his studies there. So PSI could develop a regular output of European studies, which PEP had lacked the means to do in the previous decade, and of political studies in a way which was perhaps unprecedented in PEP.

### PEP's Impact: The Balance Sheet

PEP's small research staff, never more than about 15 in number, produced much in the decade leading up to 1978. The foregoing account has tried to show what influence the various programmes of research may have had. But what was the result, seen as a whole?

In half a dozen main sectors of policy, there can be little doubt that the work had a major impact. The first survey of racial discrimination was decisive for the subsequent legislation, and the later research on ethnic minorities was probably the main source of information used by both policy makers and the public. The European studies, if the publications of the previous decade are included, did much to raise British consciousness of Community affairs to the point where membership became practical politics. The research on personal mobility gave a focus for the Copernican transition from car-centred to person-centred transport policy. The work on manpower and unemployment influenced the establishment of the Manpower Services Commission and the massive development of labour market policy. The surveys of collective bargaining and social attitudes to inflation helped to determine the shape of the incomes policy which brought inflation down from 25 per cent to single figures in the mid-1970s.

The majority of those policy sectors were at the centre of British problems during the period. PEP's work was also influential in some more specialised sectors, such as family planning; and it made a substantial contribution to knowledge about issues of public policy across the wide range of its economic, social and political research. None of this was negligible; some of it was important; some, such as the success of the first survey of racial discrimination, seemed almost miraculous. Incrementally, PEP had become a modern social science institute, using the tools of social science to help fashion better public policy. But although this was good, those who were concerned about the state of Britain in the 1970s wanted more. The weakness of the economy was becoming more and more evident. Why could we not put forward ideas for general economic policy that would help to make it stronger? The Model T welfare state was being questioned. Why could we not foreshadow the next stage of social policy, as PEP had done in 1937 with its reports on the social and health services? Political institutions were under increasing strain. Why could we not make comprehensive proposals to reform the British constitution? Or if such wide-ranging, grand reforms were not to the questioner's taste, why could we not have such an impact on other fields of economic and social policy as we were having in labour relations, manpower policy and race relations?

**Organising for Growth; Merger with CSSP**
These questions were not formulated so precisely when members of the Executive Committee and senior staff went to Dartington for their meeting over a lovely autumn weekend in October 1972. It was a happy time. Leonard Elmhirst was delighted to have PEP at Dartington again; and he had reason to be, as PEP was doing well and was embodied in a remarkable group of people. Those who made the journey included his old friends from PEP's foundation, Max Nicholson and Oliver Roskill; Eric Roll, by then Chairman of the Committee, Samuel Brittan, Geoffrey Denton, Frank Jones, Alan Sainsbury and Dorothy Wedderburn; and, from the staff, Dick Davies, Bill Daniel, Mayer Hillman and myself. Leonard's idea was that people who eat as well as work together will produce something good in a way that is not given to those who just confront each other in a committee. That was why he had quietly insisted the year before that we revive the weekend meetings; and that was why he was the perfect host for the occasion. It was almost the last time he put his mark on PEP; he died in California less than two years later. But he certainly did something to us that weekend, for events were to show the prophetic nature of our deliberations.

The timeliness of the decision to launch research on the social and institutional causes of inflation – on 'why man had become such an inflationary animal' – has already been noted. More pregnant for the future of the institute, however, was the discussion on the role of PEP. Although the questions about PEP's performance were not put in a critical way, there was a clear understanding that we must increase our capacity to respond to the problems that increasingly beset our country. Eric Roll spoke of the 'need to develop a great Brookings-like centre in Britain'; and the recently announced establishment of the Centre for Studies in Social Policy was noted, as an institute that 'seemed likely to cover a substantial part of the field in which PEP worked'.

Prophetic though the juxtaposition of those two thoughts was to prove, PEP tried to expand under its own steam into becoming at least a greater centre than it had been hitherto. It was decided to aim for a research staff of 25–30, which would require twice the current income. John Nash and Dick Davies managed to increase our industrial donations and the researchers obtained new grants as old ones faded away. But inflation ran almost as fast as we did, and the net result was that we could only offer stability for a staff of fairly constant size. Our capacity and reputation as a social science institute continued to rise. But the incoming tide of Britain's problems rose faster, and others took up the cry that a great Brookings-like centre was required.

The debate about a British Brookings was accompanied, in 1976–77, by two attempts to launch a big new institute, on the part of Derek Robinson at the SSRC, of which he was then Chairman, and Ralf Dahrendorf at the LSE. The Brookings protagonists seemed, from my subjective standpoint, to undervalue what we had done and to suppose too readily that something new would be much better. Yet they had a point (which had been made at Dartington in 1972), and we thought the existing institutes must do something about it. Hence our approach in the summer of 1977 to the Centre for Studies in Social Policy.

The Centre were also considering what to do in the future; and once the talks about merger began, they went ahead very quickly. It was agreed that Eric Roll and Frederic Seebohm would be the Joint Presidents of the merged institute, Monty Finniston Chairman of the Council and Charles Carter Chairman of the Research and Management Committee. The constitution was to be, like those of both PEP and CSSP, a company limited by guarantee. The members of the company and of the Council would be appointed in equal numbers by each predecessor institute. I was to be the Director; Michael Fogarty, whom I had learnt to know and appreciate when he worked at PEP, and who had been Acting Director of CSSP since Sandy Isserlis left after a five-year spell as Director to return to the Civil Service, would be Deputy Director; Dick Davies was to be

Director of Administration. All members of the staff of both institutes could have jobs in the merged institute. But what was it to
be called?

The staff at PEP insisted the name must be PEP, because of the
accretion of goodwill to it through the (as it seemed to us) ages.
The staff at CSSP refused to accept any such indignity. The PEP
side were shaken when Max Nicholson said that the founding fathers
knew they had made a bad choice and he had never cared for the
name at all; but we refused to allow our woad to be scrubbed off
us, even by Max. The deadlock was broken only by referring the
issue to arbitration by the Joint Presidents, who chose a name that
both staffs resisted; and this caused all concerned to unite and
rapidly agree on Policy Studies Institute. Soon after this reconcilia-
tion, the merger was consummated, on 31 March (*not*, the stage
managers were careful to ensure, the first of April) 1978.

## PSI in 1980

By the autumn of 1980, on the eve of the 50th anniversary of
PEP, PSI had embodied at least a good part of the idea of a 'great,
Brookings-like centre' that Leonard Elmhirst's benign magic had
conjured out of PEP's Executive Committee at Dartington in 1972.
The founding officers of PSI had been joined by a most distinguished Council, whose Vice-Chairmen were the Permanent Secretary to the Treasury and the Deputy Chairman of ICI. There was a
research staff of nearly 50 and a total staff of about 70, and a
budget of over £1 million a year.

There were some 50 studies in the fields of social security, personal
social services, voluntary organisations, health services, housing,
education, demographic trends (one of the latter, on population
trends in Britain, having been initiated by Max Nicholson); on labour
relations, manpower policy, technological and industrial policy; on
parties, interest groups, parliament and the European Community.
Visiting fellows working at PSI for a year or more had included
Shirley Williams, John Pardoe and, on their retirement from the
Civil Service, Denis Barnes (whose book on *Governments and Trade
Unions*, written at PSI with Eileen Reid, was published in 1980) and
Sandy Isserlis. The publications included books, reports (formerly
PEP broadsheets), three new series of discussion papers, European
papers and research papers, and a quarterly journal called *Policy
Studies* to make the research findings more accessible to non-

specialist readers. Hardly a week passed without good press coverage of a PSI publication or event.

While not quite so close as Queen Anne's Gate to Whitehall and Westminster, PSI's building in Castle Lane was only ten minutes' walk from Parliament and a number of government departments. The intention was to help bring our research and public policy closer together by enabling policy makers to come easily to the institute; and this, together with Dick Davies's pulling power, seemed to be working. The institute had been formally opened in 1979 by James Callaghan, then Prime Minister. The speakers at a new series of lunchtime meetings had included ten members of the Conservative Cabinet and people of similar distinction from other areas of politics and from the civil service, business, trade unions and the universities. During three months in the summer, one-day or two-day seminars to discuss PSI studies had been held at the rate of one a fortnight, with impressive lists of participants including two Ministers. Willy Brandt had given the annual Sieff Memorial Lecture (though this was at the Royal Institution, which is no less accessible from Bonn than Castle Lane is).

While this was all bigger and grander than PEP had ever been, those who were familiar with Upper Belgrave Street could feel at home in Castle Lane because they would still see almost all the members of the research staff who had been there in the latter years, together with Anne Blackman, Barbara Livermore and Bill and Elsie Todd on the administrative side. But what would the familiars of PEP in its heyday at Queen Anne's Gate have thought of PSI?

Britain is now undergoing a crisis in some ways comparable to that of the 1930s. The need to know the facts and draw out their implications for public policy is as great now as it was then. In contemporary society, many of the necessary facts cannot be obtained and analysed without using the techniques of social science; and PSI differs from the early PEP in being a modern social science research institute, one of the largest of its kind in Europe. We have, then, the capacity to obtain and analyse the facts on a very substantial scale. What we must ensure, in order to apply this capacity as effectively as possible to help Britain through its crisis and into better days, is that we continue to work with the blend of practical usefulness and challenge to established thought which became PEP's hallmark from the very first studies on which the founders embarked, 50 years ago.

# 8

# Plus Ça Change ...

## A. R. Isserlis

Those who have written this book so far were themselves in PEP and played a major part in making or shaping it. But there must also be many thousands of others, like me, who having merely at one time or another been members of PEP's wide-ranging readership and audience can nevertheless sense something of the same nostalgic though not uncritical recollection of intellectual and political challenge.

'Was it worth it?', ponders Max Nicholson in a burst of rare diffidence, looking back in Chapter 2 over PEP's chequered history. The record shows that it was – thanks to Max himself and his colleagues and successors and their backers. Despite many fluctuations of style and fortune PEP somehow managed never wholly to lose its effectiveness or reputation as an independent resource and forum for the clear presentation and constructive discussion of hard facts and issues for public policy. Its output and activity varied, sometimes faltered, but never ceased. For nearly 50 years it thereby made a continual and considerable contribution, often of high quality, to the information and ideas circulating amongst the thoughtful UK public and especially amongst those who made or swayed public decisions. The presence of that contribution, among others, can often be deduced and sometimes quite positively identified at successive stages in the increasingly active ferment of ideas which led from the 1930s onwards to so many potentially useful developments in public policy, structures, attitudes and practice. In a pluralistic democracy no single self-appointed institution of research and influence in public affairs can realistically or legitimately expect to achieve much more.

It was with this record behind it that in 1977 PEP made its suggestion of a merger to the Centre for Studies in Social Policy. The Centre, which had been founded and largely maintained by the generous support of the Joseph Rowntree Memorial Trustees, with myself as its Director, was then barely five years old. But already it too had established itself, albeit in a small way, as a public policy research and discussion institute of some repute, with problems and limitations but a modestly successful record of its own in terms of output and influence, and a Council and staff keen to extend these still further. It could therefore see a case, in spite of inevitable worries about scale and funding, for continuing to go it alone. I myself was returning to the public service after my five-year stint, but a successor had been sought. The Council eventually decided, however, and when I learned of it I welcomed their decision, that it would make more sense in the circumstances for the Centre to build on its five years of development and achievement by joining with PEP to form a broader-based organisation. The two bodies had fairly similar roles and interests, with experience, needs and resources which at that time were as much complementary as overlapping. It could reasonably be hoped that their union would produce even more than the sum of its parts.

The resulting merger to form PSI coincided with the demise – at least for the time being – of a somewhat grandiose proposal which for some time had been aired in various quarters and in various forms for the establishment of a UK version of Washington's Brookings Institution.

This British Brookings project was undoubtedly a well-meant one. Its backers, like the founders of PEP itself nearly 50 years earlier, were men of goodwill, concern and repute. But neither PEP nor the Centre had favoured the idea – nor, among others, had their colleagues in the two similar though more specialised independent policy research and discussion institutes, Chatham House and NIESR. Their misgivings were not only about the threat that such an attempted development might pose to their own future supplies of scarce funds and even scarcer good researchers. The proposal seemed to be based on excessive optimism about both the practicability and the utility of setting up a UK body of the kind and scale envisaged. Experience and reflection did not encourage confidence that what was being done or aspired to by the Washington organisation could either successfully or desirably be replicated on this side of the Atlantic. Even discounting some of the illusions which seemed to exist about its role and operation the Brookings Institution certainly deserved considerable respect for the range and quality of much of its work, especially in USA budgetary and international affairs. That respect was understandably enhanced among some of its admirers by past or prospective gratitude – a tradition of hospitality seldom fails to pay off – for the intellectually sustaining and psychically soothing shelter it offered from time to time to refugees, British among them, from the rigours and reverses of academic, official or electoral life. But it was essentially a USA institution, a product and feature of the USA's unique historical, geographical and political culture. The objectives proclaimed by the proponents of a British version of it, so PEP and others argued, would in the UK context be better sought by further development, improvement and collaboration – with amalgamations in appropriate cases – of the UK's existing smaller, more varied and sharper-edged institutes. And in the event that was the course followed.

Whether it will prove to have been a fruitful course can only be judged after a few more years. Meanwhile those still inclined to favour the alternative of a British Brookings will be keeping a beady and quizzical eye on the further progress of existing institutions, PSI not least among them. Charles Carter in the next chapter sets out, as Chairman of its Research and Management Committee, his own hopes for PSI's way ahead. The experience which he and his colleagues will be able to draw on for their guidance is all the richer for the record in this book of PEP's aims, struggles and achievements over nearly 50 years.

What is that record's main theme? Undoubtedly, society's constant complex interaction, which PEP's own studies and discussions reflected and sometimes helped to influence, of continuity and change – and change, moreover, of a kind itself always changing. In their respective chapters Kenneth Lindsay and others point out certain similarities, perhaps in part evolutionary, between the UK's problems in 1931 when PEP was founded and those in 1981 when PSI had succeeded it. With these similarities in mind there could be a temptation to believe that the methods and style of report and discussion which were so effective when followed by PEP researchers and publicists in the 1930s or even 1940s would be equally practicable and appropriate today. But what PEP's record also reminds us of – as witness the changing topics and content of its deliberations and output over the years and the changing interests and styles of its succession of remarkably able Directors – is the extent to which policy researchers and commentators today are dealing, and therefore obliged to take into account in the *way* they deal, with a society which for all its continuities has also become quite staggeringly different.

The difference can be seen, and over the years PEP itself documented a number of them, in the scale, complexity, speed of change, and domestic and international interdependence, of virtually all our economic, social and political activities and problems. They can be seen in the underlying scientific and technological advances which have so altered the pace of material achievement, the implications of human folly and the climate of public expectation that anything now seems technically possible yet nothing now inspires certain hope. They can also be seen in the extent and texture of education and communication, both generally and about public affairs; PEP began long before the revolution wrought by the Butler Act and the mixed blessings of post-Robbins higher education and television, and there is now a much more informed and critical public – if also, paradoxically, a more easily confused one. There have been decisive changes for good and ill in the racial texture of the population, in the influence of conventional religious beliefs, in the roles of the sexes, in the power of organised labour, in the patterns of social control and social dissent. Along with these and other enormous changes, partly as cause but mainly as effect, has gone a correspondingly vast expansion in public expectations, in the ambitions and burdens of government and therefore in its activity and intrusiveness, and in the scale, complexity and preoccupations of the political and administrative machine.

One consequence of these changes during PEP's half-century was that whereas in the early 1930s and 1940s there was an obviously pressing range of relatively clear issues about which an informed and challenging independent voice like PEP's could have good hope of being heard – and not drowned by the voices of equally audible competitors – a very different situation existed by the 1950s and 1960s, and still more so by the 1970s. By then, policy commitments and lead-times had extended; policy options were much less straightforward; value conflicts, real or factitious, were coming more into the open; government for its part was becoming more fully equipped with its own official resources of information and assessment; and outside government there was a growing Babel of publicly-aired revelation, advice, advocacy, and pressure from individuals and organisations of all kinds, some intellectually and politically reputable but many merely clothing partisan choices and presentations of policy issues and options in the jargon of garbled theory and selective compassion.

In these circumstances it was probably wise of PEP to adapt gradually its posture and practice, as the record shows that consciously or unconsciously it did, so as to distance itself a little and to give increasingly more weight to investigation and analysis rather than prescription, and to quietly authoritative persuasion rather than to more forthright propaganda.

Perhaps all the more wisely did it act thus because the euphoric atmosphere of the period of large national aims and sweeping plans and structural reforms, to which PEP itself had significantly contributed, was being succeeded by increasing public scepticism about their value, whether still on paper or in the light of experience of their results when they had been wholly or partly put into effect. It can now be only a matter of speculation as to how much of this reaction against planning was justified by insufficient realism and flexibility in the plans devised, or resulted primarily from lack of sufficient will and care and forethought about implementation and about picking up the subsequent bills – whether in financial or in other terms.

From the wry recollections of Max Nicholson and others it was evident that some unease about putting too much weight on planning was felt among PEP's founders from the start – though not by Max himself. In a comment[1] on the manuscript of the present book Noel Hall, who shared that unease, has recalled how he warned of the perennial problem that in the business of government there could be all kinds of planning from the hopefully indicative to the rigidly authoritarian, and that it all depended on what instruments you were able and willing to use for implementation. He also pointed out that a strong planning approach by any kind of government was in practice almost doomed to failure at that period for sheer lack of econometric data and techniques and manpower (to say nothing of understanding and goodwill among management and trade

[1] 'Use of the word planning in the early 1930s', 2 December 1980, PEP Archive, LSE.

unions) on which its validity and effectiveness must depend. Whether these prerequisites for real planning are available even today in scale and quality to match the increased complexities and uncertainties of modern society is another matter for speculation. But meanwhile, at the level of the policy studies institute rather than of the management of policy itself, PSI inherits from PEP and the Centre jointly a recent tradition more concerned with investigation and analysis than with panaceas.

Fortunately PEP became aware of the need to avoid pushing this trend too far. By being more uninhibitedly prescriptive the founders of PEP had taken some risks, but their work probably gained in enthusiasm and impact. It was sometimes almost abrasively positive and robust, but, by golly, in the circumstances of those times it needed to be. It is easy to overlook now what an appalling mess the country was then in, with millions suffering far more misery than exists in the UK today, and an unhealthy dominance by its ageing pre-1914 generation because of the slaughter of so many of its younger men in the first World War. It is undoubtedly true that to the non-partisan reader one of the attractions of PEP's later output was that, by contrast, it concentrated more on offering facts in a way which, as Oliver Roskill puts it, did not preclude other conclusions being reached from the same evidence. But on the other hand there was and is the danger that mere presentation of data and their analysis and the technical conclusions to be drawn from them, without frank discussion of possible policy options and implications in a wider context, can leave the reader half-informed and wholly unprotected against the temptation to interpret the results solely in the light of the latest fashion in unreconstructed conventional wisdom. The record shows that PEP's management became increasingly alert to this.

One difficulty, of course, as touched on in their different ways by several contributors, lay in the changing background and outlook of the younger research staff, in recent years increasingly made up of men and women specialising competently in their own particular interests, disciplines and techniques but either unable because of their constrained experience or unwilling because of their proper diffidence to venture beyond these into the more perilous realm of wider political and administrative discussion. On the other hand, among such staff in any policy studies organisation there could inevitably be a danger, fortunately not serious in PEP, that at times their implicit beliefs about wider political factors, unchallenged by experience or exposure, might nevertheless unconsciously influence their selection and presentation, and thus the message conveyed to their readers, of even their technical questions and data and conclusions. Perhaps the lesson to be drawn about this for the future from PEP's experience in the past is that, without prejudice to individual attribution of authorship, PSI's publications of study reports should in appropriate cases embody or be accompanied by more general comment from another hand on what the study findings and conclusions do or do not seem to signify when seen in fuller perspective.

This ties in with another theme that may clearly be found in PEP's record – its illustration of the importance of a broad base of research staff and collaborators drawn not only from the so-called social sciences but also from the natural sciences, technology, industrial and commercial management, politics and law and public administration, and indeed from among practical men and women in the informed community generally. Although sometimes PEP purported to see itself, especially in its early days, as a radical external stimulus to the Establishment, the groups of friends and colleagues who helped to formulate and apply that stimulus were as often as not themselves actual or potential Establishment archetypes. And the record suggests that PEP probably achieved its widest reputation, if not necessarily its academically most OK work, during periods when it was widely based in this way and its studies were in consequence shaped by general collaboration and politically aware discussion, not solely by the application of one or two particular techniques operating within the perceptions and parameters of one particular discipline.

It is of course difficult fully to follow this particular earlier PEP tradition in current circumstances, because of the many changes which have affected the roles and preoccupations and availability of the kind of collaborator who would need to be involved, and especially of the collaborator from Westminster or Whitehall. Party political positions seem to have hardened, and among officials the very kinds of increase and improvement in government activity and organisation and specialist resources which PEP among others had pressed for in earlier years have created in some ways an obstacle to easy access and penetration by outside bodies. But PEP's old practice of co-option and collaboration was perhaps the one characteristic that most distinguished its work and practical impact from the

doubtless scholarly but less immediately influential output of researchers and research units within universities. PSI is wise in trying
to regain or retain it.

This broad basis of collaboration with people outside who had
practical experience and responsibility was probably of particular
importance for PEP's survival in that it helped successive Directors
to safeguard the organisation against tendencies towards political or
intellectual type-casting, sectarianism or disintegration. As a result,
notwithstanding its strong interest in planning, especially in the
earlier years, PEP never became a mere mouthpiece for doctrinaire
utopianism. Despite its evident concern about perceived short-
comings in society and in the life-chances of some social groups, it
never degenerated into mere sentiment or into snarling against
society. Although its people sometimes included Fabians and others
with socialist sympathies, it never behaved like a mere research and
propaganda arm of the Labour Party. Equally, although from time
to time it also co-opted and employed Tories or Tory sympathisers,
it never became a mere extension of the Conservative Party Research Department. It avoided, unlike at least one contemporary
institute of otherwise high repute, developing such an exclusive
addiction for one particular set of economic or social theories as to
risk blunting its impact and utility. It also avoided, unlike at least
one other contemporary institute of otherwise high early promise,
allowing any faction so to manipulate its structure and operations
as to risk a withdrawal of its backers' support and esteem. It kept
its relationships with government and press sufficiently friendly to be
useful, without being so friendly as to jeopardise that usefulness. It
kept its contacts with universities and other parts of the world of
scholarship close enough for intellectual refreshment, without risking
a weakening of its practical thrust by excessive academicism. In these
ways it managed both to be and to be seen as neither a mere pressure
group for political and social change on the one hand, nor on the
other a mere agent for the intellectual justification of the status quo.

And this brings me back, finally, to PEP's essential role of challenge – responsible factual challenge to outdated conventional
wisdom in public policy and in attitudes towards it wherever there
seemed good ground in hard evidence and clear reasoning for such
a challenge to be made. The record suggests that during the earlier
part of PEP's history the conventional economic, social and political
wisdom needing challenge at a variety of points was that which had

been handed down from before the first World War. More recently, and still today, an even sharper challenge may have become necessary, but this time to the new conventional wisdom that has been handed down since the second World War. Beware, warned Max Nicholson in 1931 (and ever-youthfully reminds us of his words today, 50 years later), of the trouble caused in public affairs and public attitudes by the extended active life of elderly men with elderly ideas. May it be that too many of today's elderly men, traditionalists and trendies alike, are still preaching and practising, both directly and through the younger generation whose thinking they have managed to bemuse and dominate, false or excessive applications of the now very elderly ideas of Titmuss, Beveridge, Keynes, Tawney and even Marx? At least it would be in the PEP tradition to ask.

# Epilogue

# PSI and the Future

## Charles Carter

My own first substantial memory of PEP was of needing to use the 1955 report on *World Population and Resources,* and therefore asking my colleagues about the standing of this curiously named body. I was assured that it had kept up a remarkably high standard of work over a quarter of a century, particularly meritorious because it had very slender resources and relied heavily on the use of voluntary committees. It was, I was told, a useful sort of body, which came out with reports on practical issues which were or ought to be of current interest.

In later years I came to have a great deal of concern about the lack of practicality and relevance of much of the world's social science output, and about the productivity of the people who produce it. As a member of the Heyworth Committee, I must share responsibility for the creation of an instrument for expanding social research and training more social scientists, the Social Science Research Council. But it is sometimes forgotten that the Heyworth Committee was not at all convinced that it would be right to go for a rapid expansion, because we were concerned about the availability of people of quality to do the work. The problems about research output, however, do not arise solely from inadequate quality in the researchers, but also from their remoteness from their supposed subject matter. This has odd results: for instance, there has been a great outpouring of economic 'models', some from people of great ability, but uninformed by any careful research or appreciation of how economic decisions are actually reached. Such models appear to be concerned with real entities, but in fact they are just exercises in pure mathematics, of no practical use and (to a mathematician) trivial and uninteresting. I bear in mind as an Awful Warning an erudite piece on a model of a banking system. I inquired if the researcher had ever actually met a banker, and asked him how he did his work. He had not thought it necessary to do so.

There is a sentence of Keynes which might usefully be applied to the whole of the social sciences: 'If economists could manage to get themselves thought of as humble, competent people, on a level with dentists, that would be splendid!'[1]

In PEP in the 1950s I saw an example of humble competence applied to real and interesting problems, and it was my desire that the Centre for Studies in Social Policy should have a similar attitude. In looking forward to the future of PSI, however, it is proper to have a larger ambition: not merely competence and relevance in preparing the raw material for other people's decisions, but also a practical ability to discuss the alternative forms which those decisions might take, and a readiness to stimulate public discussion of these alternatives and to help to enlighten those who will make the decisions. This, indeed, was the ambition which PEP had in its earliest days.

Our purpose is not therefore to sit in an ivory tower, watching how other people make policies, but to be a contributor in the actual business of policy formation: of course (for we must be humble as well as competent) only one among many contributors, but ready to get our hands dirty. It would be very much safer, of course, to regard ourselves as producers of facts, leaving to others the making of such deductions about appropriate policies as the facts may justify. Many academic social scientists consider this degree of detachment to be essential to reputable work. In the terminology of the natural sciences, they are interested in research but not in development or application. The danger is, however, that the results of the research will never actually be noticed at all; indeed, will not be relevant, because it is in the process of development and application that one discovers what are the really significant unanswered questions. Anyway, there are plenty of academic social scientists, and there would be little point in having a separate institute to do the same sort of work. PSI is about application: we are technologists with an interest in policy making.

But such a purpose is open to another sort of objection. Some

---

[1] *Essays in Persuasion*, 'Economic Possibilities for our Grandchildren', published in the *Nation and Athenaeum*, 11 and 18 October 1930.

people hold that the provision of facts to be a basis of policy must necessarily be kept distinct from proposals about policy, because the latter arise from a particular political philosophy. Our neighbours at the Centre for Policy Studies can properly contribute to the business of policy formation, because they start from an explicit Conservative free enterprise philosophy. PSI's pretensions to be non-political must, on this view, be self-deception. The output will either mirror the political prejudices of individual researchers, or have behind it a common but concealed set of political assumptions.

There is obviously something in this. On given facts, the decisions of a right-wing Conservative government on (say) social security policy will differ from those of a left-wing Labour government. But the differences are by no means as great as the rhetoric of politics suggests. In some areas, the logic of the facts leads inexorably to a particular policy conclusion: in others, the public consensus is sufficiently strong to limit the conclusions to a narrow range. This is one reason why, examined *ex post*, the policies pursued by opposing parties turn out to have remarkable similarities. In other words, it can be argued that policy making is not as party-political as the speeches of MPs may suggest; and, where differences of political philosophy really do make a difference to the conclusions drawn, there is still a useful job to be done by a body which, after examining the facts, will exhibit the range of alternatives which are reasonable in the light of those facts.

So, in looking to the future, I see PSI as not only seeking to be humble, competent and practical, but also genuinely non-political. It must not be, in any sense, the 'Labour party in exile', or at some future time the Conservative party in exile, or a sanctuary for middle-of-the-road Liberals and social democrats. It is very desirable that our research staff should include people of political experience, because there is a presumption that they know more than outsiders about the actual problems of reaching policy decisions. But the purpose of having them is not to give them a sabbatical to prepare the next party manifesto, but to enable them to use their experience to raise the level of public debate about the real choices to be made.

But what is to be the range of activity? This question is a difficult one, because the number of policy issues which need study is vast. Some reduction can be achieved by keeping away from subjects which are the prime interest of other, more specialised, institutes – for instance, foreign policy and defence strategy. Yet even this means of simplification is only a limited help, because policy issues from different fields have a habit of being inter-related. It is not, for instance, possible to propose means for the rejuvenation of the British economy without taking an informed view about future relations with the European Economic Community. It may therefore appear that, to cover a sufficient range, a very large institute, with a multi-disciplinary research staff running into hundreds, would be necessary.

Such an elephantine body is not inconceivable, but we have so far taken the view (and, I hope, will continue to take it) that growth to great size would be unwise. Ideas about the optimum size of organisations are never very exact, if only because there are different optima appropriate to different aspects of the activity. We have, however, a hunch that growth much beyond 50 full-time research staff (with associated part-time and support staff) should be avoided. This hunch is based on observation of research organisations in the social sciences: beyond a very modest size, productivity seems to fall, and the organism tends to divide into disciplinary cells with inadequate contact and cross-fertilisation. These are no doubt problems which, at a cost, can be lessened by appropriate management, but we are not confident that they can be avoided.

The problem of choice of projects will therefore continue to be an acute one. Ideally we would like to know in 1981 the issues of real substance which will call for attention in (say) 1983. It is not much use starting a project which relates to some matter which, for better or worse, will be decided for a considerable period ahead by legislation next month. However, most issues of substance will not be resolved by a single government decision; the conditions of the problem may be changed while research is going on, but essentially the problem will remain.

But if one looks back at issues which have been high on the list of those thought to need attention, it becomes apparent that there are changes of fashion. There have been times at which economic success has been regarded as associated with large size, so that policy has favoured mergers into giant organisations; more recently it has been associated with smallness, and policy has gone into reverse. The changes of terminology, which have (for instance) transmuted sinners and criminals into deviants or victims of the sickness of society, correspond to changes in conventional wisdom about where the problem lies. The constraints on policy, caused by certain things being 'unthinkable' or totally unnoticed, vary from decade to decade. In 1980 it became 'thinkable' that social security benefits should no longer keep pace with real average incomes (and might even, in some cases, become smaller); in 1975 no-one in a responsible position was thinking about this option. The problem of carrying out research in a fashion industry is that one may fail to foresee the conditions of the public debate at the time when the research is concluded, and may thus be seen as hopelessly 'way out' and irrelevant, or alternatively as bound by old conventional ideas which have been abandoned.

PSI will in fact have to make a triple judgement – about the issues which will be specially important and ripe for consideration, about the assumptions of public thinking about them at the time when the work is completed, and about the sub-set of issues in which we can offer some special competence. I am not in this arguing that PSI should be bound by tomorrow's conventional wisdom – indeed, it should be one of our aims to challenge and alter the assumptions of public thinking; but we have as a practical purpose the encouragement of beneficial change in policy, and we will not be practical if the ideas we propose are totally out of touch with the general trends of thought of the time, and therefore fall on stony ground.

I have introduced in the last paragraph a further means of reducing the range of projects to manageable proportions, namely the possession in some areas of special competence – which, for instance, justifies us in taking a special interest in race relations, because of the reputation built up by PEP in that field. Even this, however, is a principle of selection which has its dangers. Doing work because we have access to leading authorities on the subject is one thing; finding jobs for existing members of staff, even if they are no longer highly productive, is quite another. Observation suggests that in middle age research institutes tend to become 'type-cast' as only interested in a particular set of subjects, and eventually doubts build up as to whether they are really productive even on that narrow set. If PSI is to go on succeeding, therefore, it must be ready to change its focus of interest and to bring in new types of skill. This is particularly important because a narrowing down of the range of interest may lose us the ability to see a problem in its entirety, using all relevant skills in its analysis.

Does this suggest that we are setting ourselves an impossible task – a wide potential range of subjects, a need to look at them from dif-

ferent points of view, but at the same time not to become too large
an organisation? A key issue here is the willingness of staff to avoid
the degree of specialisation which has become so common in
academic institutions. This is not to suggest that the job can be done
properly by a group of gifted amateurs; but equally it will not be
done properly by a group of people who think it their duty to stay
within a sub-section of a discipline. The ideal member of the PSI
research staff would be someone able to claim professional competence over a wide field, and willing to use the tools of different
disciplines in tackling a problem. Happily we have such people; it is
very important that we should continue to have them.

Because PSI is about application, it is necessarily greatly concerned
with the efficiency with which ideas can be disseminated – that is,
with techniques of publicity, of arranging informed discussion, of
reaching a specified audience accurately and economically. But the
'model' which we need to have in mind is not the simple one of
passing an idea about policy, based on research, to a puzzled decision
maker, who will then adopt it. On most subjects there will be an
existing line of policy, and a group of officials and Ministers who
are committed to defending it. It is rare that defenders can be persuaded to abandon a position by a simple demonstration that they
are talking nonsense, or that some other policy would have superior
advantages. They must be persuaded to change by degrees, preferably
believing that they have discovered a new idea themselves, or at least
co-operated in its discovery. A powerful instrument for such change
is informed public discussion; if one can change the terms in which
a problem is discussed in the media and in the talk of influential
people, the defenders of established positions are much more likely
to begin to change and adapt their ideas. Public discussion is greatly
influenced by presenting a matter in words or pictures which stay in
the memory. Boring research reports, full of appendices and long
tables of unexplained figures, are rarely worth the paper they are
written on. So PSI needs to be willing to show some sense of
drama in presenting its ideas – not by way of distorting or exagger-
ating them, but of highlighting in memorable phrases the points
which are really essential.

I believe that, perhaps by accident, the founders of PEP and
CSSP and the arrangers of their marriage have managed to find a
formula for an organisation which is competent and capable of being
effective. The interest of people in central and local government,

industry and the social services, shown by their service on Council and by their ready attendance at seminars and conferences, is an essential part of this. So is the attainment of a size which, while not too large, is enough to give advantages of cross-fertilisation; and a system of finance which gives an assurance that PSI is genuinely independent. These together create something which is exciting, and which therefore assures its own future because it attracts good people. The far-sighted people who founded and built up PEP will I am sure have grounds for continued pride in what they began.

# List of PEP Publications

PEP had two main series of publications, called Broadsheets and Reports. The Broadsheets began as fortnightly issues of *Planning*, each containing contributions on a variety of subjects; the principal subject of each issue is given in the list below. Starting during the war, the Broadsheets developed into a series of single-subject reports. After the merger with CSSP in 1978, the series was renamed PSI Reports and in addition a new series of Discussion Papers was launched, as well as the quarterly journal, *Policy Studies*.

Meanwhile the PEP series which had originally been called Reports, comprising mostly book-length studies, usually published for PEP by a publishing house, had become called PEP (then PSI) books. The list of 'PEP Reports, Books' also contains some other publications such as reports published by the sponsors of studies in their own series. The ambiguity in use of the word report, while a potential source of confusion in a historical perspective, is not a current problem because the original term of art for the PEP book-length series has not been used since the 1960s.

In addition to these two main series, there have been three series of papers emanating from three phases of European studies: Occasional Papers on 'Britain and the European Market' (1958–61); European Series (jointly with Chatham House, 1967–76); and Studies in European Politics (from 1979).

**Broadsheets**[1]

*1933*

1. Iron and Steel
2. Town and Country Planning
3. Britain and World Trade I
4. An Employment Policy
5. The Public Concern
6. Planning America
7. What the Consumer Wants
8. Agriculture
9. Planning for Liberty
10. Community Services
11. Cotton
12. What Has Been Done I
13. About the Broadsheet
14. Government Public Relations
15. Housing Survey
16. Questions for Industry

*1934*

17. The Output of Knowledge
18. The Exit from Industry
19. Cotton Reconstruction
20. The NRA in America
21. Transport Problems
22. The Entrance to Industry
23. What PEP is for
24. Britain and World Trade II
25. More or Better Agriculture?
26. A New Model for Industries
27. Future British Population
28. Housing – Some Proposals
29. The Measurement of Needs
30. A New Employment Policy
31. The Use of Statistics
32. About the Marketing Acts
33. Mapping Out Our Way
34. Employment Analysed
35. What Planning Means
36. What Consumers Need

[1] Originally *Planning Series*, now PSI Reports and Discussion Papers; this list also includes PSI's new quarterly journal, *Policy Studies*.

196. Soviet Planning in Wartime
197. Coal and the War
198. Plans for Physical Reconstruction

*1943*

199. Trade Unions in the United States
200. Two Hundredth Issue
201. British Foreign Policy
202. Retail Distribution and Town Planning
203. Nursery Education
204. Facts about Electricity Supply
205. After the Beveridge Report
206. Employment for All
207. Space for Leisure
208. International Air Transport
209. Poverty and Progress in China
210. The Gas Industry in Wartime
211. Use and Mis-use of Transport
212. Labour in the Building Industry
213. The Future of Foreign Publicity
214. A Civil General Staff
215. PEP Work, 1940–43

*1944*

216. Refugees in Britain
217. Demobilisation and Employment
218. Old Houses
219. Facts about International Trade
220. Wages and the Cost of Living Index
221. British Trade Associations
222. Medical Care for Citizens
223. Economic Development in S. E. Europe
224. Location of Employment
225. After Bretton Woods
226. People for the Commonwealth
227. Reconstruction Plans
228. British Documentary Films

*1945*

229. Export
230. Government Information Services
231. Household Appliances
232. Forward to Social Security
233. Output and the Worker

542. Personal Mobility and Transport Policy

*1974*

543. Free Trade is Good, but What About the Workers? – Trade Liberalisation and Adjustment Assistance
544. Racial Disadvantage in Employment: Summary of the Main Findings of Racial Disadvantage in Employment
545. Pre-experience Business Education and the EEC
546. A National Survey of the Unemployed
547. The Extent of Racial Discrimination
548. Reshaping Britain: A Programme of Economic and Social Reform
549. Birth Control in Runcorn and Coalville: A Study of the FPA Campaign

*1975*

550. National Voluntary Youth Organisations
551. Indexation in an Inflationary Economy: A Case Study in Finland
552. A Chance to Share: Voluntary Service in Society
553. The PEP Survey on Inflation
554. Company Responsibility and Participation – A New Agenda
555. Paying for Party Politics: The Case for Public Subsidies
556. Racial Minorities and Public Housing
557. Sandwich Courses in Higher Education: PEP Report on CNAA Degrees in Business Studies
558. Price Stability and Full Employment: A 'Neo-Keynesian' Policy for Growth Without Inflation
559. National Attitudes and the Financing of Industry

*1976*

560. The Facts of Racial Disadvantage: A National Survey
561. Unemployment *Costs* ...
562. Reinforcing Parliament: Services and Facilities for Members of Parliament: Some International Comparisons
563. Wage Determination in Industry
564. Specialist Committees in the British Parliament: The Experience of a Decade
565. Family Planning Services in the Home
566. Governments and Labour Markets: Aspects of Policies in Britain, France, Germany, Netherlands and Italy
567. Transport Realities and Planning Policy: Studies of Friction and Freedom in Daily Travel
568. The Next Stage of Incomes Policy

591. The Economics of Historic Country Houses (Jan. 1981)
592. Retirement Age and Retirement Costs

## PSI Discussion Papers

1. Discussing the Welfare State, 1980
2. Diversity and Dencentralisation in the Welfare State, 1980
3. Public Policy and Family Life, 1980

## *Policy Studies*, quarterly journal

Vol. 1, Part 1, July 1980
Vol. 1, Part 2, Oct. 1980
Vol. 1, Part 3, Jan. 1981

## PEP 'Reports', Books

1. The British Iron and Steel Industry, 1933
2. The British Cotton Industry, 1934
3. Housing England, 1934
4. Entrance to Industry, 1935
5. Exit from Industry, 1935
   (Titles 4 and 5 bound in one volume)
6. The British Coal Industry, 1936
7. The Supply of Electricity in Great Britain, 1936
8. International Trade, 1937
9. The British Social Services, 1937
10. The British Health Services, 1937
11. The British Press, 1938
12. Agricultural Research in Great Britain, 1938
13. The Location of Industry, 1939
14. The Gas Industry in Great Britain, 1939
15. Building Peace out of War, 1944
16. Economic Development in South-East Europe, 1944
17. The Market for Household Appliances, 1945
18. The Visual Arts (The Arts Enquiry), 1946
19. The Factual Film (The Arts Enquiry), 1947
20. Britain and World Trade, 1947
21. The British Fuel and Power Industries, 1947
22. Population Policy in Great Britain, 1948
23. British Trade Unionism, 1948
    British Trade Unionism (revised edition), 1949
24. Agricultural Machinery, 1949
25. Music (The Arts Enquiry), 1949

66. European Advanced Technology, 1969
67. European Political Parties, 1969
68. Youth Exchanges: The Way Ahead, 1970
69. PEP Evidence to the Roskill Commission on the Siting of London's Third Airport, 1970
70. Politics and Bureaucracy in the European Community, 1970
71. The Company: Law, Structure and Reform in Eleven Countries, 1970
72. The Member of Parliament and his Information, 1970
73. Women in Top Jobs, 1971
74. Sex, Career and Family, 1971
75. Company Boards: Their Responsibilities to Shareholders, Employees and the Community, 1971
76. State Enterprise: Business or Politics?, 1971
77. Dual-Career Families (Penguin), 1971
78. Europe Tomorrow: 16 Europeans Look Ahead (Fontana), 1972
79. Advertising Overspill: Can Advertising Prevent Urban Ghettos Developing in Britain? (Advertising Association), 1972
80. The Board of Directors: Its Structure, Composition and Role (British Institute of Management), 1972
81. Multilateral Policies for East–West Trade and Payments, 1972
82. Ten Innovations: An International Study on Technological Development and the Use of Qualified Scientists and Engineers in Ten Industries, 1972
83. The Right to Manage? A Study of Leadership and Reform in Employee Relations, 1972
84. The Fair Housing Experiment: Community Relations Councils and the Housing of Minority Groups, 1973
85. Through No Fault of Their Own: Systems for Dealing with Redundancy in Britain, France and Germany, 1973
86. The Containment of Urban England I: Urban and Metropolitan Growth Processes *or* Megalopolis Denied, 1973
87. The Containment of Urban England II: The Planning System: Objectives, Operations, Impacts, 1973
88. The House of Commons: Services and Facilities, 1974
89. Parliamentary Scrutiny of Government Bills, 1974
90. The Local Government Act 1972: Problems of Implementation, 1975
91. The Power of the Purse: The Role of European Parliaments in Budgetary Decisions, 1976
92. The Disadvantages of Inequality: A Study of Social Deprivation, 1976
93. Innovation and Productivity under Nationalisation: The First Thirty Years, 1977
94. Racial Disadvantage in Britain (Pelican), 1977
95. Planning and Politics: The British Experience 1960–76, 1977
96. Political Parties in the European Community, 1979

97. Overseas Doctors in the National Health Service, 1980
98. Governments and Trade Unions: The British Experience 1964–79, 1980
99. Britain in Europe (with NIESR and RIIA), 1980
100. The Future of Pay Bargaining (with NIESR and RIIA), 1980
101. Parliaments and Economic Affairs, 1980
102. Rational Techniques in Policy Analysis, 1980

## Series on Europe

*Occasional Papers on Britain and the European Market*

1. Agricultural Policy in the European Economic Community, 1958
2. The Free Trade Area Negotiations, 1959
3. Agricultural Policies in Western Europe, 1959
4. The European Free Trade Association: A Preliminary Appraisal, 1959
5. Proposals for a Common Agricultural Policy in EEC, 1960
6. Budgetary Control in the European Economic Community, 1960
7. Minimum Prices in European Trade in Agricultural and Horticultural Products, 1960
8. Division in Europe, 1960
9. Trade Diversion in Western Europe, 1960
10. Direct Elections and the European Parliament, 1960
11. France and the European Community, 1961
12. Four Approaches to the European Problem, 1961
13. Food Prices and the Common market, 1961
14. Agriculture, the Commonwealth and the EEC, 1961

*European Series* (jointly with Chatham House)

1. Concentration or Competition: A European Dilemma?, 1967
2. Europe and the Developing World: Association under Part IV of the Treaty of Rome, 1967
3. Agriculture: The Cost of Joining the Common Market, 1967
4. The Sterling Problem and the Six, 1967
5. Planning in the EEC: The Medium-term Economic Policy Programme of the European Economic Community, 1967
6. Taxes in the EEC and Britain: The Problem of Harmonisation, 1968
7. Towards a European Civil Service, 1968
8. The Institutions of the European Community, 1968
9. Action Committee for the United States of Europe: Statements and Declarations 1955–67, 1969
10. Trade Unions and Free Labour Movement in the EEC, 1969
11. Problems of British Entry Into the EEC: Reports to the Action Committee for the United States of Europe, 1969
12. The Transport Policy of the European Communities, 1969

13. The Proposal for a European Company, 1969
14. A Readers' Guide to Britain and the European Communities, 1970
15. Regional Policy in Britain and the Six: The Problems of Development Areas: Community Regional Policy, 1970
16. Agricultural Policy and the Common Market, 1971
17. The EEC: National Parliaments in Community Decision-making, 1971
18. The Prospects for a European Security Conference, 1971
19. External Relations of the European Community: Associations and Trade Agreements, 1971
20. The Power of the Purse in the European Communities, 1972
21. National Governments and the European Communities, 1973
22. From Free Trade to Integration in Western Europe?, 1975
23. Social Security in the European Community, 1975
24. Work and Industrial Relations in the European Community, 1975
25. The European Community's Policy towards Eastern Europe, 1975
26. Regional Management of the Rhine, 1975
27. From Summit to Council: Evolution in the EEC, 1976

*Studies in European Politics* (PSI's Centre for European Political Studies)

1. The Future of the European Parliament, 1979
2. Towards Transnational Parties in the European Community, 1979
3. European Integration, Regional Devolution and National Parliaments, 1979
4. Eurocommunism and Foreign Policy, 1979
5. Europe Elects its Parliament, 1980

# Select Biographical Data

Editing a book like this is full of pitfalls which can be avoided only by not editing it – a course which is no longer open to me. Providing the right amount of information about the people who appear in the book is perhaps the most hazardous. Without an annex containing such information, the text would be over-loaded with potted biographies and phrases like 'later Lord High Chancellor'. Yet a biographical annex poses the awful problem of whom and what to leave out.

In selecting whom to include, the most weight has been given to the part played in PEP's development. Prime Ministers who have opened buildings or unveiled plaques are not listed, nor are Home Secretaries who have made speeches at PEP dinners, unless they have also held some office or served on a committee with PEP. The choice of what to include has been biased towards the activities more closely related to what people did in PEP and to the period when they did it. Members of the staff have been included where the text gives them more than passing mention or where they worked at PEP for more than a year or so and have written PEP publications carrying their own name. This gives a bias towards those who were staff members since the mid-1960s, when the anonymity rule was abandoned, and towards the inclusion of PEP publications since then. The titles of a person's PEP publications in this period are given (or of a selection, for those who wrote more than three or four). Publications not connected with PEP are, on the other hand, not listed, with only a few exceptions. Matter relating to PEP is placed after all other matter in each person's entry, so that the reader can find it more easily. All the pages on which each person appears are given separately in the index.

Inevitably there will be errors of omission and I hope they may be forgiven.

**Mark Alexander Abrams**, 1906–
Fellow, Brookings Institution, Washington, 1931–3; Research Department, London Press Exchange, 1933–9; Managing Director then Chairman, Research Services Ltd., 1946–70; Director, Social Science Research Council Survey Research Unit, 1970–76; Director, Research Unit, Age Concern, 1976–. PEP Executive, 1963–4; Chairman, 1964–9; Vice-Chairman, 1969–1978; Member, PSI Council 1978–.

**Isobel Allen**, 1938–
PEP/PSI staff 1968–; author of *Women in top jobs* (with others, 1971), *Birth control in Runcorn and Coalville* (1974), *Family planning services in the home* (1976).

**Lord Altrincham**, Edward William Macleay Grigg, 1st Baron, 1945, 1879–1955.
Editorial staff, *The Times*, 1908–13; National Liberal MP, 1922–5; National Conservative MP, 1933–45.

**Richard Bailey**, 1916–
Economist in the fields of international development and resource management; Special Adviser, National Economic Development Office, 1964; Associate of Sir Alexander Gibb and Partners, civil and industrial engineering consultants. Director of PEP, 1954–63.

**Lord Balfour of Burleigh**, George John Gordon Bruce, 11th Baron, 1883–1964.
Banker; Chairman, Lloyds Bank, 1945–63; Chairman, Medical Research Council, 1936–48.

**Montague Barlow**, see Rt. Hon. Sir (Clement) Anderson Montague-Barlow.

**Sir Thomas D. Barlow**, GBE 1946, 1883–1964.
Director-General of Civilian Clothing, 1941–5; Chairman, District Bank until 1960; Director, Barlow and Jones Ltd., Manchester. Active Member of PEP Industries Group when working on Cotton (report 1934).

**Sir Denis (Charles) Barnes**, KCB 1967, 1914–
Deputy Secretary, Ministry of Labour, 1963, Permanent Secretary, 1966; Permanent Secretary, Department of Employment, 1968–73; Chairman, Manpower Services Commission; 1974–6. Chairman, PEP Advisory Group on study of women and their careers (main reports 1971); Member, Executive, 1970–76; author, with Eileen Reid, of PSI study of *Government and trade unions* (1980).

**Sir Gerald (Reid) Barry**, Kt 1951, 1898–1968.
Founder and editor, *Week-End Review*, 1930–34; Editor, *News Chronicle*, 1936–47; Director-General, Festival of Britain, 1948–51. Founder mem-

ber. PEP Directorate; Member Publicity Committee in 1930s; Chairman, Press Group (report 1938).

**Richard Berthoud,** 1945–

PEP/PSI staff, 1973–; author of *The disadvantages of inequality* (1976), *Training adults for skilled jobs* (1978), *Unemployed professionals and executives* (1979).

**William Henry Beveridge,** 1st Baron of Tuggal, 1946, 1879–1963.

Permanent Secretary, Ministry of Food, 1919; Director, London School of Economics and Political Science, 1919–37; Chairman of Inter-Departmental Committee on Social Insurance and Allied Services, which produced the Beveridge Report, 1941–2.

**Dr Carlos Paton Blacker,** 1895–1975.

Registrar, Department of Psychological Medicine, Guy's Hospital, 1927–1936; Hon. Secretary, Population Investigation Committee; Hon. Consultant, Royal Bethlem Hospital and Maudsley Hospital; Gen. Sec., Eugenics Society, 1930–52; Hon. Sec., 1952–61. Member, PEP Groups on British population (report 1948) and world population and resources (report 1955).

**Sir Basil Phillott Blackett,** KCSI 1926, 1882–1935.

A Director of the Bank of England; Director of Imperial and International Communications Ltd., of Marconi's Wireless Telegraph Co. Ltd.; Chairman, Colonial Development Advisory Committee; Finance Member of the Executive Council of the Governor General of India 1922–8. Founder Chairman, PEP Directorate, 1931–2.

**Hon. Mark Raymond Bonham Carter,** 1922–

Liberal MP, 1958–9; first Chairman, Race Relations Board 1966–1970; Chairman, Community Relations Commission, 1971–7. Chairman, Steering Group for PEP study of racial discrimination (reports, 1967 and 1968).

**Edward Charles Gurney Boyle,** Baron of Salehurst 1970, 1923–

Minister of Education, 1962–4; Vice-Chancellor, Leeds University, 1970–. Vice-President, PEP, 1966–78.

**Asa Briggs,** Baron of Lewes, 1976, 1921–

Professor of Modern History, Leeds University, 1955–61; Professor of History, University of Sussex, 1961–76; Vice-Chancellor, University of Sussex, 1967–76; Provost, Worcester College, Oxford, 1978–. Member, PEP Executive, 1972–8; Chairman, PEP Advisory Group on study of racial disadvantage (main reports 1974–6).

**Samuel Brittan,** 1933–

Economics Editor, *The Observer*, 1961–4; Adviser, Department of Economic Affairs, 1965; Principal Economic Commentator since 1966, and Assistant Editor since 1977, the *Financial Times*. Author of PEP Broadsheet *Inquest on planning in Britain* (1967); Member, PEP Executive, 1969–75.

**Sir Henry Noel Bunbury**, KCB 1920, 1886–1968.
Comptroller and Accountant-General of the Post Office, 1920–37; early Member of (Royal) Institute of Public Administration; Hon. Treasurer, 1923–6. Member, PEP Directorate, Executive, 1931–50; Council of Management, 1936–66; Board of Patrons, 1966–8. Hon. Treasurer during 1930s and 1940s.

**Richard Austen Butler**, Baron of Saffron Walden 1968, 1902–
Conservative MP, 1929–65; Under-Secretary of State for Foreign Affairs, 1938–41; Minister of Education, 1941–5; Chancellor of the Exchequer, 1951–5; Home Secretary, 1957–62; Master of Trinity College, Cambridge, 1965–78.

**Sir Alexander Kirkland Cairncross**, KCMG 1957, 1911–
Economic Adviser to Board of Trade, 1946–9; Economic Adviser to Organisation for European Economic Co-operation, 1949–50; Professor of Applied Economics, University of Glasgow, 1951–61; Head of Government Economic Service, 1964–9; Master of St Peter's College, Oxford, 1969–78. Member, PEP Executive, 1943–50; Board of Patrons, 1966–1978.

**Sir Alexander (Morris) Carr-Saunders**, KBE 1957, 1886–1966.
Director, London School of Economics and Political Science, 1937–56; Chairman, Statistics Committee of the Royal Commission on Population, 1949; Chairman, Colonial Social Science Research Council, 1945–57. Chairman, various PEP Groups, 1930s, and of Group on British population (report 1948).

**Sir Charles (Frederick) Carter**, Kt 1978, 1919–
Stanley Jevons Professor of Applied Economics, University of Manchester, 1959–63; Vice-Chancellor, University of Lancaster, 1963–79; Trustee, Joseph Rowntree Memorial Trust, 1966–; Chairman, Northern Ireland Economic Council, 1977–; President-Elect, British Association for the Advancement of Science, 1981–2. Chairman, Council of Management, Centre for Studies in Social Policy, 1972–8; Chairman, PSI Research Committee, 1978–.

**Professor George Douglas Howard Cole**, 1889–1959.
Fellow of University College, Oxford and University Reader in Economics, 1925–44; Chichele Professor of Social and Political Theory, Oxford, 1944–57; Chairman, Fabian Society, 1939–46 and 1948–50; President, Fabian Society from 1952.

**Sir Charles (Blampied) Colston**, Kt 1950, 1891–1969.
Chairman, 1937–54, and Managing Director, 1928–54, Hoover Limited. Member, PEP Executive, 1947–50.

**David Coombes**, 1940–
Professor of European Studies, Loughborough University, 1971–4. PEP Research Associate, 1966–72, PSI staff 1978–; author of *Politics and bureaucracy in the European Community* (1970), *State enterprise: Business*

*or politics?* (1971), *The future of the European Parliament* (1979), *Parliaments and economic affairs*, ed. (1980).

**Sir Richard Coppock**, Kt 1951, 1885–1971.

General Secretary of the National Federation of Building Trades Operatives until 1961; Chairman of London County Council, 1943–4. Consultant to PEP Industries Group when working on Housing England (report 1934).

**Frank Richard Cowell**, CMG 1952, 1897–1978.

HM Stationery Office, 1921–39; Foreign Office, 1939–46; Secretary, United Kingdom National Commission for UNESCO, 1946–58. Active PEP Working Member in 1930s, particularly on consumer affairs.

**Rt. Hon. Richard (Howard Stafford) Crossman**, OBE 1964, 1907–74.

Assistant editor, *New Statesman and Nation*, 1938–55; Labour MP, 1945–1974; Minister of Housing and Local Government, 1964–6; Secretary of State for Social Services, 1968–70; Editor, *New Statesman*, 1970–72. Member, PEP Post-War Aims Group, 1939–41.

**Geoffrey Crowther**, Baron of Headingley 1968, 1907–72.

On the staff of *The Economist*, 1932–56, Editor, 1938–56; Deputy Head of Joint War Production Staff, Ministry of Production, 1942–3; Chairman, Central Advisory Council for Education (England), 1956–60; Chancellor, Open University, from 1969. Member, PEP Press Group (report 1938).

**Lionel George Curtis**, CH 1949, 1872–1955.

Secretary to the Irish Conference, 1921; Adviser on Irish Affairs in the Colonial Office, 1921–4; writer on world affairs; co-founder, Royal Institute of International Affairs; co-founder, 'Round Table'.

**Professor Ralf Dahrendorf**, 1929–

Professor of Sociology, Konstanz, 1966–9; Parliamentary Secretary of State, Foreign Office, West Germany, 1969–70; Member, Commission of the European Communities, Brussels, 1970–74; Director, London School of Economics and Political Science, 1974–. Member of Council, Centre for Studies in Social Policy, 1974–8.

**William Daniel**, 1938–

PEP/PSI staff 1968–; author of *Racial discrimination in England* (1968), *The right to manage* (1972), *A national survey of the unemployed* (1974), *The PEP survey on inflation* (1975), *Wage determination in industry* (1976), *The impact of employment protection laws* (1978).

**Richard Davies**, 1916–

Worked for National Association of Youth Clubs, 1954–6; Industrial Adviser in UK to Marshall Aid Plan, 1957–61. PEP staff, 1962–; Director of Administration and External Affairs; author (with Raymond Clarke) of *A chance to share: voluntary service in society* (1975).

**Sir Ronald Conway Davison**, Kt 1938, 1884–1958.

Writer and lecturer on unemployment and social questions; worked at the Board of Trade and Ministry of Labour, 1912–28; retired aged 43 to write and lecture in England, Canada and the United States. Members, PEP Directorate, Executive, 1932–50; Chairman, Civic Division in 1930s; member of several Groups.

**Brigadier-General Sir Wyndham (Henry) Deedes**, Kt 1921, 1883–1956.
Military Attaché, Constantinople 1918–19; Director-General of Public Security in Egypt, 1919–20; active in social affairs in 1930s.

**Rt. Hon. Sir Geoffrey Stanley de Freitas**, KCMG 1961, 1913–
Labour MP, 1945–61 and 1964–79; Under-Secretary of State at Home Office, 1950–51; President, Assembly of the Council of Europe, 1966–9; Vice-President, European Parliament, 1975–9. Member, PEP European Organisations Group (report 1959); Member, PEP Executive 1960–61.

**Charles de Hoghton**, 1930–71.
PEP staff, 1966–71; author of *Cross-Channel collaboration* (1967), *The company: law, structure and reform in eleven countries*, ed. (1970), *And now the future: a PEP survey of futures studies* (1971).

**Lord de la Warr**, Herbrand Edward Dundonald Brassey Sackville, 9th Earl, 1900–76.
Parliamentary Under-Secretary, War Office, 1929–30; Parliamentary Secretary, Ministry of Agriculture and Deputy Ministry of Fisheries, 1930–31 and 1931–5; Parliamentary Secretary, Board of Education, 1935–6; Postmaster-General, 1951–5.

**Elizabeth Marian Denby**, –1965.
Sociologist; Specialist on low-cost housing; first Organising Secretary, the Kensington Housing Trust and the Kensington Housing Association; Leverhulme Research Fellowship into low-cost housing in Europe, 1934–5. Consultant to PEP Industries Group when working on Housing England (report 1934).

**Geoffrey Denton**, 1931–
Reader in Economics, University of Reading, 1967–; Director, Federal Trust 1973–; Professor at College of Europe, Bruges. PEP staff, 1955–9; Member, PEP Executive Committee, 1967–73; author of *Planning in the EEC: the medium term economic policy programme* (1967), *Economic planning and policies in Britain, France and Germany* (with others, 1968); *A new economic mechanism? Economic reform in Hungary* (1971).

**John Gordon Dower**, 1900–47.
Architect; Member of YHA and designer of youth hostels from 1930s; a pioneer of official town planning; in 1936 became Drafting Secretary of Standing Committee for National Parks formed by Council for the Preservation of Rural England; in 1942 joined Reith's Ministry of Planning as Head of Amenity Section; in 1945 'Dower Report' on National Parks in England and Wales published. Member, PEP Directorate, from 1932; Secretary, Group on town and country planning (first statement issued in Planning No. 2, 1933); active contributor to work of Industries Group when working on Housing England (report 1934).

**Sir Alan Alves Dudley**, KBE 1961, 1907–71.
Head of Information Policy Department, Foreign Office, 1942–9; Counsellor, UK Delegation to OEEC, Paris 1949–50; Head of UN Economic and Social Department, FO, 1950–53; Under-Secretary, Department of Technical Co-operation, 1961–4.

**Rt. Hon. (Lewis) John Edwards**, OBE 1946, 1904–59.
Staff tutor, University of Leeds, 1932–6; General Secretary, Post Office Engineering Union, 1938–47; Labour MP, 1945–59; Parliamentary Private Secretary, Ministry of Health, 1947–9; Parliamentary Secretary, Board of Trade, 1949–50; Economic Secretary to the Treasury, 1950–51; President of the Consultative Assembly, Council of Europe, 1959. As Chairman of PEP Executive Committee, 1951–9, was active in adapting PEP to new post-war role.

**Sir Alfred (Charles Glyn) Egerton**, Kt 1943, FRS 1926, 1886–1959.
Reader in Thermodynamics, Oxford University 1921–36; Professor of Chemical Technology, Imperial College of Science, 1936–52; Chairman, Scientific Advisory Council to Minister of Fuel and Power, 1948–53; Editor, *Fuel*. Consultant to PEP Industries Group when working on the British Fuel and Power Industries (report 1947).

**Dorothy Whitney Elmhirst**, 1887–1968.
Co-founder, Dartington Hall Trust, 1925. Constant backer and source of inspiration for PEP from its foundation to the 1950s.

**Leonard Knight Elmhirst**, 1893–1974.
Co-founder, Dartington Hall Trust, 1925; Founder and President, the International Association of Agricultural Economists. Founder Member of the PEP Directorate, Executive, 1931–72; Chairman of PEP, 1939–53; Vice-President, 1966–74; particularly concerned with PEP's rural and world-wide interests.

**Sir Harold Corti Emmerson**, GCB, 1896–
Secretary, Royal Commission on Unemployment Insurance, 1930–32; Permanent Secretary, Ministry of Works, 1946–56; Permanent Secretary, Ministry of Labour, 1956–9. Served on PEP Groups in 1930s.

**Sir George Evetts**, Kt 1946, 1882–1958.
Director of Public Utility Companies at home and overseas. Gas Adviser to Board of Trade Gas Division and to Ministry of Fuel and Power, 1939–45. Member, PEP Industries Group when working on Gas (report 1939).

**Sir Derek Ezra**, Kt 1974, 1919–
Member of UK Delegation to High Authority of European Coal and Steel Community, 1952–6; Chairman, National Coal Board, 1971–. Member, PEP Executive, 1962–8; Member, European Organisations Group (report 1959).

**Sir Frank (Edward) Figgures**, KCB 1970, 1910–
HM Treasury, 1946; Director of Trade and Finance, OEEC, 1948–51;

Under-Secretary, HM Treasury, 1955–60; Secretary General to EFTA, 1960–65; Third Secretary, Treasury, 1968; Director-General, NEDO, 1971–1973. Member, PEP European Organisations Group (report 1959). Chairman, Committee of Enquiry into the Engineering Profession, 1978–80.

**Sir (Harold) Montague Finniston**, Kt 1975, FRS 1949, 1912–
Chief Metallurgist, UKAEA, Harwell, 1948–58; Technical Director, C. A. Parsons Ltd., 1959–67; Deputy Chairman, British Steel Corporation, 1967–73; Chairman, British Steel Corporation, 1973–6; Chairman, Sears Engineering Ltd., 1976–9. Member, PEP/PSI Executive, Council, 1968–; Chairman, 1974–.

**Richard Sidney Richmond Fitter**, 1913–
Economist, author and naturalist; Secretary, Fauna Preservation Society, 1964–. PEP staff, 1936–40.

**Garret FitzGerald**, 1926–
Member of the Dail (Fine Gael Party) 1969–; Leader, Fine Gael Party, 1977–; Minister for Foreign Affairs, Republic of Ireland, 1973–7. Author of *Planning in Ireland* (PEP, 1969).

**Michael Patrick Fogarty**, 1916–
Fellow, Nuffield College, 1944–51; Montague Burton Professor of Industrial Relations, University College of South Wales, 1951–66; Director, Economic and Social Research Institute, Dublin, 1968–72. Led PEP study on sex, career and family, 1966–8; Senior Fellow, Centre for Studies in Social Policy, 1973, Deputy Director, 1977–8; Deputy Director, PSI, 1978–; author, with others, of *Sex, career and family* (1971), *Women in top jobs* (1971) and several PEP Broadsheets and PSI Reports.

**E. Maxwell Fry**, CBE 1953, 1899–
Town planner, architect and painter; Vice-President of Royal Institute of British Architects, 1961–2. Contributed to PEP work on planning in 1930s and 1940s, and to work of Industries Group on Housing England (report 1934).

**Sir George Henry Gater**, GCMG 1944, 1886–1963.
Education Officer, London County Council, 1924–33; Clerk of the Council, 1933–9; Secretary, Ministry of Home Security, 1940–42; Fellow, Winchester College from 1936; Warden, Winchester College, 1951–9.

**Raymond John Goodman**, 1916–
Assistant to Chairman, Marks & Spencer, 1953–6; Director, East Asian and Pacific Department, World Bank, 1968–74; Director, Financial Policy, 1975–7; Vice-President, Operations, 1977–. Director, PEP, 1946–53.

**Sir Ernest Arthur Gowers**, GCB 1953, 1880–1966.
Chairman of the Board of Inland Revenue, 1927–30; Chairman of Coal Mines Reorganisation Commission, 1930–35; Chairman of Coal Commission, 1938–46; author of *Plain words: a guide to the use of English* (1948). Consultant to PEP Industries Group when working on Coal (report 1936).

**Rt. Hon. Arthur Greenwood**, CH 1945, 1880–1954.
Lecturer in Economics, University of Leeds; Labour MP from 1932; Member of War Cabinet and Minister without Portfolio, 1940–42; Lord Privy Seal, 1945–7; Paymaster General, 1946–7; largely concerned in developing post-war reconstruction studies in 1940s.

**Sir Edward William Macleay Grigg**, see Lord Altrincham.

**Rt. Hon. Joseph Grimond**, 1913–
Barrister; Director of Personnel, European Office, UNRRA, 1945–7; Secretary of National Trust for Scotland, 1947–9; Liberal MP, 1950–; Leader of Parliamentary Liberal Party, 1956–67. PEP staff, 1949–50.

**(Thomas) Graeme Nelson Haldane**, 1897–
Electrical engineer; Partner, Merz and McLellan, 1941–57; Consultant, Merz and McLellan, 1957–71. Consultant to PEP Industries Group when working on Electricity (report 1936) and other fuel and power reports.

**Earl of Halifax, Edward Frederick Lindley Wood**, 1881–1959.
Lord Privy Seal, 1935–7; Leader of the House of Lords, 1935–8 and 1940; Lord President of the Council, 1937–8; Secretary of State for Foreign Affairs, 1938–40; British Ambassador at Washington, 1941–6. Encouraged PEP's work on Post-War Aims in 1939–40.

**Sir Noel (Frederick) Hall**, Kt 1957, 1902–
Lecturer and Senior Lecturer in Department of Political Economy, University College, London, 1927–35; Professor of Political Economy, University College, 1935–8; a founder and first Director, National Institute of Economic and Social Research, 1938–43; Joint Director, Ministry of Economic Warfare; Principal of the Administrative Staff College, Henley on Thames, 1946–61; Principal of Brasenose College, Oxford, 1960–73. Founder Member, PEP Directorate, then Member, Executive, to 1940.

**Peter Geoffrey Hall**, 1932–
Professor and Head of Department of Geography, University of Reading, 1968–. PEP staff, part-time, 1966–71; author of *The containment of urban England* (with others, 1973), *Planning and urban growth* (with Marion Clawson, published for Resources for the Future in Washington as a result of joint study with PEP).

**John Henry Hansard**, 1895–1979.
Merchant banker and Director of Lever Bros.; developed the Ford Collection of Parliamentary Papers at Southampton University. PEP Executive, 1956–66; Hon. Treasurer, 1956–64.

**Christopher Harlow**, 1939–
Management Consultant, Peat Marwick Mitchell and Co., 1975–80. PEP staff, 1967–70; PSI, 1980–; author of *Innovation and productivity under nationalisation* (1977).

**Tom Harrisson**, 1911–76.
Ornithologist and anthropologist; co-founder, with Charles Madge, of Mass Observation, 1937; subsequently curator of the Sarawak Museum.

Influenced PEP in direction of responsiveness to public attitudes.

**Geoffrey Heyworth**, 1st Baron of Oxton 1955, 1894–1974.

Director, Lever Bros, from 1931; Chairman, Unilever Ltd., 1942–60; Chairman, Committee on Research in Social Sciences, 1963–5; Chairman, Leverhulme Trust, 1941–70. Chairman, PEP Group on Trade Unions (reports 1962–4).

**Mayer Hillman**, 1931–

Architect and planner; private practice, 1954–67. PEP/PSI staff 1970–; author (with Anne Whalley) of *Personal mobility and transport policy* (1973), *Transport realities and planning policy* (1976), *Fair play for all* (1977), *Walking is transport* (1979), *The social consequences of rail closures* (1980).

**William Graham Holford**, Baron of Kemp Town 1965, 1907–75.

Architect and planning consultant; Professor of Town Planning, University College, London, 1948–70; Director, Leverhulme Trust, from 1972. Member, PEP Executive, 1943–50; 1966–9; Chairman, Council of Management, 1958–66; chaired Executive, 1959–61; Vice-President, 1966–1975; Chairman, Advisory Group on study of urban growth (main report 1973).

**James Hosken**, 1908–

Worked at British Commercial Gas Association on the industrial uses of town gas, 1930–39; Arthur D. Little, 1947–55; subsequently worked for various companies in the electronic data processing field. Member, PEP Industries Group when working on Gas (report 1939).

**Rt. Hon. Sir (Richard Edward) Geoffrey Howe**, Kt 1970, 1926–

Conservative MP since 1970; Chancellor of the Exchequer, 1979–. Co-author of *Anti-discrimination legislation: the Street Report* (PEP, 1967).

**Sir Harold Gibson Howitt**, GBE 1946, 1886–1969.

Partner, Peat Marwick Mitchell and Co., 1911–61; Deputy Chairman then Chairman, BOAC, 1943–8; Member, Council on Productivity, Prices and Incomes, 1957–60. Member, PEP Council of Management in 1930s.

**Yao-Su Hu**, 1946–

Industrial Economist, Projects Department, World Bank, 1976–8; Senior Lecturer, The Administrative Staff College, Henley, 1981–. PEP staff 1971, 1974–5; author of *National attitudes and the financing of industry* (1975).

**Guy Hunter**, CMG 1973, 1911–

Worked for Gas Light and Coke Co., 1936–8; Warden, Urchfont Manor, Wilts., and Grantley Hall, Yorks., Adult Colleges, 1946–55; Director of Studies, 1st Duke of Edinburgh's conference, 1955–6; from 1957, research and consultancy for developing countries, particularly in Africa and Asia; Senior Research Officer and then Adviser, ODI, 1967–. Drafting Secretary for PEP Report on Gas (1939); Director, PEP, 1945–6.

**Sir Peter Hutchison**, 1907–
Solicitor; Deputy Clerk of the Peace and of the County Council, East Suffolk, 1947–71. Member, TEC PLAN Group, 1931–3.

**Aldous (Leonard) Huxley**, 1894–1963.
Writer; works include *Point Counter Point* (1928), *Brave New World* (1932, written after sitting in at early PEP meetings), *The Perennial Philosophy* (1946) and *The Devils of Loudon* (1952).

**Sir Julian (Sorell) Huxley**, Kt 1958, 1887–1975.
Biologist and writer; Secretary, Zoological Society of London, 1935–42; Director-General, UNESCO, 1946–8. Founder Member, PEP Directorate and Member, Publicity Committee in 1930s; Member, Group on world population and resources (report 1955).

**Alexander Reginald Isserlis**, 1922–
Principal Private Secretary to the Prime Minister, 1970; Assistant Under-Secretary of State, Home Office, 1970–72; Director of Investigations, Office of the Parliamentary Commissioner for Administration, 1977–80. Director, Centre for Studies in Social Policy, 1972–7; Member, PSI Council, 1978–80; Senior Fellow, PSI, 1980–.

**Sir (William) Wilson Jameson**, GBE 1949, 1885–1962.
Dean and Professor of Public Health, London School of Hygiene and Tropical Medicine; Chief Medical Officer of Ministry of Health and Ministry of Education, 1940–50; Medical adviser to King Edward's Hospital Fund for London, 1950–60. Used 1937 PEP Report on health services as a basis for his work in shaping the National Health Service.

**John Maynard Keynes**, 1st Baron of Tilton 1942, 1883–1946.
Economist and author; Fellow and Bursar of King's College, Cambridge; books include *The General Theory of Employment, Interest and Money* (1936). Gave much informal advice to PEP in 1930s and 1940s, largely through Leonard Elmhirst.

**William Stephen Richard King-Hall**, Baron of Headley 1966, 1893–1966.
After a career in the Royal Navy was MP (Ind. Nat.), 1939–44; founded K-H Newsletter Service in 1936; founded the Hansard Society for Parliamentary Government in 1944. Did much to disseminate PEP material in his Newsletter and Parliamentary work.

**François Lafitte**, 1913–
Special writer on social questions, *The Times*, 1943–59; Professor of Social Policy and Administration, University of Birmingham, 1959–80. On research staff and subsequently Deputy Secretary of PEP, 1938–43; Chairman of PEP Research Groups on health services, 1943–6, and on housing policy, 1948–51; Member, PEP Executive, 1943–53, 1957–63.

**Sir John (Waldemar) Lawrence**, OBE 1945, 1907–
Press Attache, HM Embassy, USSR, 1942–5; freelance writer; Editor of *Frontier*, 1957–75. Member, PEP Executive, 1950–67; Member, TEC PLAN Group, 1931–3; worked on co-partnership study in 1930s.

**Hon. Christopher Walter Layton**, 1929–
Director, Centre for European Industrial Studies, Bath University, 1968–71; Chef de Cabinet to Commissioner Spinelli, Commission of the European Communities, 1971–3; Director, Computer Electronics, Telecommunications and Air Transport Equipment Manufacturing, Commission of the EC, 1973–. PEP staff, 1966–71; author of *European advanced technology* (1968) and *Ten innovations* (1972).

**Samuel Clement Leslie**, CBE 1946, 1898–1980.
Publicity Manager to Gas Light and Coke Co., 1936–40; Director of Public Relations, Ministry of Supply, 1940; Home Office and Ministry of Home Security, 1940–43; Director, Council of Industrial Design, 1945–7; Head of Information Division of the Treasury, 1947–59. Member, PEP Press Group (report 1938).

**Kenneth Lindsay**, 1897–
Independent National MP for Kilmarnock Burghs, 1933–45; Independent MP for Combined English Universities, 1945–50; Civil Lord of the Admiralty, 1935–7; Parliamentary Secretary, Board of Education, 1937–40; visiting professor at many American universities. Founder Member, PEP Directorate, Executive, first General Secretary, 1931–5; Member, Council of Management, 1936–66; Board of Patrons 1966–78.

**Marquess of Lothian**, Philip Henry Kerr, 11th Marquess, 1882–1940.
Secretary to the Prime Minister, 1916–21; Secretary of Rhodes Trust, 1925–9; Parliamentary Under-Secretary, India Office, 1931–2.

**James Eugene MacColl**, 1908–71.
Barrister; Labour MP from 1950. PEP staff, 1945–50.

**Rt. Hon. (Maurice) Harold Macmillan**, OM 1976, 1894–
Unionist MP for Stockton-on-Tees, 1924–9 and 1931–45. Conservative MP, 1945–64; Prime Minister 1957–63; Chairman, Macmillan Ltd., 1963–74; President, Macmillan Ltd. since 1974. Active on Next Five Years Group in 1930s, which had discussions with PEP Industries Group.

**George McRobie**, 1925–
Coal miner in Co. Durham, 1943–7; reporter and feature writer, 'Coal magazine', 1947–50; Assistant to E. F. Schumacher, National Coal Board, 1956–65; Small Industries Extension Training Institute, Hyderabad, India, 1965–7; Director, Intermediate Technology Development Group, 1967–79, Chairman, 1979–. PEP staff, 1950–56; Member, PEP Executive, 1963–1965.

**Charles Henry Madge**, 1912–
Reporter on *Daily Mirror*, 1935–6; co-founder, with Tom Harrisson, of Mass Observation, 1937; Professor of Sociology, University of Birmingham, 1950–70. PEP staff, 1942–3.

**John Madge**, 1914–68.
Architect, urban sociologist and planner; first Director, Nuffield Foundation Research Unit; Sociologist with DSIR Building Research Station for

eight years. Deputy Director, PEP, from 1960, then Chief Consultant.

**James Joseph Mallon**, CH 1939, 1875–1961.

Warden of Toynbee Hall, 1919–54; Secretary, National League to establish a Minimum Wage, 1906; Member of the first 13 Trade Boards established under Trade Boards Act 1909; on Board of Governors, BBC, 1937–9 and 1941–6; on National Assistance Board, 1940–48. Lively and unremitting friend of PEP's Civic Division activities in 1930s.

**Sir Henry (Stenhouse) Mance**, Kt 1941, 1913–

Ministry of War Transport, 1941–6; Chairman, Lloyds, 1969–72; Deputy Chairman and Treasurer, Lloyd's Register of Shipping from 1949. PEP Hon. Treasurer, 1947–56; Member, PEP Executive, 1947–59.

**Cyril Aubin Masterman**, 189(7)?–1974.

For many years was Chief Technical Officer, Gas Light and Coke Co.; in 1943 became convenor of Postwar Planning for the British Gas Federation. Consultant to PEP Industries Group when working on fuel and power reports.

**Hilda Matheson**, OBE 1939, 1888–1940.

Political secretary to Lady Astor in 1920s; joined BBC in 1926, becoming Director of Talks; maintained interest in broadcasting, becoming Director of the Joint Broadcasting Group. Member, PEP Press Group (report 1938).

**Rt. Hon. Sir Angus Edmund Upton Maude**, 1912–

Financial journalist, 1933–9; Conservative MP, 1950–57; Independent Conservative MP, 1957–8; Conservative MP since 1963; Paymaster General, 1979–81. Returned from Japanese prison camp to service PEP's manpower group after the war; Deputy Director, PEP, 1948–50; Member, PEP Executive, 1950–54.

**Lord Melchett of Landford**, Alfred Moritz Mond, 1st Baron 1928, 1868–1930.

Liberal MP, 1906–23 and 1924–8; Minister of Health, 1921–2; founder President of the Institute of Fuel; founder Chairman of Imperial Chemical Industries Ltd.; active in promoting co-operation between industry and trade unions.

**Charles Mitchell**, –1957.

Chairman, Dorman, Long and Co. Ltd.; Chairman, National Committee for the Iron and Steel Industry. Consultant to PEP Industries Group when working on Iron and Steel (report 1933).

**Gilbert Richard Mitchison**, Baron 1964, 1890–1970.

Barrister; Labour MP, 1945–64; Joint Parliamentary Secretary, Ministry of Land and Natural Resources, 1964–6.

**Rt. Hon. Sir (Clement) Anderson Montague-Barlow**, 1868–1951.

Barrister; Conservative MP, 1910–23; Minister of Labour, 1922–4; Chairman, Royal Commission on the Distribution of the Industrial Population (report 1940). Attended some meetings of PEP Industries Group when working on Regional Development (report 1939).

**Roger Morgan**, 1932–
Deputy Director of Studies, Royal Institute of International Affairs, 1971–4; Professor of European Politics, Loughborough University, 1974–8. Joint Editor, PEP/RIIA European Series, 1971–4; contributor to *European political parties* (1969); led PEP study of *Paying for party politics* (1975) and *Reinforcing Parliament* (1976); Head of European Centre for Political Studies, PSI, 1978–.

**Santosh K. Mukherjee**, 1931–79.
Deputy Head, Research and Economic Department, Trades Union Congress, 1960–65; Economic Adviser, Ministry of Labour, 1965–7; Tutor and Lecturer in labour economics and industrial relations, Department for External Studies, Oxford University, 1967–79. PEP staff, part-time, 1969–79; author of *Changing manpower needs* (1970), *Making labour markets work* (1972), *Unemployment* costs ... (1976), *Winners and losers: pay patterns in the 1970s* (with others, 1977).

**Keith Anderson Hope Murray**, Baron of Newhaven 1964, 1903–
Agricultural economist; Fellow, Bursar then Rector, Lincoln College, 1937–53; Chairman, University Grants Committee, 1953–63; Chancellor, Southampton University, 1964–74; Director, Leverhulme Trust, 1965–72; President, Agricultural Economics Society, 1959–60.

**John Edward Nash**, 1925–
Executive Director, Samuel Montagu from 1956 and Director, 1960–73; Director, Monetary Affairs, Commission of the European Communities, 1973–7; Director, S. G. Warburg and Co. Ltd., 1977–. Hon. Treasurer, PEP 1964–73.

**Lawrence E. Neal**, 1895–
Lieutenant, 1st Wilts Regiment, 1916·19; joined Daniel Neal & Sons Ltd., 1919; Director and Secretary, 1922; Managing Director, 1932; Chairman and Managing Director, 1939–63; Member, Sea-Fish Commission for the United Kingdom, 1933–6; Member, Council of Retail Distributors' Association Incorporated, 1933–65, Chairman of Council, 1949; Member, Retail Trade Committee of Board of Trade, 1941–2; Deputy Secretary, Ministry of Town and Country Planning, 1942–6; Vice-Chairman, Crawley New Town Corporation, 1947–56; Founder Member, British Institute of Management, 1949 and Fellow of Institute from 1960; first Chairman, Furniture and Timber Industry Training Board, 1965–9; Chairman of Trustees of the Industrial Training Boards' Pension Fund, 1971–6; awarded Her Majesty's Silver Jubilee Medal, 1977. Founder Member, PEP Directorate, then Member, Executive, to 1943; Member, Council of Management, 1936–66.

**(Edward) Max Nicholson**, CB 1948, 1904–
Head of Allocation of Tonnage Division, Ministry of War Transport, 1942–5; Secretary of Office of the Lord President of the Council, 1945–52; Director-General, Nature Conservancy, 1952–66; Chairman, Land Use

Consultants, from 1966; Vice-President, Royal Society of Arts, 1978–; President, Royal Society for the Protection of Birds, 1980–. Founder Member, PEP Directorate, Executive, 1931–72; General Secretary and Editor of publications, 1933–40; Chairman, Council of Management, 1953–8; Vice-President, PEP/PSI, 1966–.

**Henry Nimmo**, CBE 1953, 1885–1954.
Chief Engineering Inspector, Electricity Commission, 1929–45; Electricity Commissioner, 1945–7; Chairman, Southern Electricity Board from 1948. Consultant to PEP Industries Group when working on Electricity (report 1936).

**Jim Northcott**, 1928–
Director of a firm of economic consultants, 1966–. PEP/PSI staff, 1976–; author of *Industry in the development areas* (1977), *Microprocessors in manufactured products* (with others, 1980).

**Sir (Arthur) David Kemp Owen**, KCMG 1970, 1904–70.
Director, Sheffield Social Survey Committee, 1929–33; Co-Director, Pilgrim Trust Unemployment Enquiry, 1936–7; worked with Sir Stafford Cripps in the creation of United Nations Organisation; Executive Chairman, UN Technical Assistance Board, 1951–65; Co-Administrator, UN Development Programme, 1966–9; Secretary-General, International Planned Parenthood Federation, 1969–70. Secretary, Civic Division, PEP, 1934–6; General Secretary, PEP, 1940–41; Member, Executive, 1940–50; Council of Management, 1950–66; Board of Patrons, 1966–70.

**Sir Peter Parker**, Kt 1978, 1924–
Chairman, Bookers Engineering and Industrial Holdings Ltd., 1966–70; Chairman, British Railways Board, 1976–. Member, PEP Executive, 1964–78; Vice-Chairman, 1969–73; Hon. Treasurer, 1973–8; Chairman, Advisory Group for study of company law reform (main reports 1971–2).

**Sir Michael (Willcox) Perrin**, Kt 1967, 1905–
Assistant Director, Tube Alloys (Atomic Energy) Department of Scientific and Industrial Research, 1941–6; Deputy Controller, Atomic Energy (Technical Policy), Ministry of Supply, 1946–51; Director, Inveresk Research International, 1961–74; Chairman, The Wellcome Foundation Ltd., 1953–70. Advised PEP Industries Group on a number of technical and other problems in 1930s.

**Lord Percy of Newcastle**, Eustace Percy, 1st Baron 1953, 1887–1958.
Unionist MP, 1921–37; President of the Board of Education, 1924–9; Minister without Portfolio, 1935–6.

**John Pinder**, OBE, 1924–
Head of Overseas Department, then International Director, the Economist Intelligence Unit, 1953–64. Director of PEP/PSI, 1964–; author of 'Economic Growth, Social Justice and Political Reform' in *Europe tomorrow* (1972), *Reshaping Britain* (with others, 1974), *The European Community's policy towards Eastern Europe* (with Pauline Pinder, 1975),

'The Community as a framework for British external relations' (with William Wallace) in *Britain in Europe* (1980).

**Wyndham Raymond Portal**, 1st Viscount 1945, 1885–1949.

Chairman of Portals Ltd.; Trustee of Lord Nuffield's scheme for assistance of Special Areas from 1936; Additional Parliamentary Secretary to Ministry of Supply, 1940–42; Minister of Works and Planning and First Commissioner of Works and Public Building, 1942–4.

**John Craven Pritchard**,

Engineer, economist, designer and furniture designer, 'Plywood' Pritchard; worked for Venesta in 1920s then set up Isokon in 1931; played leading role in Modern Movement in architecture and design; Director, Furniture Development Council, 1949–63. Founder Member, PEP Directorate, 1931–1932; Chairman, TEC PLAN Group, 1931–3.

**Sir Arthur Pugh**, Kt 1935, 1870–1955.

General Secretary, Iron and Steel Trades Confederation and British Iron, Steel and Kindred Trades Association, 1917–36; Chairman, General Council of Trades Union Congress, 1925; Member, Economic Consultative Committee, League of Nations. Consultant to Industries Group when working on Iron and Steel (report 1933).

**Hugh Quigley**, 1895–1979.

Economist and farmer; Chief Statistical Officer, Central Electricity Board, 1931–43. Consultant to PEP Industries Group when working on Electricity (report 1936).

**Marchioness of Reading**, née Stella Charnaud, Baroness Swanborough 1958, 1894–1971.

Chairman, Personal Service League, 1932–8; Founder and Chairman of Women's Royal Voluntary Service from 1938.

**Eileen Reid**, 1945–

PEP/PSI staff 1976–; author of *Governments and trade unions* (with Denis Barnes, 1980), *Differentials for managers and skilled workers* (with Michael Fogarty, 1980).

**Rt. Hon. (Aubrey) Geoffrey (Frederick) Rippon**, 1924–

Conservative MP, 1955–64 and since 1966; Leader, Conservative party Delegation to Council of Europe and WEU; and Leader, Conservative Group, European Parliament, 1977–9. Member, PEP Executive, 1961–2; Member, European Organisations Group (report 1959).

**Prof. Sir (Edward) Austin (Gossage) Robinson**, Kt 1975, 1887–

University lecturer, Cambridge, 1929–49; Professor of Economics, 1950–65; Secretary, Royal Economic Society, 1945–70; President, International Economic Association, 1959–62; Director of Economics, Ministry of Power, 1967–8.

**Eric Roll**, Baron of Ipsden 1977, 1907–

Professor of Economics and Commerce, University College of Hull, 1935–46; Permanent Under Secretary of State, Department of Economic Affairs,

1964–6; Director of the Bank of England, 1968–77; Chancellor, University of Southampton 1974–. Chairman, S. G. Warburg, 1974–. Member, PEP Executive, 1960–63, 1966–74; Vice-President, 1966–74; Chairman, Executive, 1969–74; President, PEP, 1975–8; Joint-President, PSI, 1978–.

**Oliver Wentworth Roskill**, 1906–
Founder, O. W. Roskill Industrial Consultants; Director of Companies; founder Member of Council, British Institute of Management, 1947–58; President, Institute of Management Consultants, 1970; consultant on development projects to various overseas governments. Member, PEP. Executive, 1940–67 and 1969–75; Vice-President, 1975–8; Secretary, Industries Group in 1930s; Chairman, Group on A Fuel Policy for Britain (report 1966).

**Dennis Routh**, 1912–
Lecturer in International Politics, University College of Wales, Aberystwyth, 1936–9; Fellow of All Souls, Oxford, 1937–61; Ministry of Information, 1939–45 (Deputy Director, Psychological Warfare Division, SHAEF, 1943–5); Overseas Controller, Central Office of Information, 1946–68; Ministry of Education, retiring as Assistant Secretary in Education Office for Wales, 1948–73. Member, PEP Executive, 1942–50; Director, PEP, 1945.

**John Ryan**, CBE 1949, 1894–1975.
Managing Director, Lancashire Cotton Corporation; Vice-Chairman, Metal Box Co.; Chairman, British Closures' Manufacturers Association, 1942–74; Chairman, Centre for Interfirm Comparison Ltd., 1969–74. Member of Industries Group when working on Cotton (report 1934).

**Alan John Sainsbury**, Baron of Drury Lane 1962, 1902–
Joined J. Sainsbury, Ltd., 1921; Chairman, 1956–67; Joint President, 1967–; Member, Food Research Advisory Committee, 1960–70; NEDC Committee for the Distributive Trades, 1964–8; House of Lords Select Committee on the European Communities, 1978–. Member, PEP Executive, 1970–1976; Chairman, Advisory Group for study of personal mobility (report 1973).

**David Sainsbury**, 1940–
Finance director, J. Sainsbury, Ltd.; Chairman, Gatsby Charitable Foundation.

**(James) Arthur Salter**, 1st Baron of Kidlington 1953, 1881–1975.
Director, Economic and Finance Section, League of Nations, 1919–20 and 1922–31; Gladstone Professor of Political Theory and Institutions, Oxford University 1934–44; Parliamentary Secretary to Ministry of Shipping, 1939–41; Head of British Merchant Shipping Mission, Washington, 1941–1944. Member, PEP Directorate, from 1932; Council of Management, 1936–66; Board of Patrons, 1966–75.

**Herbert Louis Samuel**, 1st Viscount of Mount Carmel and of Toxteth, Liverpool 1937, 1870–1963.
Liberal MP, 1902–18 and 1929–35; Chairman, Royal Commission on the

Coal Industry, 1925; Leader of the Parliamentary Liberal Party, 1931–5; Secretary of State for Home Affairs, 1931–2.

**Hugh Saunders**, OBE 1949, 1910–

Barrister, 1933–9; Company Secretary and Head of Legal Department, Unilever, and from 1947 also Head of Public Relations, 1946–56; from 1956 Deputy Managing Director, Rio Tinto Co.; in 1963 went to Bank of London and South America to carry out an administrative reorganisation, retiring as Deputy Chairman; Saphier, Lerner, Schindler Ltd. 1977–. Member, PEP Executive, 1961–72; Chairman, 1961–4; Vice-President, PEP/PSI, 1972–.

**Ernst Friedrich Schumacher**, CBE, 1911–77.

Economist, farmer, conservationist and journalist, originator of the concept of Intermediate Technology for developing countries; academic at Oxford during the Second World War; Economic Adviser with British Control Commission in Germany, 1946–50; Economic Adviser, National Coal Board, 1950–70; author of *Small is Beautiful* (1973). Advised PEP world population and resources group (report 1955).

**Sir George Ernest Schuster**, KCSI 1931, 1881–

Economic and Financial Adviser, Colonial Office, 1924–8; Chairman, Allied Supplies, 1936–46; National Liberal MP, 1938–45; Member Select Committee on National Expenditure, 1939–45; Government Committee on Industrial Productivity and Chairman of Committee Panel on Human Relations, 1947–51; author of *Private Work and Public Causes* (1979). Member, PEP Council of Management, 1947–66; Board of Patrons, 1966–78.

**Laurence Prestwich Scott**, 1909–

Various jobs in the newspaper world before joining *The Guardian* in 1944; Company Secretary, then Director, then Managing Director of Manchester Guardian and Evening News Ltd., 1944–9, Chairman, 1949–1973; Director, Press Association and Reuter, 1948–55 and 1956–60. Member, PEP Press Group (report 1938).

**Frederic Seebohm**, Baron of Hertford 1972, 1909–

Director, Barclays Bank Ltd., 1947–79; Chairman, Finance Corporation for Industry, 1974–80; Chairman, Joseph Rowntree Memorial Trust 1966–; Chairman, Committee on Local Authority and Allied Personal Social Services. President, Centre for Studies in Social Policy, 1972–8; Joint-President, PSI, 1978–.

**Earl of Selkirk**, George Nigel Douglas-Hamilton, 10th Earl, 1906–

Commissioner for Special Areas in Scotland, 1937–9; Paymaster-General, 1953–5; Chancellor of the Duchy of Lancaster, 1955–7.

**Barbara Shenfield**, 1919–

Lecturer, Bedford College, 1962–. Member, Committee on Hardship in Rating, 'Allen Committee', 1963–4; in early 1970s various visiting Professorships in the United States; Vice-Chairman, WRVS, 1976–. PEP staff, 1965–70. Author of *Company Boards* (1971).

**Sir Robert Minshull Shone**, Kt 1955, 1906–

Director, British Iron and Steel Federation, 1950–53; Executive Member, Iron and Steel Board, 1953–62; Joint Chairman, United Kingdom and European Coal and Steel Community Steel Committee, 1954–62; Director-General, National Economic Development Council, 1962–6. Member, PEP Council of Management, 1963–66; Board of Patrons, 1966–78; Chairman, Group on growth in the British economy (report 1960).

**David Daniel Sieff**, 1939–

Director of Personnel, Marks & Spencer Ltd., 1968–72 and 1975–8; Director, 1972–; Vice-Chairman, Institute of Race Relations, 1971–2. Member, PEP/PSI Executive, Council, 1976–.

**Israel Moses Sieff**, Baron of Brimpton 1966, 1889–1972.

Vice-Chairman and Joint Managing Director, Marks & Spencer Ltd., 1926–64; Chairman and Joint Managing Director, 1964–72; President, 1967–72; author of *Memoirs of Israel Sieff* (1970, contains chapter on PEP). Member, PEP Directorate 1931–; Chairman 1933–9; Vice-Chairman 1939–1964; President 1966–72; Chairman of Industries Group in 1930s.

**Marcus (Joseph) Sieff**, Baron of Brimpton 1980, 1913–

Joint Managing Director, Marks & Spencer Ltd., 1967–; Chairman, Marks & Spencer Ltd., 1967–. Member, PEP Executive, 1968–74; Chairman, Group on human relations in industry (report 1972); Vice-President PEP/PSI, 1975–.

**Thomas Spensely Simey**, Baron 1965, 1906–69.

Lecturer in Public Administration, University of Liverpool, 1931–9; Charles Booth Professor of Social Science, University of Liverpool, 1939–69. PEP Working Member active in Civic Division in 1930s.

**Ernest Darwin Simon**, 1st Baron of Wythenshawe, 1879–1960.

Engineer and industrialist; President, Simon Engineering; influential in housing, slum clearance and town planning, smoke abatement, health, local government and university education; Lord Mayor of Manchester, 1921; Liberal MP, 1923–4, 1929–31; Chairman of BBC, 1947–51; founder of Simon Population Trust. Originator, PEP study of world population and resources and Chairman of Group (report 1955).

**David J. Smith**, 1941–

PEP/PSI staff 1972–; author of *Racial disadvantage in employment* (1974), *Racial minorities and public housing* (with Anne Whalley, 1975), *The facts of racial disadvantage* (1976), *Racial disadvantage in Britain* (1977), *Overseas doctors in the National Health Service* (1980).

**Sir Ernest (Woodhouse) Smith**, Kt 1947, 1884–1960.

Technical Director of Woodall Duckham Companies 1922–44; Chairman of Society of British Gas Industries, 1931–2; Director-General of Gas Supply, Ministry of Fuel, 1942–3.

**Sir (Joseph) Lincoln (Spedding) Steel**, Kt 1965, 1900–

Director, Imperial Chemical Industries Ltd., 1945–60; President, International Chamber of Commerce, 1963–5; Chairman, Overseas Committee of Federation of British Industries, 1950–65; EFTA Consultative Committee, 1960–69. Member, PEP Council of Management, 1958–66; Board of Patrons, 1966–78; Member, PEP European Organisations group (report 1959).

**Sir Arthur William Street**, GCB 1946, 1892–1951.

Second Secretary, Ministry of Agriculture and Fisheries, 1936–8; initiator of the Agricultural Marketing Boards; Permanent Under-Secretary of State for Air and Member and Secretary of the Air Council, 1939–45; Deputy Chairman, National Coal Board, from 1946.

**Sir Stephen (George) Tallents**, KCMG 1932, 1884–1958.

Secretary to the Empire Marketing Board 1926–33; Public Relations Officer, General Post Office, 1933–5; Controller, Public Relations, BBC, 1935–40; Principal Assistant Secretary, Minister of Town and Country Planning, 1943–6. Advised PEP on publicity matters in 1930s.

**Michael Thomas**, 1944–

Labour MP, 1974–. PEP staff, 1968–73; author of *Work camps and volunteers* (1971), *Overseas nurses in Britain* (1972), *The Board of Directors* (1972), *National voluntary youth organisations* (with Jane Perry, 1975).

**Ray Thomas**, 1930–

Senior lecturer, Open University, 1972–. PEP staff 1967–72; author of *Journeys to work* (1968), *London's new towns* (1969), *Aycliffe to Cumbernauld* (1969), *The containment of urban England* (with Peter Hall and others, 1973).

**Sir Raymond Unwin**, Kt 1932, 1863–1935.

Architect and town planner; designed first Garden City, Letchworth and Hampstead Garden Suburb; Chief Adviser to Greater London Regional Town Planning Committee, 1929–33; Chief Technical Officer for Building and Town Planning, Ministry of Health, 1918–28.

**Henry Agard Wallace**, 1888–1965.

Writer, statesman and agriculturist; Progressive Party Candidate for US President, 1948.

**Sir Edward (Redston) Warner**, KCMG 1965, 1911–

United Kingdom delegation to OEEC, Paris, 1956–9; Ambassador to Cameroon, 1963–6; United Kingdom Representative to Economic and Social Council of the UN, 1966–7.

**Dorothy Enid Cole Wedderburn**, 1925–

Lecturer, then Reader, then Professor of Industrial Sociology, Imperial College of Science and Technology, 1965–; Director, Industrial Sociology Unit, 1973–. Member, PEP Executive Committee, 1969–76.

**Anne Whalley**, 1945–

PEP/PSI staff, 1968–; author (with Mayer Hillman) of *Personal mobility and transport policy* (1973), *Transport realities and planning policy* (1976), *Walking is transport* (1979). *The social consequences of rail closures* (1980) and (with David Smith) of *Racial minorities and public housing* (1975).

**Sir Geoffrey (Granville) Whiskard**, KCB 1943, 1886–1957.
Assistant Under-Secretary of State, Dominions Office, 1930–35; first High
Commissioner to Australia, 1936–41. Member, PEP Directorate, Executive, 1931–5.

**Lt. Col. Sir Arnold (Talbot) Wilson**, KCIE 1920, 1884–1940.
Acting Civil Commissioner and Political Resident in the Persian Gulf,
1918–20; with Anglo-Persian Oil Co. Ltd., 1921–32; National Conservative
MP, 1933–40; killed in action as tail-gunner in bomber, 1940.

**Sir Geoffrey Masterman Wilson**, KCB 1969, 1910–
Served in HM Embassy, Moscow and Russian Department of Foreign
Office, 1940–45; Cabinet Office, 1947; Treasury, 1948; Under-Secretary,
Treasury, 1956–8; Vice-President, World Bank, Washington, 1961; Deputy
Secretary, Overseas Development Ministry, 1966–8; Deputy Secretary-
General (Economic), Commonwealth Secretariat, 1971; Chairman, Race
Relations Board, 1971–7. Member, PEP Executive, 1948–58; Chairman, International Organisations Group (1950–51).

**Michael Young**, Baron of Dartington 1978, 1915–
Secretary, Research Department, Labour Party, 1945–51; Director, Institute of Community Studies, 1953–; Chairman, Social Science Research
Council, 1965–8. Secretary, PEP, 1942–5; Member, PEP Executive,
1945–58; Vice-President PEP/PSI, 1966–.

**Solly Zuckerman**, Baron of Burnham Thorpe 1971, 1904–
Committee on Future Scientific Policy (Barlow Committee) 1946–8;
Deputy Chairman, Advisory Council on Scientific Policy, 1948–64; Chairman, Committee on Scientific Manpower, 1950–64; Chief Scientific Adviser
to Secretary of State for Defence, 1960–66, to HM Government, 1964–71;
President, Zoological Society of London, since 1977. Member, PEP Group
on world population and resources (report 1955).

**Michael Zvegintzov**, 1904–78.
Born in Russia, known to British friends as Zog; Research Chemist, Gas
Light and Coke Company, 1927–8; Imperial Chemical Industries, 1928–37;
General Foods Corporation of America, 1937–40; War service, eventually
taking charge of German chemical industry in the British Zone of
Germany, 1940–46; Unilever, 1946–50; Technical Adviser then Chief
Adviser, Planning, National Research and Development Corporation,
1950–71, Consultant 1971–8. Active Working Member of PEP in 1930s
and 1940s; contributed to work of International Trade Group (report
1937) and drafting of statement on *European Order and World Order*
(1939).

# Index